HEROES at SEA

DON WALL

Cover by Clem Seale

By the Same Author

Singapore and Beyond

Sandakan – The Last March

Abandoned?

Published by D. Wall

98 Darley Street West

Mona Vale NSW 2103

Australia

Printed by Griffin Press, Adelaide, S.A. 5000

Typeset by Deblaere Typesetting, Dee Why NSW

ISBN 0 646 03578 9

DEDICATED TO THE MEMORY OF
AUSTRALIAN PRISONERS OF WAR AND CIVILIAN INTERNEES
LOST AT SEA DURING WORLD WAR II

AND A TRIBUTE TO
THE CREWS OF THE UNITED STATES SUBMARINES
PAMPANITO
SEALION
BARB
QUEENFISH

INTRODUCTION

During World War II some 1800 Australian Prisoners of War and Internees of the Japanese lost their lives while being transported to Japan. The Japanese rescued some of those who survived in life boats and the POWs and those rescued believe many more were massacred in the water by them. United States submarines rescued 136 Australians and British from rafts after they had survived, without food and water, floating in a heavy oil spill for up to six days.

When these survivors arrived in Australia in October 1944, General Blamey said:

"The rescue of these Australians is one of the great stories of the war, but even greater is the story of the courage, endurance and the unflagging loyalty of the men themselves, during their period of imprisonment and while battling for their lives in the China Sea.

"These men have set an example to the whole of Australia by the manner in which they sustained their morale under almost impossible conditions. They were always on top of the Japanese, they never bowed to their temporary victors, nor did they accept their capture as a defeat, or as the end of the war for them."

It was not until the war ended in 1945 that the story of a greater tragedy at sea unfolded – the loss of the MONTEVIDEO MARU sunk by a U.S. submarine on 1 July 1942, en-route to Japan with over 850 POWs and 200 Internees on board. There were no survivors to tell this story.

HEROES AT SEA tells the story of some of these survivors, of their ordeal and ultimate rescue.

The Honour Roll names those lost.

SCHEDULE OF EVENTS

February 1942	Singapore falls. Japanese take large number prisoner of war including some 16,000 Australians.
March 1942	The Australian cruiser, HMAS PERTH, sunk off Java. Allied Forces surrender in Java including some 3,000 Australians.
May 1942	3,000 Australian POWs sent to Burma.
January 1943	Japan decides to use Allied POWs to construct a railway line from Burma to Thailand. Large number of POWs sent from Java and Singapore to work on Railway.
November 1943	Railway completed. 2,800 Australian POWs die.
January 1944	Imperial General Headquarters decide to transport 10,000 of the fittest Allied POWs to Japan to work in industry. Most of these were now located along the Railway. Orders were given to move "Japan No. l Party" to Saigon for transportation. U.S. Submarines taking heavy toll of Japanese shipping.
June 1944	Party of Allied POWs leave Singapore, their ship TAMAHOKO MARU sunk 24 June 1944 off Nagasaki. SS WAERWIJCK sunk in Malacca Strait.
July 1944	Japan party arrives from Saigon for shipment to Japan.
September 1944	Some 2,200 British and Australians leave Singapore. 1,319 British and Australian POWs loaded on RAKUYO MARU. 900 British POWs loaded on KACHIDOKI MARU.
September 12, 1944	Code-breakers advise convoy departure. U.S. submarines lay in wait. USS GROWLER opens attack sinking the lead destroyer at 5 a.m. 5.30 a.m. Tanker sunk lights up convoy. RAKUYO MARU hit by two torpedoes – Japs abandon ship and POWs. No POWs killed in attack – throw rafts over and abandon ship. By late afternoon Japanese rescued. After their

	rescue Japanese officer calls out to POWs "Goodbye Goodbye – we hope you all die!" By evening of day 1,300 POWs floating around in boats, on debris and many in life-jackets. About midnight PAMPANITO sinks KACHIDOKI MARU carrying British POWs. POWs occupy 11 lifeboats left by Japanese; that night break into two parties.
September 14, 1944	Brigadier Varley party of six boats believed massacred by Japanese. Duncan's party of 4 boats carrying 135 men rescued by Japanese.
September 15, 1944	Hundreds POWs clinging to rafts, debris, spread out over large area. First sighted by USS PAMPANITO. Rescues 73. Requests SEALION for assistance rescues 54. Leave area; advise Pearl Harbour many more survivors still alive.
September 17,1944	QUEENFISH and BARB arrive in search area; rescue a further 30.
October 1944	Australian survivors arrive in Australia
September 1945	Australians learn Japanese transport, MONTEVIDEO MARU carrying over 1,000 Australian POWs, lost July 1942 off Luzon.

CONTENTS

POWs DESTINED FOR JAPAN

An American submarine, the USS PAMPANITO. under the command of Lt.Cdr. Paul Summers, returning to the scene of an attack on a Japanese convoy, sighted a raft. Believing it carried Japanese, a party armed with automatic weapons was ordered on deck. As the submarine swept past the raft the crew heard the occupants calling out; Tony Hauptman, a crew member, noticed two of the men appeared to have curly hair, he knew Japanese didn't have curly hair – "Who are you?" he called out and back came the reply, "We are Australian prisoners of war! Please pick us up!"

An officer standing on the conning tower held up one finger – one man – and a rope was thrown out. Frank Farmer swam to the submarine and reported, "We are Australian POWs part of 1300 British and Australian POWs sunk on the RAKUYO MARU four days ago."

Lt.Cdr. Summers ordered, "Take them aboard!" and so began one of the most remarkable rescues of World War 11. These were some of the first Australian POWs rescued by U.S. submarines in September 1944.

After the completion of the Japanese thrust into the South East Asia area in 1942 they had captured 21,000 Australian POWs and a few hundred internees, of these just under 8000 died in captivity, 2800 died while working on the construction of the Burma Thailand Railway, 1800 died at Sandakan, where only six survived, and some 1800 died at sea.

When they were facing defeat early in 1944, the Japanese Imperial General Headquarters issued orders to ship 10,000 of the fittest POWs to the homeland where they were to work in the war industry.

The major portion of the POW labour force was concentrated in Burma-Thailand recovering from the inhumane and brutal treatment meted out to them by their Japanese guards during the construction of the Railway. The remnants of 'F' and 'H' Forces, which had suffered heavy losses on the railway, belonged to the Singapore POW Administration and were now put to work on the construction of the Changi Airfield.

The men in Burma were told they were being sent to Japan – some liked the idea, like Bill Mayne who said perhaps they would be treated in accordance with the Geneva Convention and not like rabble as Colonel Nagatomo often described them.

During the medical examinations, the POWs were tested for dysentery and other contagious diseases, the Japanese also seemed to be concerned with race and colour – some Australian Aboriginals were rejected for the draft to Japan on the grounds of colour.

The movement of the POWs began early in 1944 – they were told they were to proceed to Saigon where they would be shipped direct to Japan. Japanese troops en-route to the Burma Front told the POWs they would be 'fish food' – because many of them had been torpedoed on their way from Japan. As the POWs travelled through Thailand they received encouraging news of the progress of the war from the native people.

In early April this group, now known as "Japan No.1 Party", arrived at Phnom-Penh in what was then French Indo-China.

Brigadier Varley was the only senior Allied Officer to lead a POW working party. Soon after 'A' Force went to Burma in 1942 the Japanese decided all officers above the rank of Colonel would be concentrated in Manchuria or Formosa. Now Varley was travelling with the party as far as Formosa. Captain Arthur Sumner, an Infantry officer, respected by all those who served with him, was in charge of the party and assisted by Lieuts. Campbell-Smith, Stupart, Phillips and Burke. The senior Medical Officer was Major Chalmers, assisted by Captain Rowland Richards. The Japanese officer given the command to get this party to Japan was Lt. Yamada, best described by POWs as "reasonable" -

In 1941 when France collapsed the Vichy French Government collaborated with the Germans and ordered its Colonies to do likewise. This arrangement allowed the Japanese to move military forces into Indo-China during 1941, giving them a base to launch their drive to Singapore and Java; however, many of the French there remained loyal to the Allied cause.

During the POWs' stay at Phnom-Penh they found the French friendly and helpful, surreptitiously they supplied the POWs with food, medical supplies and even musical instruments. Reg Bullock had made contact with a local native while endeavouring to 'flog' a pair of boots – the contact suggested he might provide names of all the men in the party, this was soon reported to Brigadier Varley, he decided nothing could be lost by providing the list. At the same time many other approaches were made to the POWs, message pads were thrown over the fence of the compound, some men suspected these motives, others complied. One such was Wal Williams, his father later received a message picked up on a Perth radio that he was well. This nominal roll eventually reached Australia and was used as the basis to check the name of those believed to have been lost when the RAKUYO MARU was sunk.

The party was moved down river by ferry to Saigon. The first sign of Allied air attacks were the remains of many ships sunk in the river. Some had mixed feelings about Saigon – the Allies were getting closer but the chance of a sea voyage looked grim.

Here the Australians met up with British POWs who had been in Saigon for some time; they were well-dressed and well fed and were surprised to learn of the hardships the Australians had suffered on the Burma railway. The British POWs told them no ships had been able to get out of Saigon for some time because of U.S. submarine activity.

The POWs were surprised when they were marched to their camp to find it was one used by the French Foreign Legion and provided amenities they had not seen since Changi. However after a few days they continued their journey down river where they were to embark for the voyage to Japan.

This was to be a false start – the next day they returned to Saigon; here they remained until June, in the meantime their morale had been somewhat lifted by the news the French had passed on that the Allied Forces had landed at Normandy.

The POWs voted Saigon as the best camp of the war and now they were on their way back down the line to Singapore where new arrangements would be made to transport them to Japan.

They arrived at River Valley Transit Camp in early July, 1944.

Rear Admiral Richard H. O'Kane (Ret.) Commander of USS TANG when it sank four ships including TAMAHOKO MARU with six torpedoes on the night of June 24, 1944. He is credited with having sunk the greatest tally of ships during World War II. TANG was lost on her 5th patrol when one of her own torpedoes malfunctioned in a circular run and struck TANG. There were several survivors rescued by Japanese, O'Kane spent the rest of the war as a POW.

TAMAHOKO MARU

A few weeks before another party destined for Japan had vacated the camp. Most of the draft of POWs on this ship were taken prisoner at Timor in 1942 and were moved to Java on the DAI NICHI MARU in September 1942. During the voyage they were attacked by a B17 Flying Fortress. Arriving at Sourabaya at the end of September, after several months they were transferred to the notorious "Bicycle Camp" near Batavia, where they remained for some time.

It was in the early part of 1944 the order was given for all "fit" POWs to be sent to Japan when space was available. The draft, now comprising the Timor party and a number of other men from the 2/2 Pioneer Battalion, 2/3 Machine Gun Battalion who had been abandoned in Java, together with Medical personnel, 268 Australians and British, American and Dutch POWs, totalling 777 men.

They reached Singapore on 22 May 1944 where they were taken to the bare and bug-ridden Staging Camp at River Valley Road. Here medical tests were carried out for dysentery, reducing the party to 772 men.

Lance Gibson, surviving officer of the TAMAHOKO MARU, recorded: "Minni Sam, the Western-educated, friendly, Korean guard, decided to throw a party the night before the ship sailed. He smuggled five officers out of River Valley camp to a Chinese house where they were treated to roast suckling pig and Chinese brandy. Next morning, bearing tremendous hangovers, they were loaded on the BIJOU MARU. It would be Minni Sam who later would be responsible for insisting the POWs be rescued."

Norm Segal: "The first night out of Singapore one of our leading boats was torpedoed (no prisoners aboard this boat) so all prisoners were battened down below decks until the danger had passed. We arrived in Manila on 11 June 1944, and the next day I celebrated my 21st birthday, with the usual fare.

"On 14 June 1944 we left Manila and ran slap-bang into a typhoon. Prisoners were again battened down below, as it would have been impossible for any number to have survived had they been on decks, waves which I would estimate to be at least 30 ft. high crashed down and completely covered the boat at about one minute intervals.

"Conditions down below were appalling, sweat rose off 772 bodies stacked in this single hold like sardines, condensation on the cold deck above fell back as rain. Latrines were out of the question, and had been washed away anyhow. So consequently we were forced to relieve ourselves where we were, this did not improve conditions.

"The heat and sweat rashes were unbearable, there was absolutely no way this condition could be relieved, as neither could we relieve the suffocating air we were forced to breathe for 24 hours on end without any ventilation other than a shaft about 8' x 6' up one end of the hold, which let more water in than air.

"The cookhouse, which was situated aft on deck, was washed away and neither prisoners nor captors ate from 15 June 1944 until we struggled into Takao, Formosa, on one engine (the other broke down during the typhoon) on 18 June 1944.

"Here we were transhipped to a much larger boat, the TAMAHOKO MARU, with more livable and spacious conditions. We were now allotted two holds and below us was stacked a cargo of sugar – thanks to a sympathetic Formosan, one of the manhole covers was left unlocked."

As the convoy came in sight of the land, the guards were jubilant, saying to the prisoners, "Tomorrow I'll be home" –

They had no idea three U.S. submarines were waiting for the convoy just at Japan's back door. The three submarines were operating in the East China Sea – all these boats at some time would have played a role involving Australians – Donald Weiss of TINOSA took a commando party into Borneo – Eli Reich in SEALION II will feature in the sinking of the RAKUYO MARU and rescuing British and Australian POWs – and Richard O'Kane in TANG in a matter of days would sink this ship.

The boats operated independently off the west coast of Kyushu along the principal shipping route to Nagasaki, Sasebo and Shimonaseki, and kept in touch with one another. On the night of June 24 they sent their executive to a meeting with Donald Weiss, the senior skipper on the TINOSA for a strategy meeting. Generally it was agreed to call one another should contact be made.

Richard O'Kane, an aggressive skipper, was previously executive officer on the famous WAHOO with 'Mush' Morton. It was the WAHOO which went to Wewak and while investigating the Harbour a Japanese destroyer charged her. WAHOO attacked and, after missing with four torpedoes, the fifth torpedo was a 'down the throat' shot at 800 yards. The following day he found a four ship convoy – two freighters, a large transport and a tanker. Morton fired two torpedoes at the last of the freighters and three at the transport, the torpedoes failed to explode, he fired another torpedo and she blew up. The transport, fully laden with combat troops was destined for New Guinea – thousands of soldiers jumped overboard. When WAHOO surfaced, deck guns manned, she sailed through the bobbing heads determined to kill every one, after an hour they believed they had sunk all the boats, rafts and most of the troops. Morton then continued the chase for the tanker and freighter which had escaped. The tanker was hit and the freighter sunk.

Much discussion took place regarding the cold-blooded killing – apparently there was no policy in this regard, it was left to the discretion of the skipper. Many found it repugnant. But Morton had no qualms about killing combat soldiers who could be rescued, armed, and sent into battle.

O'Kane, now with his own boat TANG and on his third patrol, picked up a large convoy heading for Nagasaki on the night of June 24. He sent signals to the other submarines but they were unable to close. The convoy consisted of six ships with many escorts – O'Kane attacked a freighter and tanker, sinking both – he was not to know at the time that he had sunk four ships with six torpedoes – including the TAMAHOKO MARU –

Lt. Lance Gibson: "I was between decks in the hold, and the Australian officers were all lying with our heads to the forward mast – we were in the forward hold – the ship was loaded with sugar and pumpkins – we changed the colour of the ship with the effects of the sugar and pumpkins! The officers were worried about the pilfering of the cargo and we put over ten empty bags at night. We were all asleep and at midnight the ship ahead of us was torpedoed. I only had time to get to my feet, I was sleeping in singlet and jockey underpants and I grabbed my shorts and shirt and had almost got to my feet when there was a tremendous blast! My C.O., Major John Dudley Morris, C.O. of the 2/2 C.C.S., A.A.M.C., and Lt. Richard Hamilton of 2/3 M.G. Bn., were next to me and I heard John say, "I'm going to try and get some clothes on" and that is the last I heard of him. The water just came in and we were knocking against the top of the hold; I don't know whether I was knocked out

Above: Lt. Lance Gibson – 2/3 M.G. Bn. Nanneela Vic. Only surviving Officer from TAMAHOKO MARU

for a second because they reckon she only took two minutes for the boat to go, but I remember kicking along the roof of the hold, I must have had enough nous to go at right angles because the hatch covers had all been blown off. Earlier we had had permission from the Japs to get people out on deck because it was getting so hot in the holds and there would have been something like 80 men on the hatch cover and not one of them survived. The torpedo hit right under us and it blew the hatch cover up and they went right down, some said the deck just crinkled. I made the surface just in time, I'd nearly lost my breath but I made it to get a gasp of air just in time to see the tail-end of the ship going down. I got tangled up with cables and I went down again – I don't know how far but it seemed a long way and I made a lot of swimming straight up when I got untangled. When I made the surface I was terribly sick; it was pitch black and a reasonably rough sea, I swam around and I thought I was the only survivor because you can't see far when you are in the water and then from the top of a wave I could a dark mass over in the water, I swam over to it and it was the bridge of one of the boats. The submarine had got the boat ahead of us, then us, then the one behind us, and then when we were in the water they got another one. A bit of the bridge was a support and we virtually fished other people out of the water, there were no Australians, every bloke I seemed to fish out was a black Dutchman.

"With the phosphorous and starlight we could see a bit but it got pretty rough towards early morning. The piece of the bridge was only a support with your head sticking out, it turned over and the Dutch panicked. There were three Dutch doctors, one elderly bloke, a senior man from Java; he passed out and I hung on to him, put my legs around him and held his head out of the water and kept him alive until I was nearly exhausted. At daylight the Japanese came back with a destroyer, lowered a boat and collected all their own men.

"It wasn't until they picked up the interpreter, a Korean, Minni San, who had been friendly towards us, that the Japs began to pick up prisoners. At daylight earlier there were a couple of our blokes picked up in the dark and when they were identified on the destroyer as being prisoners they were put back over the side again at daylight. One bloke couldn't swim and I couldn't help him. Anybody who tried to get into a boat got the boot for a start and it wasn't until they finished up with a little whale-chaser that they picked us up.

"The wreckage seemed to be in an area where it did not move very much, we were only about two hours out from Nagasaki. It was a fast boat which picked us up, they also rescued civilians and one poor little Japanese girl had a little baby which she had managed to hang on to – it was dead of course – and when we were on the way in one of the Jap sailors took a look at it, saw it was dead, took it from her and heaved it over

Jim Barnes, R.A.A.F.: "During the afternoon of 24th a group of us were sitting on the foredeck and I thought I saw a periscope away on the port beam. That night, just before midnight, I was awakened by a terrific explosion. We all stood up in alarm and I remember our O.C., Major J.D. Morris, saying, "It's alright chaps, settle down." The next minute our ship was torpedoed and began sinking immediately.

"I had been sleeping one deck down alongside Sgt. J.J. Green, R.A.A.F., of course it was quite dark but we couldn't have been too far from No.1 Hold which had had its cover blown off. I was trying to reach up to the coaming of the hold but it was too high for me, a tall lad had just managed to reach it and get out and I turned to Jack Green standing beside me and said "It's a wonder somebody doesn't stop and give us a hand" but the next thing I knew the water in the hold was rising so quickly that I managed to float up with it.

"But my troubles were not over then as I was mixed up in the winches etc. on the foredeck. Managing to find a stay to the mast I pulled myself up and saw which way the ship was lying so I swam off at right angles. Sadly, I didn't see Jack Green again. Another R.A.A.F. lad, Sgt. Brian Toohey from Warracknabeal in Victoria, was drowned; he and I had slept every night on deck until we boarded the TAMAHOKO MARU when I elected to go below as it had rained every night. Brian and some others, including C.P.O. Cedric Mellish, ex HMAS PERTH, were sleeping on No.2 hatch cover, and unfortunately were blown up by the force of the blast.

"Meanwhile I managed to get on to a raft with some others then spent the rest of the night paddling around keeping clear of any Japanese survivors. I was picked up the next day at 1100 hours by the whalechaser which was one of our convoy escorts. I believe I was the last person from our raft to be rescued, by this time the whaler had gone past but fortunately I was a good swimmer and I went as fast as I could so that I wouldn't be left behind. It was rather surprising to find out later that some of the survivors could not swim, one lad told me that he had just bobbed up on the surface right under a raft.

"Probably the biggest fright of my life was just after getting out of the hold, I was treading water when suddenly the great bow of a ship seemed to be going over me – in fact it was another ship sinking."

A.E. Long: "About 11.40 p.m. on the night of 24 June 1944, a torpedo hit on the starboard side abreast of the bridge. There were about 500 in the forward hold, the remainder sleeping on deck. I was in the hold when the torpedo hit and this immediately filled with water. I picked myself up as soon as I could after the explosion and already the water was round my ankles.

"I held on until the rush of water stopped and, as soon as the hold filled, I let go and rose immediately to the surface. All that was showing of the ship was the stern and propellors turning. This took 1½ minutes. I swam away from the ship's location and eventually reached a hatch cover board where two of us spent the night. Next morning there seemed to be Japanese all round, we kept as clear as we could of them.

"At about 10 o'clock, a Japanese escort vessel picked up about thirty POWs, mostly Australians. After half an hour they were made to jump back over. Pte. G. Ashman of 2/3 M.G. Bn., was made to jump back and he later drowned.

Left: Survivor. Frank Fitzmaurice. Tea Gardens, NSW.
Right: Allan Pollock, Gosford, NSW, Aged 18 at the time of rescue.

Left: Reg McConnell, Gosford, NSW
Right: Jim Barnes, R.A.A.F. Survivor.

The order of picking up was: Jap Army, Jap women and children, then POWs. One chap who thought he would be cunning saw a Japanese child on a raft so he swam over and nursed her thinking he would get a priority, he was one of the last to be picked up.

"All the POWs were picked up by a Jap whaler. I was greeted with a smart kick in the ribs for not being able to walk. When the torpedo hit, Major Morris went back into the ship to retrieve the POWs' money and was not seen again. Squadron Leader McArty (R.A.F.) was with him at the time but he survived."

Allan Pollock: 'Shorty' Porter, a Merchant seaman, was sitting up in the forecastle giving us a running commentary of the two torpedoes coming at us; one hit directly under the hatch cover I was on, the other hit mid-ships, and she literally sailed under – the ship really just blew apart and went straight under.

"I was half asleep when a vivid orange flash and the next I knew I was going through the air but I landed back in the hold. She filled up that quickly and I got washed against the side and hit my head on the decking, I was just about to take one gulp of water when I shot to the surface. I must have gone in the right direction but I hit my head on a raft when I was coming up. I was on the raft on my own for twelve hours then I was picked up next day."

Reg McConnell: "The Japanese agreed to allow a number of men on deck, so I suggested to my mate, 'Slim' McCurdie, "How about coming up on deck and we'll sleep on the life rafts and if we get hit all we have to do is to float off" – it sounded feasible but the torpedo hit the hold. I remember coming up in the water amongst cables and later climbed on to a piece of the bridge with two Japanese and a Dutchman where I spent the night. I was bleeding from injuries received from the blast and affected by the depth charging. The Dutchman wouldn't speak to me, he sat there in a daze.

"Eventually the deckhouse broke up – the two Japanese went one way and I remained with the Dutchman. When we were being picked up a rope was thrown to us – and the Dutchman spoke for the first time, "Can you swim?" he asked in English."

Bill Atkinson, 2/40 Bn.: "I was on deck when the torpedo struck, there was a ball of fire and my first thoughts were of my sister –

"I was struggling to the surface and popped out near a raft which I grabbed. I was naked and shocked – there was turbulence and depth charges exploding. There were seven men hanging on to the raft including one Japanese.

"There was one Jap hanging on to the raft with us, I wanted to drown him but the others said, "No – the raft can't support any others, what happens if one of our mates comes along – he'll have to go then" but there was never another. I grabbed a box floating by, it contained Japanese clothing and we divided it up.

"Before the torpedo hit the men were discussing the weather, the fact that it was getting colder, and a couple said, "Well I'll go down below and get a good night's sleep" – never saw them again.

"When we arrived at Nagasaki we were still in shock and talked a lot about the memory of the men in the hold – it was not until a bombing raid came that we stopped discussing it."

John Prosser: "My mate, Dave Lewis, and I were on the deck. I reckon the ship went down in a few minutes. I managed to swim to a raft with several others, after about 14 hours we were picked up by a small Japanese naval craft. We were taken to Nagasaki."

Frank Fitzmaurice, Harry Magnusson and Ted Wellington, all from the same Unit, arranged that one of the group would remain on deck to warn their mates in the hold of any torpedo attack. Fitzmaurice was in the hold, Magnusson and Wellington were on deck. When the attack occurred Magnusson never made it to the hold – he saw the torpedo coming and raced to warn the others, it was too late, he went up with the blast. Others in the group included Bruce Wall, John Nangel and Ian McIntosh of Brighton, Victoria. Fitzmaurice did not remember anything till he landed in the water clinging to the wreckage, he was later able to join the others on a raft.

Peter McGrath-Kerr: "On the morning of 24 June, land was sighted, at first several Islands and finally the mainland of Kyushu, which was still in sight when night fell. Shortly before midnight, men on deck were roused by a brilliant flare of light and the sound of an explosion as a ship to starboard blew up and sank. Some ran to that side in time to see the wake of a torpedo heading towards our ship.

"There was a crashing explosion as the torpedo hit just below the bridge, tearing a great hole in the side of the ship which began sinking immediately. Many of the men on that side of the ship were killed by the blast, while those sleeping on the hatch cover were blown into the air with the shattered remains of the planking, killed instantly or fell back into the hold and drowned.

"Survivors on deck rushed to throw overboard rafts or any give support before jumping into the water to get as far away as possible from the drag of the sinking ship.

"Down in the hold, there was pandemonium – where the explosion had smashed the side of the ship men sleeping there had been killed, including most of the Japanese guards. Water poured into the hold and in a little over a minute after the explosion the ship went down, carrying hundreds of men with her.

"I was in the hold and couldn't get out, I went down with the ship. As the water filled the holds the lights went out, increasing the confusion below, as more and more men scrambled to try and reach the deck before the ship went down. Fortunately, I managed to escape from the hold and shot back to the surface; I had gone down so deeply and came up so quickly that my lungs were almost bursting and all my clothes were dragged from me by the rush of the water. When I reached the surface I was naked.

"After clinging to some floating wreckage for a while a mate and I reached an upturned lifeboat where, as the night passed, we were joined by six other POWs. The night seemed to last a lifetime to the men struggling to stay afloat and hold together the makeshift rafts which the waves threatened to break apart. We clung to the inverted boat until we were picked up by a small Japanese boat early in the afternoon. A passing survivor threw me an old pair of Japanese sailor's trousers, which was my only clothing. Fortunately the day was overcast and sunburn was not a worry but we were very cold.

"The rescue took several hours because the survivors had been spread over a large area by the wind and seas, but eventually all those still living were picked up and the ship headed for Nagasaki."

Lt. Lance Gibson: "There was inadequate life saving equipment on board the ship, the three or four lifeboats were not available for POWs and the rafts were quite inadequate. Of the 772 POWs on board 560 were lost.

"No efforts were made to provide for the safety of the POWs. When a submarine or aircraft attack warning was sounded all POWs were forced to go into holds and guards were posted on the hatches. Lifebelts were not issued. After many attempts to persuade the guards to issue some, a stack of old, torn, useless belts were stacked in the hold, their only effect being to make the overcrowding worse. POWs were not allowed to collect them individually.

"As we entered Nagasaki Harbour the sailors made us face in, we were not allowed to see anything – you can imagine how interested we were! We pulled in to the wharf and one of the Rules state that when a ship docks the first thing to do is to wash down the decks, this they did and everybody was hosed down thoroughly. Then a Jap doctor and nurse came on board, I don't think they had any bandage dressings, they had mercurachrome.

"We stayed around on the ship, then we were on the wharves, then we were taken to this mainly Dutch camp in the centre of Nagasaki – Fukuoka 13. The camp was a factory building with every second tooth out – this was the barracks. It had a big heavy wall down the front of it with a passage way and we were put into a couple of rooms. None of us moved for a while.

"Pneumonia was almost contagious, of the 72 Australians who had survived, there was a number who died of pneumonia and related things."

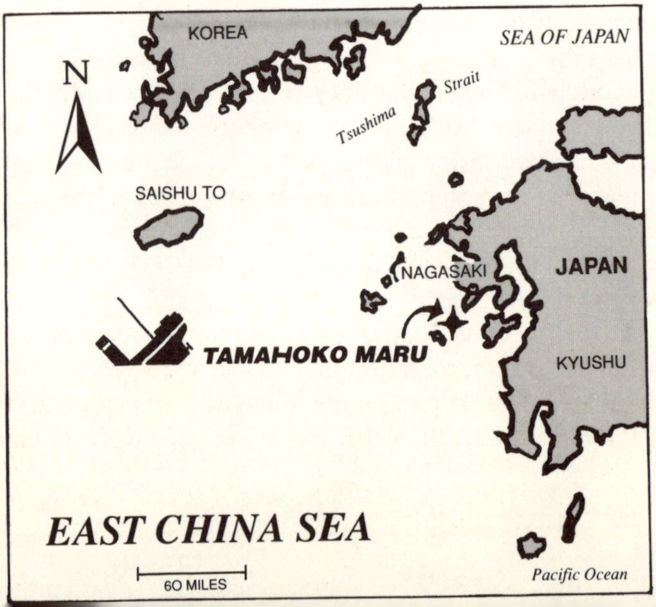

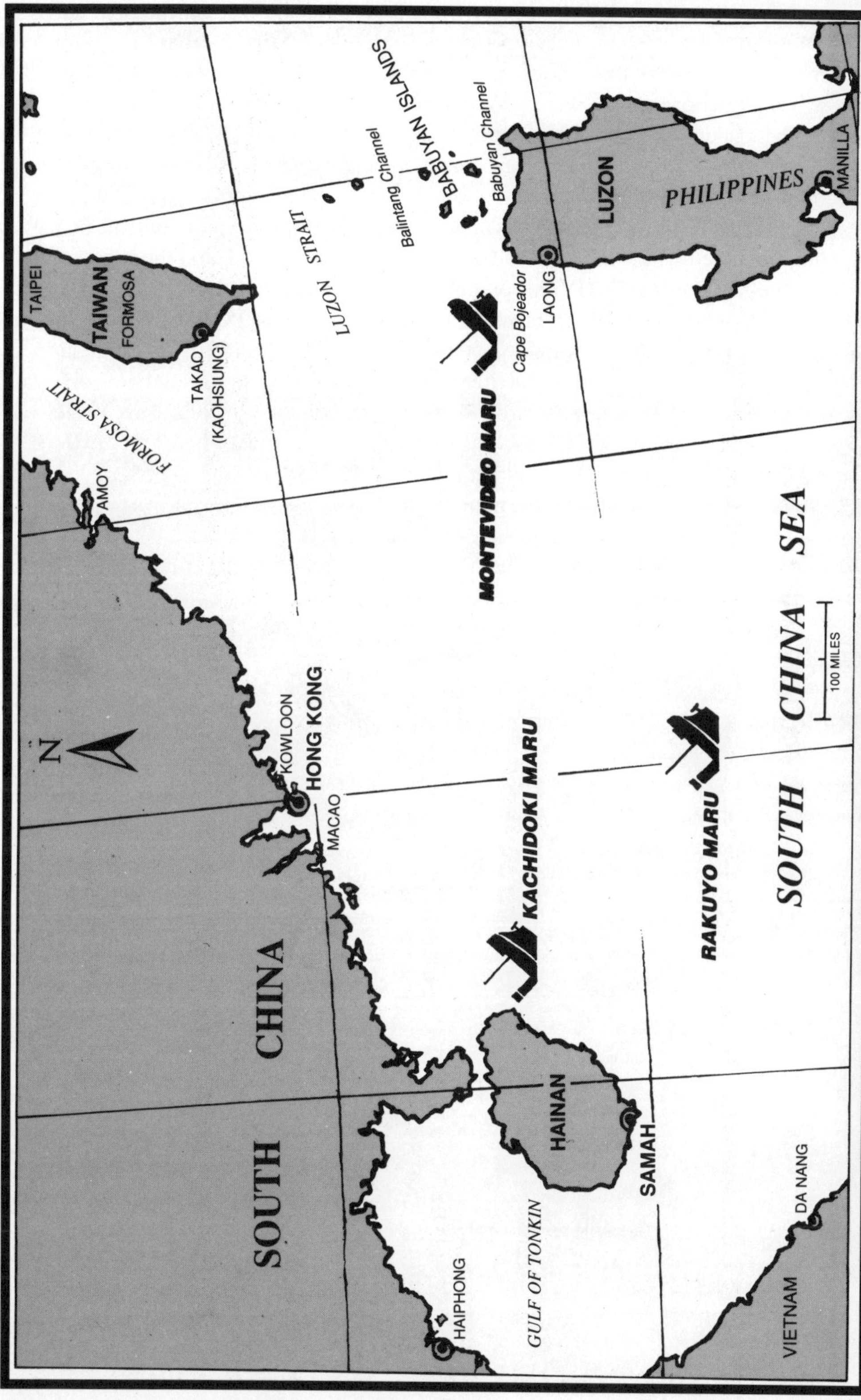
N
SOUTH CHINA
HONG KONG
KOWLOON
MACAO
AMOY
FORMOSA STRAIT
TAIWAN
FORMOSA
TAIPEI
TAKAO
(KAOHSIUNG)
LUZON STRAIT
Balintang Channel
BABUYAN ISLANDS
Babuyan Channel
Cape Bojeador
LAONG
LUZON
PHILIPPINES
MANILLA
MONTEVIDEO MARU
KACHIDOKI MARU
RAKUYO MARU
SOUTH CHINA SEA
100 MILES
HAINAN
SAMAH
GULF OF TONKIN
HAIPHONG
DA NANG
VIETNAM

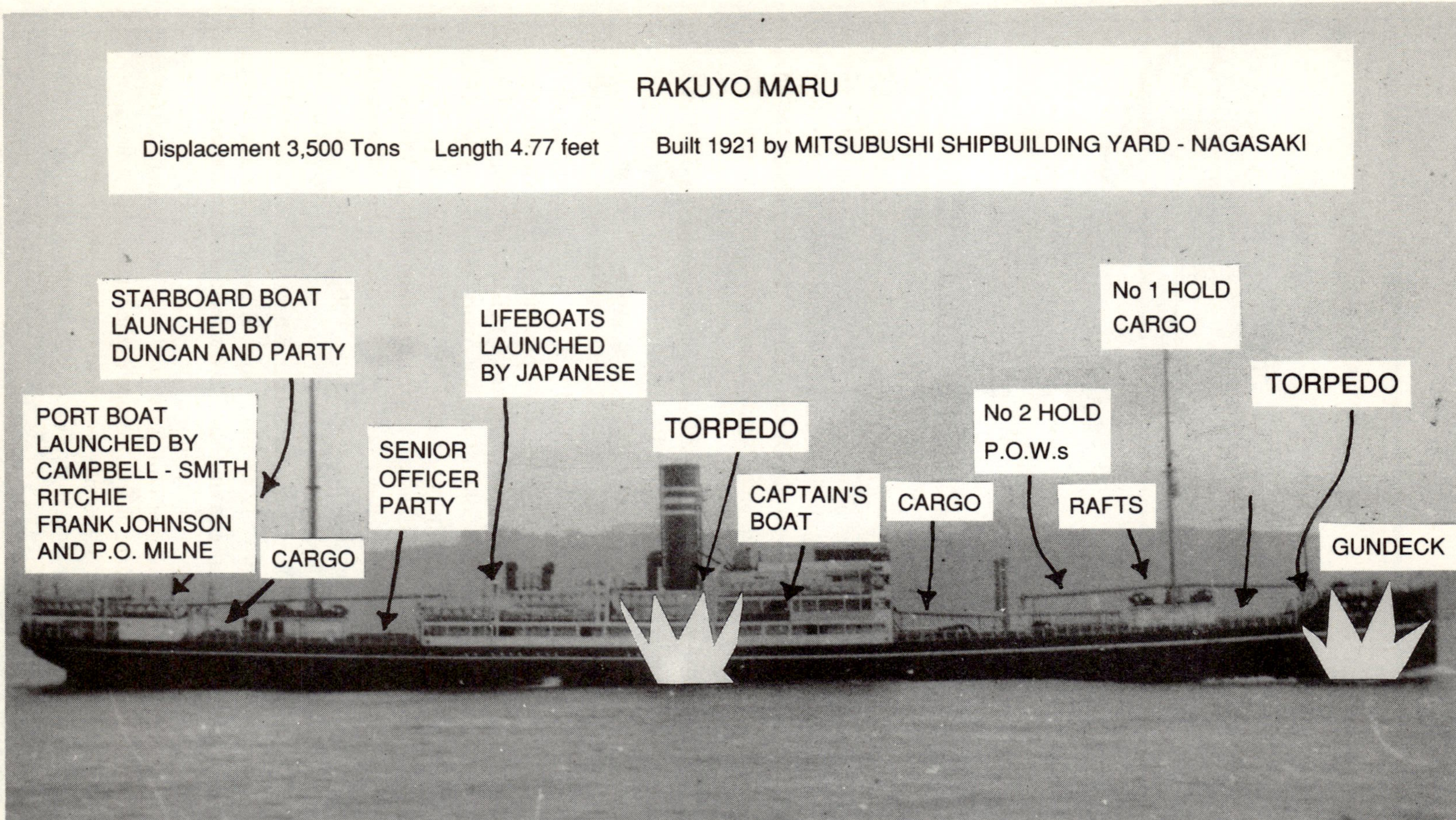

RAKUYO MARU Pic. – U.S. Navy.

SINGAPORE 1944

Back in Singapore it was about July 1944 when the Japan party at River Valley Road Camp first got wind of submarine activity close by; survivors from the S.S. VAN WAERWIJCK – an old Dutch steamer carrying about 1500 Dutch, British, and 49 Australians was sunk together with two tankers in the Malacca Straits.

A British officer, Major Campbell, was in charge of the draft under the command of a Japanese officer, Lt. Doi. Lt. Charles Baerertz, who was captured at Padang on 11 March 1942, stated there was no provision for the prisoners to escape in the event of the ship being torpedoed – no life-saving equipment was supplied and the only ventilation in the hold was by way of removing one hatch plank. in conformity with Japanese practice the prisoners were on reduced rations.

The survivors were picked up by a Japanese tanker and taken to Singapore.

According to Otto Cheal, one of the survivors, the convoy left Belowen near Medan in Northern Sumatra on 25 June 1944. The POWs were forced into the holds by way of rope ladders, there was standing room only and the heat made conditions unbearable. The only toilet facility was a bucket passed around. They remained in this hold, under dreadful conditions, until late in the day when the ship moved out and hove to just off shore.

They were escorted into Malacca Straits where they were joined by two tankers and several cargo ships. Early next morning two tankers and a transport were seen sunk, the transport carrying the POWs received two torpedo hits, she broke in two with the stern part lying on its side. Many of the POWs were able to escape, however there were approximately 200 men lost. Valiant efforts were made to save the sick who were unable to cope in the water.

Fred Norden was one of the survivors and he was taken, along with others, to Singapore and placed in the trans-shipment camp at River Valley Road. Suffering from malaria, he was later taken to Changi Gaol.

The news of the sinking of the ship in the Malacca Straits soon spread throughout the camp; the men worried about their chances and many left diaries and letters with mates remaining in Singapore to be passed on to their relatives.

The Japan Party remained nearby until early September, when they were ordered to prepare to move.

Bill Mayne: "The party of about 1,300 strong, four abreast, looked a very sad sight indeed as we marched down to the docks, with all our worldly possessions that we could carry. Some had packs, others had bags and others had their gear wrapped in a blanket rolled up like a swag. Along the streets Chinese and Malays eyed us enquiringly and with pity as some of the boys were still weak and unable to do a hike like that, we just ambled along without that vim and vigour that we had had."

Back in 1942, men marched from the same camp down the same road with military precision, whistling 'Colonel Bogey', and on full stomachs – at that time there was plenty to scrounge. Now the stragglers, weakened by their two years on the Burma Railway, were pushed along with rifle butts.

Bill Mayne: "After what seemed a long walk, was indeed about two miles, we arrived at the docks and to our surprise we found another bunch of troops, English, on the offside of the street.

"We were told we could sit down and smoke, but not allowed to move from our position or yarn with our fellow captives. After about three hours we were on the move again and the foremost of the party were moving up the gangplank of a dirty looking ship, the RAKUYO MARU. When we were about to climb the gangplank, we were instructed to pick up a bundle of rubber, it had a handle and shaped like an attache case, only much heavier of course.

"Our fellow captors helped us up the gangplank with their boots and rifles and directed us to a hold, told us to get down there and sit down. A few of us had designs of staying on deck, but the bloke with the rifle had been told to get us down below, he did a good job once more with his rifle butt.

"When we got down into the hold only one hatch cover was off, therefore the light was very bad and the air was foul. We eventually got all the hatch covers off and that was much better; underneath the decking a two-tier woodwork decking had been erected to accommodate the 1,300 men who were allotted to the ship.

"The hold appeared to be bursting with sweating bodies and still no sign of the end of the line, when our officers made enquiries as to how many were to be put down there the answer was, "Everybody must go below." The allotted space was 12 square feet 12 men, and that was for eating, movement, as well as sleeping.

"Captain Arthur Sumner had a talk with the Japs and explained that the men were fainting and some had diarrhoea; soon after the ship moved out to sea and anchored, they allowed 200 men up on deck. While all that was taking place the medical orderlies were hauling the sick chaps out of the hold with a rope tied around their middle and around their armpits. Men were fainting everywhere, we just had enough room to stand up, we could not move, perspiration flowed in rivulets down over bodies and the stench was fast becoming sickening.

"After permission to allow 200 men on deck at a time there was a much better feeling below because the 200 fluctuated up to 800 up on deck, but down below we still had that feeling of being trapped."

Sgt. Bill Cunneen was big enough and tough enough to control the kitchen in Burma, able to pick up with ease a four bushel bag of rice weighing 200 lbs. and, with a mate, carry half a 44 gallon drum of water up through the mud from the river to the cook house on the railway. He was without boots for two years and acquired the name, "Big Foot".

Everyone knew the cooks and those who worked in the kitchen because everyone watched them. Sick men needing building up were often allocated 'light duties' to get a bit of extra but strong men were needed to do the heavy work.

Now, coming on board the RAKUYO MARU, Sgt. Cunneen and his off-siders had control of the rations and the cooking arrangements. The English started complaining why the Australians got the good jobs. The Japanese stored rice and sugar in large bags around the Bridge to cushion and protect it from shelling; to placate the British a couple of their number joined Cunneen's staff and remained on deck.

C.P.O. Vic Duncan of HMAS PERTH was in charge of one group of 150 men: "We trooped up the gangway, along the upper deck and shuffled reluctantly into a dark doorway from where we made our way down a staircase which could be more felt than seen.

"As we moved into the light again we could see that we were in a hold which ran from side to side of the ship about 50 ft. and from the forward to the after end extended over a distance of about 60 ft. The deck-head (or ceiling as the land-lubber would call it) was seven feet six inches from the deck and was broken in the centre by an opening or hatch 24 feet by 18 feet, the walls of which rose a further four feet six inches making the hatch planks over this opening a full twelve feet from the deck on which we stood – much too high for a sudden exit if the necessity arose. The only other way out was back up the narrow staircase which would be out of the question with about 1300 men set on the same idea. It was obvious that the only solution was to devise a quick method of getting the men up through the hatch."

"Kitch" Loughnan: "The issue of food was a problem. The majority of the POWs were fed below decks, rice and sloppy, watery soup which was lowered in buckets down through the hatchway, on an average we received about three-quarters of a pannikin of very inferior rice per meal, twice daily, plus a little weak tea and watery stew. The waterbottles were filled once every two days and, due to the excessive heat and the fact that the rice and stew was cooked in seawater, the men were constantly calling for water. This was worsened by the fact that it was known that the Japanese guards, including Lt. Yamada, were using fresh water to bathe in. In spite of all this little, if any, provocation was given the Japanese guards to reprimand or punish any POWs. This was mainly because of the threat by Lt. Yamada and the ship's master to force all personnel, including the very sick, below decks should a number in excess of the number allowed by the Japanese attempt to remain on deck.

"At no time was the hold illuminated and the night was indeed a nightmare. We were forced to lie upon one another which meant that, if anyone did actually fall asleep through sheer exhaustion, he would invariably fall upon his neighbour who would be forced to waken him to obtain relief from the additional weight. It was impossible to see and consequently the diarrhoea cases, and there were many of them, who tried to get up to the latrines on deck were forced to tread all over their companions."

The chances of the RAKUYO MARU reaching Japan seemed slim. The Japanese at no time requested safe passage for any ships carrying POWs or internees. Brigadier Varley also felt the chances of reaching Japan were not good. When he visited Changi, on the pretence of receiving dental treatment, he was able to bury his Diary. Varley placed a number of sailors and soldiers who were former members of the Merchant Marine in position and rank in order they could assist the Army personnel in the event of having to abandon ship. One of these was Bob Collins of the HMAS PERTH.

On 6 September 1944 as Paul Summers, Commander of the USS PAMPANITO, one of the new submarines to come into service, was celebrating his 31st birthday in the China Sea, the convoy comprising the RAKUYO MARU, KACHIDOKI MARU, two other passenger cargo vessels, two fully loaded tankers, escorted by a 'Kamikazi' type destroyer, the SHIKINANI, and three frigate escorts, took up position in the convoy; overhead cover was provided by two float planes – the entire convoy proceeded north west. Changing position every seven minutes they used flags for communication during the day and at night they used red signals and the convoy would move into closer formation and increase speed.

Soon after leaving Singapore the POWs observed an incoming convoy from the southern oil fields, this convoy comprised several tankers escorted by a fleet destroyer and an aircraft carrier of an unusual design with a flat deck, no funnel visible and carrying several aircraft on deck. Most believed it was a converted passenger ship.

During the period 1943-44 U.S. submarines sank over 1¼ million tons of Japanese shipping. These heavy losses forced the Japanese to shorten their transportation routes and thus concentrated their shipping which made targets easier for U.S. submarines and shorter turn-around time for missions.

The Japanese were no longer able to ship adequate oil to maintain their war effort. The tankers were prime targets and these were usually placed in the centre of the convoys and shielded by merchants ships or ships carrying POWs.

The code-breakers were well informed on the movement of shipping and in most cases the cargo the freighters were carrying. It is reasonable to assume if Command knew a ship was carrying bauxite it would also have known it was carrying troops or POWs. It is unlikely SUBPACCOM would have disclosed this information to submarine Commanders. POWs were expended, their job was to sink ships – Admiral Lockwood was now introducing the pack policy of attacking enemy convoys. in August 1944 two packs were sent to the Luzon Straits. The first comprised Gene Fluckey in BARB, Elliott Loughlin in the new QUEENFISH and George Pierce in TUNNY.

Later, in August, the second pack comprising Ben Oakley in GROWLER, Paul Summers in PAMPANITO and Eli Reich in SEALION, reached their destination in Luzon Straits on 29 August 1944.

12 SEPTEMBER 1944 – SOUTH CHINA SEA

On the night of September 11-12, the convoy was proceeding northward in three columns, three ships to a column, the destroyer SHIKINANI leading the centre column and three small escort vessels protecting each flank.

"Ben's Busters" pack, comprising GROWLER, PAMPANITO and SEALION, moved 300 miles and took up position for the expected arrival of a north-bound convoy which ULTRA advised had left Singapore earlier on 6 September. Ben Oakey, the Pack Commander, was given the approximate position and in GROWLER he opened the attack at 2 a.m. by sinking the main escort vessel, the SHIKINANI. (Most POWs described this destroyer as a "cruiser"). This explosion woke the POWs.

PERTH sailor, Arthur Bancroft (known as "Blood" because of his red hair): "For half an hour the convoy zigzagged furiously and depth charges were dropped by the dozen. All men were hunted down below but there was no panic among the prisoners. As things quietened down the men wandered back on deck again and went off to sleep immediately."

Reg Harris: "Everyone burst out of the hold, Japanese were screaming and yelling and forced us back down the hold, however many remained on deck, including Duncan and Cunneen's groups."

By 5 a.m. the Americans attacked again, this time the SEALION fired six torpedoes at a tanker which burst into flames and lit up the whole area. Eli Reich had also hit another transport, NANKAI MARU. The POWs now realised they were sitting ducks –

"Kitch" Loughnan: "The blast was terrific and naturally most of us tried to get up on deck to see what had happened and, if necessary, to escape. We knew at the time that there was a great risk of being torpedoed. The Japanese and Korean guards, under instructions from Lt. Yamada, forced us back into the hold by beating us with the butt ends of their rifles, aiming blows at any portion of the body, whether it be the head, shoulders, shins or buttocks. A number of men were consequently injured in this manner and the guards threatened to shoot. It was quite light, although the night was dark the blaze from the escort gave enough light for us to see Lt. Yamada and his guards. We realised it was useless to attempt to stay on deck so we remained below until about two and a half hours later when two other explosions quite close to us occurred and then shortly after our own ship was torpedoed. This time there was no attempt to keep us below. By the time most of us had scrambled on to the deck the Japanese had disappeared over the sides of the ship into the lifeboats which they had lowered."

Arthur Bancroft: "At approximately 5.30 a.m. a tanker only a few hundred yards off our port bow blew up within a couple of minutes. At the same time another tanker was hit and she too exploded into flames. Our transport, which was on the tail-end of the convoy, was silhouetted beautifully against the two burning tankers. Screams from the Japs on the bridge heralded the approach of a torpedo from the starboard side. It struck a little abaft of amidships and shook the ship from stem to stern. A minute or two later another explosion rocked the ship as yet another torpedo found its mark. Water from the explosion poured over the ship and down the hold in which the prisoners were standing. It was not a very pleasant sensation. Luckily the second torpedo hit the already helpless ship right up in the bows and did very little damage except for a large gaping hole through the bows. The Jap gun crew fired three shots which were apparently timed as the captain of the gun had a watch in his hand, and as he raised his hand a shot was fired. The gun was trained on an after bearing on the port side but at no visible target. They then abandoned ship and the general opinion was that it was a distress signal."

PERTH C.P.O. Vic Duncan: "We expected to be torpedoed and expected to be sunk, so before we sailed a party of Army men from the 2/2 Pioneer Bn. we had first met in Java were trained in advance. The main object of the training was to get the men out of the hold quickly; when we first went aboard I measured up the hatch cover area and the intermediate deck and had a plan to put into operation."

Reg Harris: "I was with Bill Smith and we saw this torpedo coming for us and I remember saying, "This is ours!" and she hit right in the guts. It lifted the ship right up and plonked it down. It was pandemonium – the Japanese raced for the lifeboats – some said there were many sitting in the boats soon after the tanker was hit."

The first torpedo sent a great cascade of water to come over the ship and this caused a number of casualties among the POWs, as far as it was known, no one was washed overboard. Some panicked and jumped overboard.

Ross Smith: "I was on the hatch which was set up as the R.A.P., after the second torpedo hit the bow we were blown against the winches. Soon after Vic Duncan, assisted by 'Jock' Turnbull, one of three brothers who had met his other two brothers, ex-Middle East, after the sinking of the PERTH, took control and directed the men out of the hatch and how to abandon ship. I went over with ten other men soon after a raft was thrown over – Duncan had told us to get away from the ship. I had no life jacket and lost my water bottle and hat when the torpedo hit. There were eleven of us and it was not long before there were squabbles about taking it in turns to sit on the raft – some refused to do their stint in the water and not everyone could swim. The first day seemed endless."

The convoy was dispersed and with PAMPANITO and SEALION in pursuit.

Frank Farmer: "Eddie Anderson and I were sleeping on the lowest tier of one of the platforms surrounding the forward hold of the RAKUYO MARU. We lay naked, hip to hip, in complete darkness, in the thick fog, barely conscious of the drama unfolding above us. I remember checking the whereabouts of my few possessions, what little clothes I had, a straw hat, my carefully filled waterbottle, and a kapok lifejacket which had been issued when joining the ship, and mentally retracing the way out, the position of the ladder and ventilator shaft which earlier we had decided would be the quickest way out.

"I slept through the first explosion, so Eddie Anderson woke me with the news that a torpedo had struck the ship somewhere aft of where we lay. Eddie was already sitting up and minutes later a second torpedo struck the ship, this time forward of our position and sending a wave of water through the cargo deck below us. Men began scrambling on all fours towards the ladder where more men struggled to gain a footing. We sat in the dark assessing our situation, it was apparent the ship was not sinking because our sleeping platform was still on an even keel and there was no discernible rise of the water in the hold."

Bob Collins of HMAS PERTH: "I was instructing a group of men on how to prepare for abandoning ship when a Lieutenant ordered the men to abandon ship immediately. We had a stand-up row, the officer insisted the men jump; I told him it was too soon to make that judgement as the ship was steady on the water, there was no sign it was going to sink quickly. I told the officer the less time the men spent in the water the better. The officer insisted and this caused a lot of men to jump unprepared – "As a commissioned officer I'm ordering you to carry out my orders!" "Look Sir, I've been sunk before!"

"After the destroyer was sunk in the early hours we knew the submarine was still about and would be manoeuvring for a better shot at the prime target – that came when the tanker was hit and it was just a matter of minutes before we got it.

"One of my men pinched my life jacket which was clearly marked in a cross with red lead. The man later admitted he had stolen it and explained he was married with a family.

"At the time one of the Cobon twins, John, was on deck and I said to him, "Stay with me" and he replied, "No, I've got to find Burke." They were a couple of terrific fellows, the only way I could identify the difference between them was that John had a mother-of-pearl face on his wristwatch.

"When I left the ship I went over with the Cobon brothers without a life jacket. Later on a raft a couple of English blokes asked for a sip from my water-bottle – they drank the lot!"

Noel Day, No.l Squadron R.A.A.F., came from Byrock, N.S.W. A man of the Outback, hard worker, competent and able to look after himself, possessing country integrity – when you nod at a Sale your reputation goes with the nod.

For some unknown reason he and Bob Collins of HMAS PERTH hated one another's guts, until one dark night up in the Burma jungle Collins had a small fire going and was boiling up some burnt rice scrapings from the kwali for 'coffee'. It looked like coffee but still tasted like burnt rice, but up on the line it was 'Coffee'. A bloke approached the fire, Collins, without looking up said, "Care for a cup of coffee?" "Sure", said Day. After a couple of sips, Day said, "You're not a bad sort of bastard." They yarned for a while; Day was without boots and a Pommie had died, his size was right but Day had no money. Collins said, "I'll lend you the $3." and Day replied, "I'll pay you back some time when I can."

Gnrs. Burke and John Cobon, Crows Nest, Qld. Twins, aged 26.
Last seen 12.09.44.
Pic: Sister, Mrs. McLaughlin.

Now, Collins, swimming around looking for something to hang on to, saw Day appear on a hatch plank about 2'6" x 8' long – there was a rush to grab the plank but Day held them off, he said, "I'll take Collins." Later he asked him why he took him and Day said, "Don't you remember the $3. you loaned me?"

Cliff Farlow was with Geoff Millard, hanging on to the winch under the cascading water: "The Japs panicked and tried to get us down the hold – then the other torpedo hit her right in the bows – you could feel it going. The Japs were running for the lifeboats while we took the covers off the hatch and put them down the hold to enable the men to climb out. We pulled everyone out – there was a dark-haired bloke by the name of McNamara, with an injured leg – but no one was killed."

Tom Moxham and his brother, Harry, were on the ship. Tom had met up with Harry at Saigon and became separated during the morning. Another brother, Bill, was to be one of the six survivors from the 2,500 lost on the death marches in Borneo. They belonged to a family of pastoralists – their father had them all placed on station properties and when war broke out he was preparing to put them on their own properties. They were all able and experienced survivors. Earlier, when the Japanese Captain of the RAKUYO MARU left the ship, Tom reckoned his best chance of survival would be with the Captain so he followed him down the rope to a small boat tied up below. He observed it was well loaded with supplies – Tommy decided it would do him! He took the officer's sword, cut the boat

Left: Brigadier Arthur Varley, M.C. Mentioned in Despatches. Inverell NSW
Right: Captain Arthur Sumner, Mentioned in Despatches. Geelong, Vic.
Pic: Austin Ellerman.

free and tossed the Captain overboard and drowned him. Tom later had second thoughts about staying on the boat – "The Japanese will want to know what happened to the Captain", he said, "they probably will bump me off!"

Captain Arthur Sumner was injured when the first torpedo hit the ship and created the water cascade over the deck; despite this injury to the face he continued to assist the men in getting rafts overboard and telling the men how to jump. As the men floated around Sumner used much of his energy endeavouring to keep them together, particularly those who were ill and suffering from the effects of depth charging. Bill Cunneen met him in the water during the morning and found he was depressed because of a broken jaw – he thought he had let his men down because of his injury.

Wal Williams was sleeping on rafts on the deck when the first torpedo hit: "The torrent of water washed us off the rafts and over the winches and we finished up on the bulkhead where the Bridge had been."

While the men were throwing rafts and hatch boards over the side, Williams said to his mate Max Campbell of HMAS PERTH: "What do you think Max, do you think we should leave yet?" He replied: " I don't think we should leave yet, I've got a feeling she won't go down for a while." So they hung about and watched most of the men go over the side. Campbell advised not to put the life jacket on until you're in the water, it might break your neck. Both Campbell and Williams were good swimmers and members of the Northbridge Swimming Club, they had met up with each other on the Railway when members of the PERTH came up from Java.

Frank McGovern had been sunk before on the PERTH: "The first torpedo just missed the hold where all the Australians were held. When the second torpedo slammed into the ship only seconds later debris was blown all over the ship and many of our men were injured, but as far as it is known, no one was killed.

"My mate, Gerry Parkes, was down in the hold so I went over to the hold and by this time we were getting the hatch covers down and the blokes were coming up on their bare feet and I straddled an iron beam going across the hold – the one that carried the hatch covers – and Gerry Parkes down below was yelling out, "Get off there you silly bugger!" but I said, "She's right mate!" We got them all up from there and Gerry and I said, "What are we going to do?" – the ship didn't seem to be going down too quickly and it was pretty level because it seemed the rubber ingots we loaded at Singapore were keeping it afloat – so we decided to scrounge around again, like most blokes; down to the galley looking for some food but it was half full of water and we didn't get much. We came up on deck and saw a couple of dead Japs there, then up on to the next deck then up on to the Bridge, it was getting a bit light by this time and we pulled a couple of charts from the Wheel- house. I grabbed two charts, one of them I thought might be able to help us and the other one I used as toilet paper in the corner of the Bridge, that gave me a bit of satisfaction! We started to wander down aft and saw a lot of our fellows."

Jack Flynn: "The Japs in their panic lowered themselves away in the lifeboats, leaving us to fend for ourselves. Our Major Chalmers addressed us and he said "Well, men, we are free. But it's a doubtful kind of freedom. It's going to be pretty tough, and I'm sure you all realise the position is grim. Throw everything overboard that will float, and swim out clear of the ship or she will suck you down when she sinks – which won't be long now. Good luck!"

Bill McKitterick: When I jumped there was a raft about 20 ft. away and I managed to get to it. There were two men on it, I learned later one was Norm Nutley. I asked them if I could come on the raft, they replied, "You can't come on!" I said, "Well I can't swim!" and Nutley said, "Well you better get on!"

"I knew the danger of a sinking ship, the only light came from the flames of the burning tanker which used to flare up occasionally; we had no means of propelling the raft other than our hands, the flames seemed to be creeping across the water. By daylight we were some distance from the ship and had become separated from a lot of the men who left the ship about the same time. We managed to tie on to a refrigerator door with an opening handle on it.

"Over the water came a group who were singing the "Recessional" – "Oh God Our Help" etc. etc., and "Abide With Me" and I thought to myself that won't help us at this stage! and it could have a depressing effect on the men.

"Present was John Hunt, a lifesaver from Clovelly, a tall, strapping, handsome bloke, skipping around on a plank like a surf ski, didn't seem to have a care in the world. Nearby was another mate, Jack Skene, they said, "Come and join us" but I just settled with what I had, I knew if I left it I was a goner. Jack was worried about his family of six."

John Langley: "I was down the hold when the first torpedo hit and a great cascade of water came over the hold. I must have been knocked out as when I came to I was alone. I found a rope and climbed up on the deck where I found Sgt. Moynihan organising a raft. He said, "What are you going to do "Butch"?" and I said, "I've never been in this situation before!" Moynihan said, "Well you better throw that roll of bamboo over and jump and hang on to it." I jumped and caught the bamboo roll and drifted away from the ship.

"Soon after the depth charges commenced (this would be about 7 a.m.) and every time a charge went off it was like a terrific kick in the stomach – you vomited and your bowels opened and that went on for some time. You get a tingle down the spine – it was horrific. I felt like screaming when this happened. I just hung on to the bamboo raft feeling very depressed.

"Nearby was a large group of rafts tied together, with a Japanese officer sitting on the high point of the raft. One of my mates said he was their insurance – the best hope of being rescued."

Claude Longey: "Some of the men went back onto the boat and took a large manilla rope that had held the latrines on the side of the ship and with it they tied the rafts together.

"There were a lot of rafts tied together and they veered and jammed my legs, so I asked if any one had a knife and I cut nine free, then I said who was coming with me on the rafts – about forty men joined me. If we saw any pieces of board we swam and picked them up, anything like hatch planks we pushed them under the rafts to get them higher out of the water. At night we sat back to back on the rafts to try and keep each other out of the water."

Norm Nutley: "I spoke to my mate Harry Hodgson who was ill with malaria and dysentery, he was with the sick gathered together with Capt. Richards on the night before we were torpedoed – he was too sick to eat his meal so he gave it to me. After the torpedoing I asked him to come with me and he replied he was too crook and would go down with the ship. (He remained on board and was recovered with the Duncan boat).

Doug "Tony" Mayer and his mate Bernie Davies, VX.30002 of Coburg, Victoria, were in the hold and managed to climb out on large rope netting someone had dropped down: "We went over the side fairly early and swam round, Bernie was a small bloke and not a good swimmer. We caught a box floating by and Bernie was able to get on it. The depth charging had weakened everybody who was in the water at the time. Bernie later slipped off the box and drowned."

Reg Harris: "We met one senior officer and he said, "Hop up on top and throw off anything that will float." So we went up on top and threw off anything

Left: Spr. Andrew John Skene, Woy Woy, NSW. Father of six. Lost 14.09.44.
Pic: Betty Carter
Right: Cpl. Joseph Sargent, West Ryde, NSW
Last message to his two small girls - "Give the little darlings a kiss."

that would float – old Carley rafts and things – I met the guard I had had an argument with and I reckoned I'd throw him overboard but I didn't have time. I thought we were sinking fast but nobody could have foreseen she would stay afloat so long. Lt. Les Stupart said, "The C.O. said every man for himself!" so I jumped over the side and I went down and down – I didn't think I was ever going to come up but we must have been higher out of the water than I thought, it took so long, but when I came up to the air the surface of the water was burning from the spillage from the oil tankers. But we got round that and Miscamble and I grabbed a raft and we tied together with Charles McKechnie on his raft. I had a waterbottle, an old green coat and a pair of shorts and a life jacket. I gave the waterbottle to a Pommy to hold but he dropped it – someone else said he drank it and then dropped it.

"We wanted to get away from the burning oil so we swam and pulled the rafts – there were a few who couldn't swim so they just sat on the raft. Then we got the oregon planks from the hatch covers, spread them out and tied them down, one man picked up a rope ladder which we unravelled and used for lashing – and we were going to paddle to China – we didn't know which way though!"

Frank Jesse: "With Jack Turner and Dave Flinn I jumped into the water. Although the ship did not appear to be sinking at this stage we paddled as fast and as far away as we could. The shock waves from the depth charges from the Japanese destroyers could be felt in the water even though we were some distance away. Most of us were vomiting.

"Owing to the crowding of the rafts I straddled a plank for the first two days, my legs became lacerated from the rough board. We were in groups of approximately 100 but had to spread out to avoid injuries due to the boards smashing into the men's bodies when the sea was rough. We were covered with oil which saved us from shark attacks, although the fear was ever present.

"On the afternoon of the first day we drifted away from the RAKUYO MARU, close enough to watch it sink. I was told some men had returned on board for supplies before the sinking. I helped to return men to the rafts, many were affected through drinking seawater, it proved to be a hopeless task.

"By the third day ample room became available on the rafts due to men disappearing. The rafts became waterlogged and were always under water level."

Harry Weigand: "Lots of men were going over the side. There was a great crowd forward so I decided to go aft and go over the side from there. Then before I went I remembered my wife and boy's photo which was in my pack tied to one of the derricks. I rushed back to get their photos, saying to myself, "Chicko, you and Bill will bring me luck", and then I made aft. By this time the decks in the alley way were 2 feet under water, I waded aft to the galley and had my final drink of water before going over the side. Believe me, it gives one a very lonely feeling when you go over the side and leave the ship behind. I swam out to a raft and climbed aboard, there was plenty of rafts in the water and timber of all descriptions to hang on to. These rafts were just flat pieces of timber nailed together, about 7 ft. x 4 ft. x 1 ft., with ropes all around to hang on to. Four men could sit on them comfortably and they would float. In no time there was nine men on our raft and it settled down about a foot under the water."

John Hocking: "After we were hit by two torpedoes at 5.30 am, a fellow 2/2 Pioneer, Hec Matthews, and I made sure there were no POWs left behind in the forward hold where the majority of the POWs were housed. We arrived topside about 6 a.m. and looked about for anything that would help us keep afloat when we had to get into the water.

"The ship listed to port at 6.30 a.m. Hec and I looked at each other, tossed two hatch covers overboard and joined them. My wristwatch, not waterproof, stopped at 6.30 a.m. On board my hatch cover I found I was drifting back toward a burning oil tanker, I paddled around the stern of the RAKUYO MARU, down the starboard side and joined a number of POWs.

"After jumping into the water I never saw Hec Matthews for some years. He was eventually picked up by the Japanese and taken to Japan where he was recovered in September 1945.

"I stayed with the group who had one of the ship's rafts. On the first night there must have been a couple of dozen of us sitting on and clinging to the side of the raft; taking it in turns to sit on or cling. By morning the numbers had decreased, apparently some had weakness through illness, had had enough and drifted off to a lonely grave.

"I had seen an officer drinking seawater and his condition deteriorated swiftly. lt was this incident that remained with me for the 3½ days before rescue, and I made certain I only sipped enough seawater to moisten the mouth, and to swallow as little as possible."

Ross Dunbar, Ernie Wade and his brother John, Bert Wall, Titch Lemin and the injured Cpl. Richards were together and hanging on to the raft when Dunbar and Ernie Wade decided to return to the ship during the day to see if they could scrounge some food and water. lt was a long swim of about 1½ miles but once back on board they were rewarded by finding some food, water and cigarettes. They returned to the raft where they all enjoyed a cigarette or two. Everyone was very optimistic despite suffering from the effects of the depth charging.

Reg Stewart, better known as "Jungle", remained on the ship with Vic Duncan. He was so impressed by the way Duncan took charge and directed what should be done in the event of the ship being torpedoed: "When the Japs were leaving the ship I remember seeing Frank McGrath, 2/2 Pioneers, belting them as they came down from the bridge." Up on the Burma Line Frank McGrath had been bashed by a Jap guard who had had to stand on a box so he could reach McGrath and after that bashing he vowed to his mates "he'd get square with them". As Stewart went overboard McGrath was seen still bashing the Japs.

In the water Stewart lost contact with his mates Jack Baguley and F.B.T. "Jock" Ryan – the currents were strong and unpredictable – the first night he drifted into the oil slick and was still in it at daybreak. "During the night we were cov-

Dvr. Henry Thomas Hounsell, NX.72064. Urana, NSW. Aged 36.
Dvr. Arthur James Hounsell, NX.72062. Wagga Wagga, NSW. Aged 36.
Pic: Keith Hounsell.

ered in thick oil and as soon as the sun came up the oil melted in the heat and got into our eyes, we had to keep our eyes closed, we had nothing to clean our eyes with.

"We could see sharks beyond the oil slick but they wouldn't come into the oil. At night we lay on our backs, looked at the stars and wondered and dreamt of home. Some would say, "I'm going to have a coffee over the road" and they would just float off.

"The continual "pit-pat" of the water lapping against my stomach irritated me more than anything, to be able to get out of the water was a great relief."

Les Bolger: "It was dark when Captain Sumner ordered men to abandon ship, there was no panic, men were throwing rafts over then so many would jump, I jumped with my mate, Bill Scarpella, a big strong fellow of Italian descent. During the jump I lost my hat and I grabbed a raft which I was to remain on for four days.

"It was just daybreak when a Japanese escort vessel which was picking up survivors from a blazing tanker was hit by a torpedo and exploded. Other escorts commenced dropping depth charges, which was one of the worst experiences I have ever endured – it was like being hit in the stomach with a sledgehammer. It weakened everybody considerably, causing vomiting and diarrhoea.

"There were fifteen on our raft, we were close by when the Japanese picked up their own survivors, they told us we could stay there and die, the men in the water responded by singing 'Rule Brittania'."

Charles McKechnie: "Not being sailors we didn't know when it was going to sink so we thought we'll get out of here before she starts to go down and take us with her. I had one of those kapok life-jackets on, a green Dutch hat and an old shirt and a pair of shorts. I was not a good swimmer, after we had clung to the ladder for a while Clarrie decided to go back to the boat – I didn't see him again." (Unbeknown to either of the men they both were picked up.) "After a few hours on my own clinging to the bamboo a raft floated near and I got over to it and there was Reg Harris, Ron Miscamble, Reg Stewart, Bill Cunneen, Frank Holcroft and Alex Petherbridge off the HMAS PERTH."

Roy Cornford: "I was with Glen Gollan, Darcy Lynch, Norm Calvert and Pat Linnane and we went looking for water and headgear, so Glen Darcy and Norm minded a raft while Pat and I went looking. By this time everyone had jumped into the sea from our end of the ship. We met others looking for food and water, we filled our waterbottles and went back to the raft where we all had a bellyful of water. We then tossed our raft over as the ship was listing badly; all the other rafts had paddled or drifted away from the ship. You could hear men singing out, "What's it like to be free!!" Claude Longey and an English bloke joined us so we all jumped over. We had not been in the water long when a Jap Naval vessel came back towards us blinking lights flashing when there was an explosion, either it got sunk or depth charges going off but was that close it made us sick from the explosion as we were in the water, we could not get on the raft, so we lost all the water we had drunk."

Frank Farmer: "It was now dawn and the ship's decks were almost deserted. Odd POWs scrounged for food and water or looked for any crew or guards left behind. The ship was steady on an even keel and it was clear to us that for the moment she was the best place to be. But our fellow POWs had already cast themselves on the mercy of the sea so we set about throwing anything and everything that would float or give support to men in the water. We tore off the tarpaulins covering the hatches and threw overboard the heavy wooden planks beneath them. There were stacks of square wooden rafts which we also threw over. Aft, a couple of life-boats dangled from their davits but they were too heavy for us to move.

"We were suddenly alerted by a cry of "She is sinking aft!" Looking back we should have perhaps checked the warning cry but afraid of being sucked down with the ship we made a hasty departure over the side. Eddie and I found a couple of planks to support us. The ship drifted slowly away and to our discomfiture remained very much afloat."

At about 7 a.m. most of the men were in the water and one group had drifted towards the burning tanker – within several hundred yards Japanese escorts were picking up their own survivors – one escort was still in the water. The USS GROWLER, which had returned to the scene, selected the escort, fired, and the HIRADO immediately blew up.

Tom Moxham observed the group of rafts and many men hanging on to them. "One moment they were there, next minute there was no one hanging on to the rafts." The explosion had a devastating effect on the men; then the other Japanese escort commenced depth charging to locate the submarine. Max Campbell advised Wal Williams: "Get on your back, it won't have such a bad effect."

Ron Miscamble suffered from the depth charging, he said Reg Harris, his best mate, supported him for four or five hours. Tony Clive's father had always advised him to get as far away from a sinking ship as possible so he left the ship on the port side soon after the hatch boards were thrown over. As an experienced surfboard rider, with three others, he paddled one of these boards measuring 18 ft. x 2 ft., well clear of the ship; there were people milling around in the water and hanging on to debris. Suffering from an injured arm which he received when the first torpedo struck the ship, he asked a medical orderly to look at his arm, he said it was okay.

Once feeling secure away from the ship the men started calling for their mates and grouping together; there was a feeling of exhiliration according to Charlie McKechnie: "We were free – we had no water with us – nothing to eat – the only clothes I possessed I was wearing – but we were free! We were no longer POWs, the Japanese had abandoned us!"

However, those who drifted towards the burning tanker found the time on the water frightening. Harry Weigand wrote: "There were clusters of rafts everywhere, our raft joined up with about ten more rafts. We tied them all together, the current was drifting us down on to the burning ships and burning oil floating away from the ships. The next few hours was very hard work for everyone, using pieces of wood as paddles we rowed for our life to keep away from burning oil. There was plenty of Japs on rafts with our boys and one Jap officer had all his clothes, boots, spurs, sword strapped up his back, he was sitting there with the fear of the water on his face. The Japs that were in the lifeboats kept about a mile away from us all the while, I think that they were frightened of us taking the lifeboats from them."

Reg Harris: "After the Japanese left the ship and those who realised the ship was not going to sink quickly, collected the lifebuoys and threw them over and hatch boards and then jumped.

"Fred Mills didn't know he could swim until he hit the water. We were all milling around in the water when Bdr. Rex Standen (NX.52286 of Abbotsford, NSW) yelled out an order to get some organisation into the group. There was a count made of this group of 164. Mates joined mates – at this time everyone seemed optimistic but many were feeling the effects of the HIRADO blowing up and the subsequent depth charging."

Frank Lawrence: "Sgt. Moynihan did a great job exhorting the men in the holds not to panic and make it easier for the men to get off the ship. My mate, Sgt. Arthur Wright from 2/18 Bn., scrounged a couple of life jackets and said "we should not get off the ship until she had lost way". Arthur had been in the Merchant Navy in England before the war and I believe his knowledge of the sea saved both our lives. We were the last of the POWs to leave, we found a float about 3 ft. square, threw it over then jumped into the water. Not long after we got off we saw one of the escorts torpedoed and it just seemed to disintegrate. We floated around, paddling to keep us as near the ship as possible, often people hung on to our raft and when they saw any of their friends they'd join them."

Lloyd "Darby" Munro, one of the younger members of the HMAS PERTH, left the ship early – there were so many who appeared afraid to jump that he jumped to demonstrate to them there was nothing to it.

He joined a large group hanging on to a raft and went with the current. The oil caused considerable pain and discomfort and greatly affected the will to survive. Those whose eyes were not damaged found the oil insulated them from the hot sun and acted as a shark deterrent against them – the sharks could be seen out on the fringe of the oil slick.

Bill Mayne: "Boats were being lowered right beside us but the Japs would not allow any POWs to get aboard. Harold Ramsay, my mate, suggested we go aft but I asked what would be the use, the boats would be the same there as where we were, so we held fast for a moment until we noticed a small flat bottomed skiff, a craft that is used by the Japs to scull between ships and shore whilst in port.

"This particular skiff was about 8 ft. long with 3½ ft. beam and was manned by two Jap Army officers, so Harold and I went over the side and swam to the side of this craft and climbed aboard. The officers did not object to us getting aboard. Several of our mates tried to clamber on but the officers did not want any more, we had about six inches freeboard then, we helped our mates aboard and by this time we had drifted quite a distance from the ship.

"While we were busy preparing to leave the ship the submarines were still in the area. It was not until we were in this small skiff did we realise the havoc being made with the rest of the convoy. We felt the percussions right through the water when an escort was sunk and from near and far could be heard explosions and screams of men who were either about to drown or those aboard the burning oil tanker.

"Our craft was drifting toward this particular oil tanker which was aflame from bow to stern. We could distinguish the Japanese crew running about or sometimes blown off by exploding drums of oil. It was an unpleasant sight to watch, as we were slowly drifting nearer. The oil from this tanker was spreading at a great rate and I believe this is why the English boys were so choked up with oil in their lungs; we could hear the screams of the men trapped in the burning oil, some of our lads jumped before we did, with nothing to hang on to, could have drifted towards the burning tanker.

"The Japanese officers of our craft were alarmed at our drift towards this tanker, because in their eagerness to get the boat under control and underway one lashed his sword to the oar and tried to scull, but that was impossible, the number

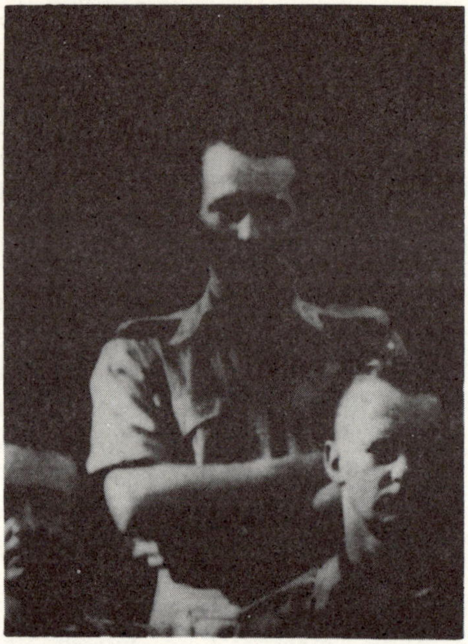

Sgt. Frank Tome, NX.32743. Inverell, NSW. Lost 12.09.44. His brother, Cpl. Mark Tome, was drowned the following day.
Right: Sgt. Stanley Claude Melbourne Du Ross, NX.24909. Manly, NSW. Lost 12.09.44. Pics: 2/30 Bn. Assn.

we had aboard for the size of the craft left barely room to crouch. About this time we were very close to the burning tanker, apparently the screams of their fellow men did not appeal to the Nip officers – one of them stood up and stepped over the side of the boat. He had full uniform on, sword, kneeboots and no lifejacket, that movement caused the boat to upset and of course turn completely over, but all our boys got hold of it some way or another. Not one of us knew what happened to the other officer, he did not come to the surface.

"Some of the lads could not swim so I suggested we cling to the boat and try to push it towards the RAKUYO MARU as it had not sunk yet. We managed to get the boat to within 50 yards of the side of the ship but could get no further, try as we did, the swirl from the bow caused a strong current.

"Leaving the rest to fend for themselves, Harold Ramsay and I swam the remaining distance and climbed up the Jacobs ladder which was conveniently slung over the side. On deck we found several of our lads endeavouring to hoist a boat over the starboard side, and another group, under directions of our officers, throwing rafts, hatch covers and anything that would support a body, over the side, then jumping over themselves trying to clamber on these supports.

"Owing to our previous experience, my mate and I were not very keen on the idea of the planking, so we set to with several more under the direction of Petty Officer Vic Duncan to launch a boat."

Norman "Shorty" Calvert: "I was with my good friend Bill Jinks who helped me as a POW, and he said, "Don't panic, we will be okay". Most of the men had gone overboard when we jumped into the sea. We both jumped at the same time, it seemed to take a long time before we came back up to surface.

"The initial exultation at being free at last – afloat in an oil slicked sea – soon gave way to a desperate struggle as thirst and hunger took its toll. Our water-bottles were from World War I and only had a cork stopper, these became contaminated by seawater.

"Bill and I joined a crew that had bound two rafts together, which made a party of thirteen. Some of the men were very sick, vomiting, one had malaria. Bill had gone to No.l raft to help out the sick and asked me to help out on raft No.2."

Arthur "Blood" Bancroft, H.L. "Lofty" Nagle, and Edward Clark, known as "Marcus", were inseparable up to the time of selection for the Japan Party – Clark was left behind. Bancroft and Nagle, both seaman from the PERTH, made a pact that they would stick together come what may. The burning ships provided the only light, not enough to see what you were throwing overboard or light enough to recognise your mates.

Arthur Bancroft: "Irrespective of orders from others we had decided to leave the ship after assisting all the men from the hold, she seemed to be drifting towards the burning tankers so we jumped over the port side. Because of the sound of the water pouring through the bow we didn't think it would last long. We hit the water about an hour after the explosion, just about the time it was starting to get light, and got on to planks that we had thrown over. I was dressed in Dutch shorts, jacket and carried a Dutch waterbottle I had exchanged for a tin of milk in Burma. We hung on to the plank and when light came the Japanese escorts were still around dropping depth charges – you could see all the percussion of them through the water. We did see one Jap destroyer signalling away to another one and up she went with a bang (HIRADO) so the submarine got that one but up till that stage everybody was just drifting in one great big pack, hanging on to what was available including the latrines which had been thrown over the side; we had one Jap officer in our midst, everybody was wondering whether we were going to drown him or what to do with him but with the Jap destroyers whizzing around we considered he might be a very good life-saver – so we got him to stand up and signal to the Jap destroyer, which he did, and the destroyer came over and dropped a boat – rowed over – held us off – took him and they went back. That was the time when I thought we might have bought it because after they picked up the Jap officer the destroyer took off and did a great big sweep and came steaming back towards us. You've all heard those stories of dropping depth charges amongst survivors – it looked very suspicious but as they got within a few hundred yards of us they just veered away. They were just cat-calling and yelling out from the destroyer, so we gave back just as good as we got – "You'll get yours you yella bastard!" – things like that – and we started singing 'Rule Brittania'."

Norm Nutley remembers: "Someone yelled out, "You dirty rotten yellow bastards – you don't appreciate good workers when you have them!".

Bob Farrands: "An empty cargo ship came in and they put out their motor launches and came round looking for their own. I remember Kevin Altshuler (Sgt. Evsick Altshuler, NX.38958), a Jewish boy, studious type of bloke, not really robust, he spoke some Japanese, and they had this Jap on their raft and we said, "Drown the bastard drown him!" and he said, "No, he'll get us home in a boat" – and they came over and picked him off the raft and just left the others. They just took their own out of it and left us – the Japs offered us cigarettes but we had no matches."

Bill McKitterick: "Later the Jap escort came round and started picking up survivors, some of my mates swam towards the Japs hoping to be picked up and called out to me, "Come on over!" but I said, "No – I can't leave the raft, I'11 stay here". He remained alone all night, a rough night of despair, hanging on to the ring of the door of a refrigerator.

Arthur Bancroft: "It was by midday before the sea seemed to be clear of vessels, there seemed to be merchantmen coming across the horizon but then was diverted somewhere and by early afternoon the sea was absent of all ships and clear – with all these heads bobbing around.

"Hard to tell how many drowned that day, we saw bodies floating past for a lot had swallowed the oil – very thick oil – which was in our eyes and throats and everywhere, we had to be careful not to swallow it.

"About midday my mate "Lofty" said, "Hey – how's that water bottle going Blood?" and I said, "She's still here Lofty" and he said "What about a little sip?" so I said, "Okay, we'll have a little sip each." So I took a sip and handed it to him – and it was all covered in oil and it slipped out of his hand – so I lost the water-bottle on the first day. All my planning did not achieve much with the waterbottle.

"The situation became worse by men drinking seawater and going off their minds a little. I got to know very well four Army fellows in the Camp, Jack Lihou and Bill Smith from Queensland, Jack Pearson from Sydney and Lindsay Nunan. They said to me, "You're the sailor, so where's the nearest land?" and I said, "Well, we joined the convoy in the Philippines so I suppose that's the nearest." and they said, "Well let's start heading for the Philippines, it's better than doing nothing." I said to Lofty, "Which way is the Philippines?" and he said, "lt should be over that way". I said to Lofty, "We're going to break away from this big group, come with us – we'll gather a few rafts and off we'll go." He was sitting up to his waist in water on one of those big rafts and he said, "I'm right, I'm okay here" so I said, "Well I'm going and I don't want to leave you but it's your decision." "No", he said, "you go Blood, I'll be right." So that's where Lofty and I parted, it was just by good luck I made that decision for if he'd come with us he would have been alright. He didn't make it.

"We picked up one of the smaller rafts and started pushing it away, there was a lot of debris floating by and we picked up bits and we joined them together, then we tried to lift one on top of the other to get out of the water but with the oil it would slip off so we gave that away."

John Langley: "I kept on drifting alone. During the afternoon one fellow came paddling up and said, "Do you mind if I have a rest?" I replied, "No, you're welcome." It was good to talk to someone; this fellow said, "I'm swimming back to the ship, do you want to come?" – "No – I couldn't swim that far", looking at the ship on the horizon. He was a young fellow, I was 35 then, anyway, he swam off. I continued drifting then Bill Webb came by, he was believed to be about 50 years old – an old man – and he said, "Do you mind if I have a rest?" and I replied "You're welcome". He asked me why I didn't come back to the ship with him and I thought if this old bloke can do it I should be able to, so I said,"I'll give it a go!" – well, I was flat out keeping up with him!

"We arrived back on the ship late afternoon, scrounged through the cabins, found waterbottles and a raft and got back in the water. It was not long after that the RAKUYO MARU sank stern first, the huge hole in her bow was evident as she went down with the sounds of a dying ship."

Wal Williams: "The ship must have been a good mile away by this time and Max Campbell said, "We may as well go back to the ship and get out of the water. There was one young bloke – I was only young myself! – and he said he would come back with but he was not sure of the swimming. Max and I were good swimmers so we said we would stick with him and if he does what we tell him he would be right, we would get him back to the ship. The three of us got back to the ship and climbed up the Jacob's ladder, there were blokes on the ship that had never been off it. There were two lifeboats which had not been launched; Vic Duncan with some Army fellows and others, was trying to manage this lifeboat that had been jammed in the davits by the Japs in their panic to get away. It took us a couple of hours to get it free. There was a Jap lass there, she was part of the entourage they had down aft for their blokes, she was crying her eyes out sitting there, she was probably scared to death with all those wild-looking POWs around the place. Bert Harper tried to comfort her, he was telling her to sit down, that everything would be alright when I said, "Have a look at yourself Harper! you're stark bollocky naked!" Harper whipped off his hat and covered his privates – he was so embarrassed!

"We got the lifeboat out clear from the ship to lower and some of the halyards were broken and had had a couple of other ropes tied on to them but the knot was too big to go through the pulley, that fouled that up and the boat went down stern first into the drink, sprung a couple of the planks but they managed to float it alright. This Jap lass, we put a rope around her and lowered her over the side and she got in the boat. A lot of our blokes were in the water and fellows that were up on deck, they never even got their feet in the water. But we slid down the ropes, and by that time a lot of the blokes that were in the water piled into this lifeboat and I was hanging on to the halyards on the outside of it because of the fact there was about two inches of freeboard."

Bill Mayne: "The boat was half full of water at this stage, so with roughly

65 aboard we started to bail, I knew a boat had a bung in the bottom to allow water to get away while it is beached and thinking this may have been jolted out when the boat was unceremoniously dropped on the water I felt around for the bung hole and found the water flowing in rapidly. I asked everybody to keep a look-out for the bung and we found it and it was put in the hole; but the water was still coming in and we found yet another bung hole with the bung missing, that was found and fixed too.

"Then when we were clear of the ship an English chap jumped in and started screaming he could not swim and to help him, the boat was overcrowded and men were hanging onto the ropes around the side. We helped him to the side but he did not want to be left in the water, so we pulled him and to our amazement he had two lifejackets about him."

Vic Duncan: "She didn't sink for quite a few hours but we actually took off in this boat with quite a lot who couldn't swim. I managed to get some rice skin, like a roll of linoleum, on the sides of the Japanese kwalis, they had saved it. So we had that and we got two barrels of water into the boat from the Japanese galley and we took off.

"We had no rollocks, we had oars and I wanted to get away from the ship because we still didn't know how soon she was going to go. She sounded very dangerous. She was creaking and making a lot of noise, trying to sink. We were being blown away towards the flames and the tankers, so the idea was to get those oars in the water and start getting mobile. Very smartly we got rope, made grummets, and the blokes said, "But I can't row!" and I said, "Well you better bloody well learn right now!" – and we started rowing.

"We managed to row away with blokes hanging on the side and being towed, we started picking up everybody who was within reach. My idea was to keep them afloat and to stay not too far away from the Japs, I reckoned they would come back and pick up the survivors."

Frank McGovern: "We got away from the ship as far as we could and all the Japs were about a quarter mile away, just waiting around to be picked up. We were there until midday, some blokes went back on board, some were floating past on bits of debris. We called out to the Japs that there was the Jap lass there and they said, "Oh she can wait!" and we said, "Bugger it! she is taking up room in the boat." Eventually they came over, they were probably getting thirsty, we had two tins of water and some burnt rice from the kwali, so the Japs came over with their bayonets fixed, took the lass off and also they spied this keg of water so they grabbed that, we told the other bloke to put his feet over the other keg and they didn't see it, so they went off and left us again. I managed to get into the boat when the lass shoved off, up into the stern sheets right up on the gunwhales of the boat, that was the best I could."

Vic Duncan: "Late in the afternoon towards sundown, two frigates came back and they were picking up the Japs from the sea boats. I swam across and grabbed the first boat they abandoned. Prior to this, the Jap coxswain on this destroyer, he

Left: Sgt. William James Moynihan, NX.32703. Moss Vale, NSW. Lost 12.09.44.
Right: Cpl. Thomas Kenneth McLeod, NX.20550. Concord, NSW. Lost 12.09.44.

thought I was trying to get my 135 men aboard. He threatened me with a great black Luger, I remember saying to him, "I don't want your bloody boat!"

"We were safe in a sea boat, and we were free, so we spread our 135 into four of these clinker built boats. I had spoken to Petty Officer Milne and Ldg. Seaman Johnson earlier and they were doing the same thing; Brigadier Varley was apparently somewhere in amongst this crowd and they were doing just what I'd done, collecting people from the water and getting Jap boats as they were abandoned. I didn't trust the Japs, I reckoned that if they had spare time they'd turn nasty. So as soon as I got my three boats loaded I said, "Let's head for China as fast as we can get out of it!" We had sails at the time and we all headed west-nor-west. West-nor-west was a big target because if you went the other way you might miss the Philippines – and there were plenty of Japs in the Philippines."

John Langley: "The sun was well down when we set off to join a boat we could see in the gloomy distance. We could see they were paddling – Bill Webb said, "Come on – we'll give them a Cooee!" The wind was now getting up and the water was becoming choppy with white caps on the waves – we continued to paddle and "Cooee!" and in the distance we made contact with Vic Duncan's boat with Frank McGovern aboard – there were at least ten boats now in the group."

Wal Williams: "Max Campbell and I were sitting around the gunwhales, the boat was crowded, there must have been 60 on board; the English blokes were scared stiff of the water, you could see the fear of it in their faces. Max and I decided to get in the wooden latrine which was being towed along and I said to Max, "I'm the only bloke who had commanded a shit-house at sea!"

Ross Dunbar found the boat too high in the water to climb into, so he climbed on the shoulders of one of his mates and was able to reach it.

Many men were pulled aboard. Duncan searched the lifeboat and found a small axe and a rusty knife, without consulting anyone he threw them overboard. "What did you do that for?" some asked, "we might need them when we hit land." Duncan replied, "You fellows have no idea what shape you'll be in by that time, we don't want anyone going beserk with an axe or a knife!". The explanation was quickly accepted.

Frank McGovern: "Late afternoon the escorts were still picking up Jap survivors, they slowly moved through some of our blokes and didn't pick any of them up, we wondered what they were going to do. Then they started to move away and we thought, "You beaut!" because they could have machine-gunned or rammed us. But they moved away slowly and then a Jap officer came down on to the quarter-deck and, through a loud hailer, shouted out, "Goodbye – Goodbye!" and waved his hand – so we really gave them a sailor's farewell as they moved off over the water. We thought, "You bastards – they are just going and leaving us here."

"By this time the sea was getting a bit choppy, it was dark, a storm was coming up – so we split up over the other boats – there must have been six or seven other boats."

Ian MacDiarmid: "When the Japs vacated their boat we claimed one and put half the complement on the other boat, we had a gallon of water and remained in "cooee" range of the other boat."

On this boat was a British corporal who could not swim, he endeavoured to use his rank to command the boat but this failed. Then he wanted more water, the situation became dangerous and the others considered tossing him overboard. It was then the three A.I.F. took command, Mullens knew a bit about sailing and the others had plenty of common "nous" to do the right thing.

Nearby they spotted their mates, the Cobon twins, at this time there was quite a lot of turbulence and the currents seemed to be going in all directions. MacDiarmid threw a rope to the Cobons but it failed to reach them and they were not seen again.

Clarrie Wilson: "We rowed during the night, I was in Vic Duncan's boat with other PERTH crew, they knew more about the sea. The waves were really coming up now, they got up as big as houses and these boats were about 30 ft. long and 8 ft. across, but we kept on rowing and when you collapsed another bloke would take your place.

"Things sort of calmed down and we put up sails. We were free and it was a tremendous feeling – we were free! and we were heading for the China Coast!".

During the day the American submarine, USS PAMPANITO, tracked the remnants of the convoy, and at 1508 hours spotted one large transport, two large freighters and a small freighter. PAMPANITO kept tracking and at 1930 hours, when 52 miles from Hainan, she submerged and prepared for a night attack. She lost sight of the convoy for a short time then sighted it again, now with escorts and in two columns, KACHIDOKI MARU leading the first column, one escort on the port side of each column and two to the rear. At 2152 an escort fired a green flare which Lt. Cdr. Summers could not interpret. The convoy's course remained unchanged.

At 2240 hours PAMPANITO fired five torpedoes – three at KACHIDOKI MARU and two at a large freighter. Lt.Cdr. Summers did not know the KACHIDOKI MARU was carrying 900 British prisoners of war.

DAY 2 – 13 SEPTEMBER 1944

Humour and the joy of being free yesterday now disappeared. During the night many had disappeared, mates were enquiring about their mates, everybody was realising they were on their own, the Japanese seemed to have completed their rescue.

Frank Farmer: "The first light of dawn revealed how wretched was our plight, particularly of those already blinded by the oily scum. I decided that my survival lay elsewhere. It would be this decision that ultimately led to my rescue. I swam away and was soon in sole possession of yet another plank. Later that second morning I came upon another lone swimmer, a fellow from my own Unit with whom, while working on the railway, I had had little contact. He was Harold (Curly) Martin, formerly of Esperance, W.A. His fair hair would later be the second significant factor in our rescue. Still relatively fit, both of us able swimmers, we swam around gathering the biggest rafts and planking we could find, tying them together with rope that somehow had come to hand, while regretfully leaving to float away some 44 gallon drums which were far too buoyant to handle. At intervals throughout the day we were joined by other lonely castaways who sought our company."

Ken Williams: "The morning was spent collecting anything that would float and we could put under our planks to make us more buoyant, we also collected a large box which was covered with malthoid or rubberoid which we stripped off and made a sail, not much time to think about anything else but to make us as safe as possible. Hunger and the hot day made it bad for thirst, I tried to rinse my mouth out with seawater but it made the thirst worse."

Fred Mills: "Next day the current had dispersed the survivors in all directions and our group now comprised L/Bdr. Dick Howse, NX.27995, of Orange,

NSW, and Milton Farrell, NX.33866 of Lakemba, NSW; however we were later separated and didn't see them again.

"There were now Vic Cross of Geraldton, W.A., Harry Bunker, WX.9223, from W.A., and myself on the one raft, there were others tied to adjacent rafts.

"On the second day we lost Gnr. Lang Campbell, who came from Quirindi, NSW. He was floating away when someone said, "Hold him" and they removed his lifejacket. Before he disappeared one of the others recited The Lord's Prayer."

The kapok was removed from the jacket to use to try and clean the oil from the eyes of the men who were screaming in agony. NX.33124, Bdr. Victor Frederick Heaseman of Homebush, NSW, showed great bravery in endeavouring to overcome the effect of eyes burnt from contact with the oil. He died the next day.

The numbers were now dwindling away and the rafts concentrated in small groups, still within calling distance.

Harry Weigand wrote: "Dawn came and I was hoping the sun would soon rise as I was shivering with the cold. After it got properly daylight we could see little black specks bobbing up and down on the ocean as far as the eye could see. Most of the rafts had broken away during the night with the choppy sea. During the morning, just as if we had a wireless message, everyone started waving and shouting and giving signals and all the rafts started to close in. It took us all day of pretty hard paddling with sticks and hands to get in among the main body of rafts. Almost everyone was there that I knew off the ship and some were in a pretty bad way. By then I could see that if we didn't get picked up a lot of the men would soon perish."

Bill McKitterick: " At daybreak I came up to many other rafts and one of my mates called out, "You were Merchant Navy, what do we do?" The rafts were tied together with trailing ropes tied to a large boom. That evening there were sixteen men on the rafts together."

During the day the men baked in hot oil and went into the water for relief. Wearing only his singlet and using his underpants to protect his head from the sun McKitterick found the sea lice were attacking his body and the bites were beginning to create sores. The group discussed whether they should try and row somewhere.

Bill McKitterick: "We were taught to remain at the site of the sinking because usually someone survives to get a message out – anyway that's what we did.

"By this time our tongues were swollen, much discussion had taken place on the subject of drinking seawater, some of the men had disappeared overnight."

Roy Cornford: "When daylight came the sea was a mass of floating rafts and men, debris, lots of hatch planks and a few dead Japanese still in life jackets, which the POWs who did not have a life jacket soon removed. During the first day the rafts gradually separated and we collected pieces of board to use as paddles, thinking we could row to the China coastline as we thought we were only 200 miles from it. But we started paddling and came across a big floating ice chest full of dried fish, we got a few crates out but could not eat it as it was too salty. Sitting on top of this ice-chest was an Aussie. He would not leave the ice-chest and join us on the raft, but he did tear a 3 ft. square sheet of thin flat iron off and give us which we took in case it rained."

Reg Harris: "We had little jobs to do among ourselves, getting all the floating material we could for the raft; Miscamble spent his time trying to catch a fish, it had got itself up on the painted boards and Miscamble said, "Don't move I'll catch him!" but he had no hope of catching it with his bare hands. We thought about what we were going to do when we got home. I was never going to walk past a tap, I was going to drink out of every tap I came to. And I was never going to give up smoking come hell or high water. I only started to smoke seriously in Changi and I resolved in that water that when I got out and got to a place where there were cigarettes I'd never give up smoking – I haven't smoked now for ten years. Some poor bloke would go off drinking the briny and we'd try and stop him and somebody would say, "Well, he's gone poor bloke" and you know, it could be your best mate – there was nothing in the world you could do about it."

Arthur Bancroft: "By next day we were out of sight, we were on the ocean by ourselves."

Cliff Farlow: "We were still confident, we had sorted out our raft and our mates, we depended on one another, we were much more confident. Many exchanged places from raft to raft, others just wouldn't give up what they already had, they felt they had survived the first day on their raft and didn't like to take the risk elsewhere, it might not be as good.

"Many of us were suffering from hallucinations from the heat, I reached the stage of not being conscious of thirst but still possessing a strong feeling that we would make it. I was from the land and my life had been dairy farming and I remember at one time I was out there milking cows – they were walking around on the ground."

Ross Smith: "We tried eating a fish which had been killed by the depth charging, it was oily and we couldn't hold it to get our teeth into it. Later I acquired a hat, life jacket and a waterbottle from one of the men who died. Many had suffered from the effects of the depth charging. Every one was having hallucinations – "The island over there where there was plenty of food!" – they would leave the raft and swim about 20 yards and disappear."

Bob Farrands: "Alan Edwards was with me until that night. We said we've got to find something better than what we have got, we can't lie down with our feet in the water so we struck this raft with six Englishmen aboard and we asked them if we could come aboard and they said no, this was theirs and they were full up! – so we said we'll just wait till dark. Then we into them, fists flying and we pushed them off. I tangled with Curly Wiles, anyhow we pushed them off and we got on and then we said, "Now it's ours, you can come back on if you are good and behave yourselves!", which they did, but only Curly and I survived on that raft."

The rafts were now dispersed over a wide area.

* * * * * * * * * *

Bill Mayne: "Meantime three boats were tied one behind the other, our original one we got from the RAKUYO MARU being last with the doctor and about 20 sick men, they still had to bail 24 hours a day. The middle boat was ours, holding 70 to 80, skippered by two Navy boys, Pat Major and Syd Matson and the lead boat was skippered by C.P.O. Vic Duncan with Frank McGovern.

"As darkness set in the wind rose with such a fierceness only to be experienced on the water, how we lasted the night we don't know but we managed to keep together. We did not have a sail so we rowed the best we could under the cramped conditions. Later in the night our skipper asked if anybody knew how to rig a sail. I did, so he asked could I rig a blanket up to take the place of a sail.

"By lashing two corners on to an oar and tying pieces of rope to the remaining two corners we were able to catch a little wind, so we could keep a better course. Wherever we moved in the boat bodies could be felt everywhere. Sleep came easily to some but not to me, the skipper and his mate got tired and asked me to take over the tiller and a more trying job I have never undertaken, our boat would buffet the front and then the boat behind would buffet us, one would swing to the starboard whilst the other to the port and so that went on until morning.

"The sun coming up out of the sea was a pleasant and very welcome sight, for now assessments of our stores could be taken and perhaps some biscuits for breakfast; after being soaked all night the warmth cheered us up a little. Breakfast disposed of we got down to how this boat should be run and get some of the tired chaps who hadn't done any rowing the night before up from under the seats and organized in Watches. Although our boats were still tied together we had separate men in charge that meant a complete crew, our skipper formed three Watches, Red, White and Blue, taking Red himself, assigning White and Blue for his mate and myself respectively.

"While this was going on two sails were seen and expectations were of Chinese junks, but they turned out to be some more survivors. They were well equipped compared to us, sails, fair quantity of water, about 8 gallons, and a crew of about 30 each."

Arthur Wright: "We were on a raft and during the night there were various 'cooee's', we 'cooee'd' and we got closer and closer and we found it was a party of Englishmen who had been rowing for the Japs who had been picked up and they left them with the boat. They helped us on board and we could hear different 'cooee's' and we would row in the direction, sometimes we would find them or the voices would fade away and we would hear calls from different areas but we picked up all we could find.

"Then the various boats came together that night. Brigadier Varley was in one, and we lashed the boats together but during the night the sea became very rough and the boats were crashing together. I said somebody is going to get killed or limbs broken so we cast off and the other boats were forced to do the same.

"In the morning we found there were two boats together, another three together and gradually getting further and further away from us there were about seven other boats."

Frank Lawrence: "When the rescue ship came to pick up the Japs they made the POWs row them to the ship but would not allow any of our boys on board, some being refused at gun point and others being knocked back with pieces of wood. Fortunately they didn't try to take the lifeboats on board, so our boys rowed around picking up as many POWs as possible. Arthur and I were picked up just on dark, we were very lucky."

It was decided one boat would join the Duncan group and the other boat, with Lt.Campbell-Smith and PERTH members, Ldg.Seaman Frank Johnson, Ritchie and Milne, would head for the Philippines. It was decided to transfer the injured Cpl. Richards to this boat.

Frank McGovern remembers Ritchie called out, "We've got room for two more" but by the time he stood up to go the place was filled. That boat was not seen again.

The original Duncan boat was set adrift and those on board were transferred to the boat in which Duncan had placed the two PERTH sailors, Pat Major and Syd Matson. The doctor, Rowley Richards, was on this boat where there was more room and he was now able to stretch out and get some sleep. The two other boats were under Eddie Anderson and Arthur Wright.

Bill Mayne: "After consultation, during which we had quite a tropical downpour and we tried to catch as much water as possible, they took a few of our men and left us a piece of canvas whereby we were able to rig a better sail.

"Once we had this sail arranged to catch as much breeze as possible when it blew, we did not row. The Watch on duty sat in their respective positions, sixteen men on the oars sitting on seats across the boat, the skipper on the tiller and his mate up forward doing Watch, the skipper's job was to keep his back into the sun. Although two boats were still together drifting along following the other boats, we could not keep pace with them.

"Drifting along that day the sailor in charge of the boat, Pat Major, who had an infected foot, found that he could not handle the job any longer so he lay down under the seat, this left the other sailor and myself to handle three Watches between us. Knowing that seawater would do Pat's wound good to bathe it in, we persuaded him to do that and I think that stopped it from becoming worse.

"Our ration of food and water, which was meagre, did a lot to revive our spirits, it was only a mouthful from a measuring dip and five very small biscuits each the size of a half inch cube, this issue we had twice a day, in the morning and at night, we planned on a three week trip.

"Life jackets proved very handy and comforting; at night they would be kept around us for warmth and in case of being knocked overboard, and in the daytime they helped keep the sun from blistering a great proportion of our body.

"The following day was much the same as the first, except late in the afternoon we sighted on the distant horizon this convoy of boats, planks and rafts; just on dusk a few of our chaps said they heard gun fire. I did not hear any shots at all.

"A number of our boys seemed to me to be sleeping to a great extent, as for myself I could not sleep at all, I did not close my eyes for sleep the whole three days on the water and did not have one issue of biscuits and water, but smoke, I was craving for and they were rationed also, one half a cigarette per day.

"I held the tiller for the greater part of the night, following the other boat and keeping a star dead ahead."

Frank McGovern: "Brigadier Varley's six boats were all tied together, they were heading in a northwesterly direction to what we were heading so we had a council of war and said, "Well, what are we going to do?" Present was PERTH rating Tommy Johnson of Randwick, he was suffering from malaria, Vic Duncan, nominated by the majority to be in charge of boats, there was myself. Syd Matson was in charge of another boat with Pat Major, the doctor, Rowley Richards, was in this boat, and there was another boat. We headed towards China in a west-by-northerly, we thought that would be the best. It was a heavy, following sea and a strong current, we thought we made pretty good progress, maybe we did and maybe we didn't! We were aqua-planing that night – I sat on the tiller in the stern sheets that night because Vic had had it, he had done a big job organising things and he was exhausted by that time."

Eddie Anderson said Duncan's boat passed him like an 18 footer during the night.

Frank McGovern: "So I said to Vic, "I'll stay on the tiller at this stage." When the clouds parted a couple of times you could see a few stars and you could steer by them. We thought we were going westward all the time, during the day we kept our backs to the sun. Rowley Richard's boat was tied up with us and their boat seemed to get the surf a bit quicker than we did, at one time I was trying to steer our boat a bit slower and their boat would pull us and swing her away. I said, "Hey! keep your boat clear or we'll have to take the rope off!"

"Anyway, we got through the night. It rained a little and we sucked the water off our arms to conserve the water in the keg. The following morning it was pretty still, we had a sailmaker on board, Mullens, and we rigged up this old blanket on the mast; we found an old empty cigarette tin on board, the sort that used to hold fifty cigarettes, and towards sunset we would eke out about a quarter of that tin per man, a couple of mouthfuls. We had that just on sunset, we decided that would be the correct time rather than during the day when we would sweat it out in the sun. During the day we would look out for sharks and then we would lower ourselves over the side to try and stop the dehydration and the water would cool us off, then we helped the blokes back in the boat again.

"Two boat loads with Matson, Major and the other crew, were about a quarter mile ahead of us, we were coming up astern of them. That night – we went through it again. I would estimate we might have made China in about nine or ten days provided we got a favourable breeze because it wasn't very windy at the time."

Wal Williams: "I reckon we would have struck Varley's crowd about 5.30 p.m. or 6 p.m. in the evening, there was a bit of light but it was starting to go off. We rowed over and he said, "What course are you on?" We said we were heading due west because we thought China's a big land, with the currents we got to hit something. He said, "We are heading north-west, do you want to come in with us?" and Duncan said, "No we'll be right, we'll go on our own."

"At night, we just hove to, they had blokes sitting there holding the oars to straighten her, we had a bit of a leg-o-mutton sail but we kept within hailing distance of each other.

"Next morning, it would not have been a very great distance between us at night because we were all drifting in the same current, and my first recollection was this machinegun fire, 'pom pom' and the Navy blokes said, "Christ! she's on!". in the lifeboat you are so low in the water the range of visibility would not be far.

"The first we saw was the mast of a ship coming over the horizon, she got closer and closer, half a mast, then up came this corvette, and the sailors were swinging around on these pompoms – Max Campbell said to me, "If you believe in Jesus Christ pray – if they open up on us we're history!"

Vic Duncan: "Each time we'd see a Jap ship I told them to pull the sails down. Some of them saw our sails down and they pulled theirs down.

"On the third day there was an aircraft circling at a height overhead, I think it was passing on information because late in the afternoon up came this warship, with a very sharp bow. I didn't think he would pick us up, I thought he would just blast us and carry on. But he must have had a streak of humanity and he picked us up on the run, he actually hit us doing about six knots and the boat skewed. I thought he was going to ram us and I yelled to the fellows, "Toss your oars and bear off!" – there were a few sailors in there – they tossed their oars and as he hit we hit too and of course that takes part of the thump. The boat actually slewed savagely and the next minute the scrambling nets of this frigate were rasping past the gunwhales of our boat and there were two Jap faces up above and they were yelling out "Hyaku! Hyaku!" (Quickly! quickly!). We didn't have any option really, so I hung on to the net with somebody else to keep the boat with it while the fellows got up the scrambling net. We were the last up, back on the upper deck."

When the frigates appeared on the horizon where the Varley boats were last seen, the men in Arthur Wright's boat said they heard machine-gun fire. He made them remain quiet and listen – they all heard it again – they were convinced those two Japanese frigates were responsible for the massacre of Brigadier Varley's party.

The third escort vessel approached and challenged them, Vic Duncan's boat was the closest. The Japanese wanted to know the nationality, American ? "No", replied Duncan. British ? "No" was the reply, "We are Australian". The escort then came by on the move with scrambling nets lowered.

According to Arthur Wright, who was one of Varley's Sergeants, Varley had met a British ship's Captain in Changi when he returned there on the pretence of receiving dental treatment who told him that the Japanese submarine had rescued only the Captain and was on orders he was not to rescue any British or American personnel. There was no definite order about Australians – the decision to rescue Australians was left to the discretion of the Captain.

Wal Williams: "..: but they came alongside and threw out the scrambling nets and we went up onto the ship and a sailor hopped down into the boat and belted the bottom out of it and let it sink. They put us on the forward bow of the ship, we had no water and they would not give us any. Rowley Richards took all the waterbottles and obtained a little water from the Japs, he rationed the water out on the deck, gave each bloke a sip.

"Max had a saltwater sore on his foot, it blew up like a blister, I had a jack-knife and I asked Richards if I'd lance it and he said, "That's all you can do." I was down there just going to do it when a Jap came along and took the knife off me, probably as a souvenir for himself.

"We travelled all night on that corvette, we struck a ship that had been sunk and was still on fire. (This had been sunk by the USS PAMPANITO). We came right up close to it and I thought we are sitting ducks for a submarine, silhouetted as we were against the flames.

"We were taken to Hainan Island."

DAY 3 – 14 SEPTEMBER 1944

Jack Flynn: "About the third day in the China Sea, covered in oil, with the seas getting rougher – I was blind in the left eye – every time we went up on a wave we would have a look around. I saw what I thought was a raft about 200 yards away and decided to have a go at getting it. I got it alright. It was about 4 feet square, filled with cork, and a rope on it. I towed it back to our group and we took turns to sit on it, out of the water about up to our waists.

"About this time, there were not many of us left, most of them had been drinking seawater and having hallucinations. Dick New, from South Australia, said, "Strewth, there's a dragon fly." Having a fair knowledge of the bush I knew that dragon flies were only to be found on creeks and pools on land. I said to myself, "Dick's a goner." He had two good eyes – then I saw it and thought, "I've had it too!" I knew I had not been drinking seawater and I said to Dick, "If that is fair dinkum, land can't be far away." He said, "No, about a mile." I reckoned I could swim that far, taking it easy, so I said to him, "Which way?" and he pointed with his thumb and said, "Straight down Jack!". I could have killed him.

"There were only three of us left, Dick New, Murray Thompson and myself. The seas were getting really rough by now and our hopes were fading. The only things I had left were my rosary beads, which our Aunt, Sister Mary Loreto, gave me before I came away, and my old slouch hat. I pushed in the top of it and managed to catch some rainwater.

Jim Campbell: "Not long after sunrise on the third morning the raft to which we were clinging drifted slowly towards a large group of men who had built a raft similar to ours. We paddled furiously to reach the larger group and joined them after a :ew hours' effort.

"We thought that our chances of a rescue party sighting us would be much

S/Sgt. Arthur Davis Connan, VX.14855. Aged 33. 2/2 Pnr. Bn. Coburg, Vic. Lost 14.09.44.
Pte. Richard Camm, VX.51879. 2/2 Pnr. Bn.Launceston, Tas. Lost 14.09.44.

greater if we were together than if we were scattered. The idea was a good one, but it became too heart-rending as the day progressed the sun rose higher the misery of the weaker ones increased. It was terrible for us to see our comrades dying one by one and knowing that there was nothing we could do to save them. Some were delirious and kept calling for loved ones at home, until their cries became weaker and weaker and at last they slipped silently beneath the waves.

"The sights of that day made some of us realise that the sufferings and the mental state of the many dying men were lowering our own powers of resistance. It was impossible to do anything for those whose sanity had deserted them. We all experienced mirages, which took the form of fleets of vessels sailing across the horizon and the forests of masts of other ships whose hulls were beneath the edge of the sea. Some of us knew them for what they were, but found it quite hopeless to try and convince many of the others who insisted in swimming off to be rescued.

"Twenty of us decided to drift away and take our chance. We had two makeshift rafts tied together with ten men on each, and still clinging weakly to the sides we just let the waves and tides take us where they would. Our bodies were numb from continued immersion, yet we were suffering the agonies of thirst.

"The nights passed still without sleep. To sleep was to die. Counting of heads in the morning showed that two of our number had slipped silently away during the night. Horror filled the day. Six died before nightfall after what seemed like years of suffering. Most of them had gone mad from the sun or from the terrible consequences of drinking seawater."

Frank Farmer: "We had found a large empty wooden box-like structure floating by only partly submerged and after tying our raft to it we took it in turn to rest and dry out on its sloping top. During the night it served as a very efficient sea-anchor. Next morning it was noticed that the canvas covering its wooden roof was only lightly tacked down, and possibly could be made into some sort of simple sail. With this in mind, we set about removing the canvas, carefully safeguarding the tacks. By dark we had rigged a makeshift sail and using an oar as a mast this jury rig, supported by ropes and in turn by Martin and myself, worked quite well and our flotilla of rafts moved steadily through the water in line astern. Curly and I were certain we were making progress, and hopefully westward to where we thought the nearest land lay, and the chance of offshore fishing boats. That same night rain storms swept over us and we had caught some of the precious drops in our open mouths. Morning found two or three of our number missing, one of them, an Australian, who, blinded by oil, had earlier asked us to untie his life- jacket."

Arthur Bancroft: "Day 3 morning when we woke up we couldn't see another person, we saw bodies drifting past although they were drifting at a quicker rate than we were. We had no water, we were talking about drinking seawater and I said, "Well when Captain Bligh took his ship on his famous voyage, when they ran out of fresh water he rationed seawater out to a man a few teaspoons at a time." I remember reading that as a kid and I said "I think we can do that" so we decided to give it a go and we just took a mouthful of seawater, whizzed it round and round our mouth and spat it out and allowed just a couple of drops to go down our throat.

"There were five of us, Ray Wheeler was drifting past alone on a lifejacket, so we swam over to him and got him back to the raft. He was in a bad way and covered in oil, so we just tied him on to the raft and said, "You're just gonna have to stay there buddy", and that ended up with six of us. We were on the raft when it was daytime and if it got too hot we would slip into the water and at night when it got too cold we'd get back in the water. We used to do all sorts of things, told stories, told each other about our lives, made up menus with all sorts of wonderful dishes, that's the sort of thing that went on. We were pretty confident, we had not given up hope, we really thought a Japanese ship would come along and pick us up."

Charles McKechnie: "Although we started off with about 12 or 14 in our group by Day 3 we would have been down to about six or seven, there would have been Reg Harris, Ron Miscamble, Reg Stewart, Bill Cunneen, Frank Holcroft and myself – it was a repeat of Day 2 really.

"On this deckhouse wreck we were on there was a plank missing, you could look down between and you could see little fish swimming round, we were trying to catch them but we never got any. Frank Holcroft and I were on this deckhouse, the other fellows paddled off on their raft to try and get some help.

"When we first started off on this raft we were towing a case of tinned fish behind us on a rope but we soon lost that, we reckoned it would have been good to trade on the mainland for something."

Harry Weigand: "Third day in the water – everyone looked very despondent and a sorry sight, it was impossible to recognise the man next to me unless he spoke because of all the oil on his face, everyone was smothered in it. During the night a lot of men had died or drifted away, they were beginning to thin out very quickly now. I was feeling pretty weak and getting bad cramp pains in the stomach. The sun came up very hot and strong on the third day and it almost roasted us with the oil on our bodies. During the day lots of men drank seawater and became raving lunatics and a menace to everyone, they threw their life jackets off and sank. You couldn't do anything with them as it took everyone all the strength they had left to hang on to the raft.

"It was now almost an impossibility to sit on the raft. They were smothered in oil and we kept slipping off them. Men were begging for water, saying "Oh God, give me water!" I said it too, but in prayer. Men out of their minds would shout at me, "Give me water!", all I could say was, "Wait a little while." Our mouths were burnt with the oil and my tongue was swollen and I had great difficulty in speaking. I must have been beginning to go delirious as I was seeing ships wherever I looked. I still had my senses but I could see ships, ships and ships, but I knew that I was just seeing things. I had Chicko's and Bill's photos in my pocket so I got them out, they were wet and smothered in oil, I kissed Chicko and Bill goodbye and said goodbye to all my people thinking that I wouldn't have my senses tomorrow.

"There were only four men left on the raft I was on and it was all of our four opinions that we couldn't last out another day. Pat Smith and I shook hands, I said to Pat, "You are a young man and I hope that you make it alright and if you do will you go and see my wife for me." He said, "Yes Harry but I think you are as strong as me and if I make it so will you."

"It was a relief that day when the sun went down. We had all blistered with the sun and oil on our bodies. After dark it came over very cloudy and how we all prayed for rain, and it did rain about midnight. I think I must have caught about a spoonful in my mouth and it gave me great relief. The night wore on."

Roy Cornford: "By the third day there was only 7 men of the 18 left, and the Aussie who shared his waterbottle had gone. My best mate, Pat Linnane, was gone also. We did not see them go, they just floated away. You could now sit on the rafts but still in the water. Our lifejackets made of kapok had swollen and most had busted, we used the kapok to wipe oil from our eyes. I discarded my life jacket as it was chafing me, even though I had a hat and a sort of T-shirt I was burnt by the sun and the oil. I swam 10 feet away from the raft that morning to get a piece of timber and was nearly too weak to get back. I remember Claude Longey going for me, telling me to pull myself together. That day we saw shark fins but no sharks attacked us even though our legs were hanging in the water and there were many dead floating around."

Bob Farrands: "Alan Edwards died on the third day. At one period we saw a big lot of rafts all hooked together and to us it looked as though they had kegs on them and Alan said, "What say we swim over Bob?" so we started off and after a while I said, "Hey it's further than we thought Alan let's go back to our raft", which we did. I finally let him go, he'd slide off and I would swim and bring him back and I don't know how many times I did that and Wiles finally said, "He's dead" so I let him go.

"I met up with Geoff Millard from Young, N.S.W., on the third day – every now and then you would meet up with rafts. I swam over to Geoff from my raft and pleaded with him to come over with me but he said "No, I'll stop with this one, I'11 run the risk." He was still carrying a waterbottle that we filled before we jumped off the boat and he gave me a drink out of his bottle, then he wanted me to stop with him but I wouldn't and I said, "No, I'll go back to my own raft." He was seen after we were picked up."

Norm Nutley: "I left the ship with Hugh Campbell of Wooroonden, Qld., and grabbed a couple of hatch planks which we tied together with straps from our life belts and got clear of the ship. My mate died on the third day. My waterbottle had become contaminated with seawater so I threw it away in disgust. Being alone with no one in sight made me think my position hopeless. My eyes were affected by the oil, forcing me to keep them closed most of the time. My thoughts were of home and family."

Charles McKechnie: "It is known you should not drink sea water but you can't stop blokes doing it. A lot drank seawater and went off their head and they died. I tried my urine, which is an awful taste, I wouldn't recommend it as an after-dinner drink at any stage of the game! but that's all I could think of – I cupped my hands and urinated in them then tried to sip it, I had one or two mouthfuls and that was enough for me, it's an awful taste – salty and oh well – I vomited. It must have rained a couple of times and all we could do was to lie there with open mouth, nothing to catch water with. I don't know how but I think we absorbed water through our skin. I never really and truly felt over-thirsty, not a matter of life and death thirst. The second or third day, there were about six or eight of us, maybe ten, and one fellow I remember saying to Ronnie Miscamble, "Well Ronnie – where's your horse?" and we thought, "Geez – where do you get a horse in the middle of the South China Sea?!" and this fellow says, "I'm going to go and get your horse and I'm going to ride away and get you fellows some water." We said, "Oh well, go for your life" but he got over that alright whatever it was. But the blokes who drank seawater ended up seeing things. A lot would drink it at night so you wouldn't see."

Ken Williams: "We got the sail rigged, and then the great debate which we had to go to sail to the China Coast. None of us knowing much about navigation, so went by the sun, moon and stars. Still not much time to give any serious thought to anything but our safety. Hunger seemed to have passed us by – thirst was getting to us."

Pte. Vincent Patrick Peter Linnane, NX.43764. Lismore, NSW. Lost 15.09.44.
Sgt. Colin David Dick, QX.14602. West End, Brisbane, Qld. Aged 24. Lost 12.09.44. Pic: Norman Dick.

BOAT PARTY

Frank McGovern: "They took us back to Hainan and we then got on board a tanker, there was an air raid warning and it didn't look too good because she would have been a priority target. The wind was blowing off the land and I remember telling the fellows, "If you go that side you will all be fried, swim against the wind." But it passed off alright.

"There were British survivors from the KACHIDOKI MARU on board too and they were in a terrible mess, they were black with fuel oil, many were badly burned and some had broken arms and legs and you could see the bones sticking out through their flesh. We helped some of them to wash down with seawater but the pain must have been terrific, they would scream and yell with the pain. They were demoralised.

"The tanker was pretty full and we were in the forward well deck, they gave us some rice in our hands which was hard enough but we couldn't eat the rice, it was like sawdust, so dry. We went over to the steam winches and got some drops of condensed water and moistened our rice so we could eat it. While we were there there was an air raid on and we thought bloody hell but the air raid was only on the shore installations, we saw some planes but it did not last long. Pat Major was near the side of the ship and he said to Matson and I, "Bugger it, I'm going over!" – but the Japs must have read our thoughts for they had two machine guns on either side of the bridge and one fellow said, in English, "If anybody tries to escape we will machine gun you!".

Arthur Wright: "I said to Frank Lawrence, "I'm not travelling on any tanker, we'll swim ashore tonight." Frank said he was not a good swimmer and I told him we would pinch a lifejacket and I would tow him, it was about a mile to the shore. However it was a bright moonlight night and there was no chance of getting off without being seen in the water. Next morning, the Commander who had been on the RAKUYO MARU with us, Lt. Yamada, came aboard and he literally turned white when he saw it was a tanker.

"There were also some English troops with us, they had been on the KACHIDOKI MARU and had been confined below decks, when she was torpedoed they were blown out by the air in the hold of the boat, one man had his arm badly torn by one of the guy ropes during the blast. We were only given one meal on board, a small ball of rice.

"The Commander made it clear he was not sailing on a tanker and we were taken off and put on board a whaling mother-ship; there were about 300 British and Australians and we were all put down in the hold.

"When we first went aboard this ship the Japs used to come and look down the hold. I was standing at the head of the gangway when a Jap Warrant Officer came up, saw me and called, "Kura! Kura!". I went up and did he abuse me – it appeared I was wearing his shirt, trousers and belt, which he took off me leaving me with nothing to hold my trousers up with except my hand. He also gave me a couple of clips across the ear for taking his clothes – the fact that he had abandoned them when the ship was sinking did not register."

Vic Duncan: "This ship would have sunk very quickly because down below where they put us there were no bulkheads, she just ran right through. Underneath us again there were tanks for the whale oil. Apparently they were carrying fuel oil, or maybe even petrol, it was a tanker and we didn't know it, she was a real bomb.

"We were put down below and there was one long wooden ladder coming down so here again we looked like being in the hold when she got hit. The Japs had two sentries on the top of the ladder, when it got dark and they had retired I made my way aft – I found a door with the catches down, I took them off, opened the door and made my way up on to the upper deck of the ship where I spent the night. Before dawn I went below again. So, I knew how to get out and I knew the routine. I got hold of Frank McGovern and two or three other sailors for I reckoned they were the best in the dark for getting the door catches off and we worked out our escape routine; here again it had to work to be alive for we would have to go up these ladders to the upper decks and the two guards would be up on top, armed, and wouldn't let us out."

Arthur Wright: "In the hold there were quite a few of our men, sick and wounded; those that had been in our boat all grouped together and we shared out amongst ourselves what food we had – a few biscuits, some of which had had brandy spilt over them and made me sick and we shared out what tobacco we had. The only Australian officer was Rowley Richards. The Japs said there had to be a guard on the gangway which lead to the toilet, the 'benjo' – which was only a box over the side; there was a British officer and there was to be two Australians and two British NCO's, they would take it in turns to see that only one man used the 'benjo' at a time, while the others waited on deck – this was very trying for the men with dysentery.

"From the top of the gangway every morning we could see the crew drilling to music, sometimes there were survivors from other ships in the convoy which had been torpedoed, the convoy was by now down to only the whaling mother-ship and two frigates. When another ship was torpedoed the Japs would rush to the side of our ship in panic, holding rafts over the side ready to let them go and they would have as many as three lifejackets each on their shoulders.

"None of the POWs were allowed up on deck while the torpedoing was going on and I do not know how to describe the experience of standing at the top of the gangway, knowing you could not allow them up or even on to the gangway at all, and you would be holding your breath, waiting for a torpedo to hit or something to happen, all the time knowing that you would have to try and regulate the men so they would get up on deck without any panic and you would be looking down and all you could see was a blotch of white faces – all staring up at you – not a sound from them – everybody staring and tense – waiting to see what would happen – "

Bill Mayne: "I cannot remember how we got from the tanker to the mother or butcher whaling ship.

"We were herded down below to the butchering area, a vast area under the main deck, but once again very little space per body, we had to occupy only half the area that was there.

"This part of our journey to Japan I felt was the worst, we left Singapore reasonably fit and well morally, the rescue to the tanker still the same, but this whaling ship was one of the most degrading experiences we had seen. I was lucky but a lot of the boys had their eyes closed and gummed up with oil, coughing up blood, mucous and oil, diarrhoea was rife among us and only 20 were allowed up to the toilets at one time, a job to get up the ladder to deck with men coming and going. The stench from unwashed bodies and ones that could not hold their motions was unbearable. Up on deck the toilets were wooden frames constructed out of timber and just hung over the sides of the ship.

"As we approached the Japanese Islands we lost one of our escort vessels on our starboard side, I was below on my spot when this happened, a loud bang on the side of the ship and we all thought, "Here we go again"; there was quite a scurry for the ladder which was forward and I was well aft with my mates about midships. A Jap officer from the engine room came running up from below and assured us everything was alright.Those on deck were ordered immediately below (daytime) and they told us, one minute this man-o-war was there and then there was a puff of smoke and it was gone."

"Kitch" Loughnan: "We sailed on 17 September 1944 in a convoy of sixteen ships and reached the northern part of Formosa after being subjected to another Allied submarine attack during which three more ships were sunk. We remained in Formosa during the day and sailed again that night but again we were attacked and five more ships were sunk. We returned to Formosa and remained there for about four days. During the whole of this time we were forced to remain below decks and it was little wonder that men began to die. Five Englishmen died a few days before the trip eventually finished and several died before they could be carried ashore at Moji.

"We sailed again on 25 September and again the convoy was attacked on 27 September. This time a Japanese corvette was sunk a few hundred yards from us on our starboard. Prior to this attack the Japanese had dropped heavy drums above us, each time one was dropped we thought we had been torpedoed and by the time we reached the port of Moji on 28 September we were living on the last dregs of our resistance."

DAY 4 15 SEPTEMBER 1944

THUNDER IN THE WATER

Jim Campbell: "On the fourth night a cyclone raged in all its fury. As the wind increased the seas mounted and our ears became numb with the drumming of the gale which seemed bent on tearing us from the few flimsy planks which were our only hope of salvation.

"Each succeeding wave threatened to pound us to pieces. If ever men fought for their lives we did that night. One minute we would be on top of a wave with the wind tearing at us, the next moment sliding down – down – into a bottomless trough with nothing around and above us but black mountains of water. Then up again spluttering and gasping as the fury of the elements unleashed another attack.

"Some of the men were swept away and even their cries were lost in the angry roaring of the gale. The raft was like a live thing, twisting and bucking through the waves.

"My hands were raw from the friction of the rope, and my body was bruised and aching with the crashing of the boards against my chest and ribs. But I clung on with every ounce of my strength, unconscious of any feeling other than a futile and whimpering rage at the incessant howling of the wind.

"At last the gale died as quickly as it had begun and the seas, released from the awful pressure, gradually became calmer until towards morning the mountains of water were reduced to long rollers and we were able to relax and rest our elbows on the raft while we tried to regain a little strength."

Frank Farmer: "The fourth day of our tribulation dawned calm and clear.

We sprawled listlessly on our wooden platforms, those with the strength to do so occasionally slipping into the sea to cool off. Unwittingly this served to assuage our growing thirst. Curly and I pondered our chances of rescue, agreeing that perhaps we had the physical resources to remain active and alive a further two or three days. Heat, hunger, and thirst were taking their toll, and we could see that for some of our beleagured party, it would not be that long.

"Suddenly our interest was aroused by one of the party who had earlier been hallucinating, claiming that he could see a ship. Without my glasses I was unable to confirm this and thought it must have been another of his apparitions. Then Curly saw it !!!

"I struggled to my feet, and with the advantage of height, I could clearly make out what appeared to be the masts of an approaching craft. With Curly's help I remained standing upright for some minutes waving along my 'lady's hat'. I soon became aware of two things – the masts were the twin periscopes of a submarine, and my thankfulness that we had been sighted. It was approaching fast and we were soon able to see figures on its conning tower. They were not Japs; our hopes rose.

"No longer able to stand up I slumped down on the raft, and moments later the huge vessel powered past, leaving our flotilla of rafts jostling in its wash. Rescue had miraculously come – and gone. Meanwhile, on the disappearing submarine, someone mentioned that among us he had seen a fair head, creating some speculation as to our identity. Others aboard were sceptical, and it was probably the desire of the captain to relieve the monotony of his crew by providing them with a little headhunting that really brought them back. As the noise of the submarine's engines receded, each man suffered his own peculiar agony. For me it was a terrible resignation, a feeling that there would never be a second chance. Then it was seen that the submarine was turning back. It was beyond our comprehension that it should do so; our excitement mounted. As the sub. came closer we could see a number had come on deck and were carrying guns. Our rising euphoria quickly gave way to a feeling of suspicion. Every one of us reacted in his own way to this unexpected development; some shouted and pleaded, others sensing the danger slid off the raft into the sea, while others like myself sat transfixed, mesmerized by the sight of the guns. I gave the only signal that I knew would declare us to be either friend or foe; the 'V' for victory sign. We were as yet unsure of their intentions, but there was little we could do about it. By the conning tower stood a man with arm raised, one finger pointing upwards, beside him another ready with a heaving line. Suddenly the line was curling outwards and in that instant I saw that it was falling short. I plunged into the water and with a few desperate strokes I managed to grasp it. Hanging on grimly, I was then slowly dragged on the casing alongside the submarine's waterline, and from the deck above a strong hand reached down and hauled me up to safety. My earnest 'thank you' brought to his face a look of complete surprise that I shall always remember, and his shout of "They're English Sir!" confirmed that we had been found by friends. Taken to the conning tower I spoke to an officer, quickly identified myself, and to his total dismay, informed him that the original party had numbered over 1300 Australian and British POWs. The Captain ordered "Take them aboard!"."

Harry Weigand: "Fourth day in water – 15 September 1944. The sea was very choppy, it was making it extra hard to hang on and I was very weak. God answered my prayers and gave me strength and courage to hold on. That morning we could see a great big box away in the distance, it turned out to be the ice box from our ship. There was a man on it and he was waving like the devil. We paddled over to him and he was an Englisman, he was delirious, so we said, "Righto, jump off and get on one of the rafts that we are towing behind us." He said, "No, I can't leave this island and Betty, I love her and she loves me, I can't leave here." He wouldn't get off by coaxing so we took sterner measures and he soon got off. The raft he got on broke off some hours later in the day and I don't know what became of him. in the end we wound up with three rafts, four on the one I was on and five men on the other two rafts.

"About 5 p.m. on the 4th day Frank Coombes sighted a ship on the horizon, she first looked like a small oil tanker and then with the help of the other three men on the raft I eventually managed to stand up with the others supporting me, the raft was so slippery with oil and we were just about all in with the effort, but then did I wave or did I. The ship eventually came within a mile of us and we could see quite plainly that it was a submarine, we could hear the diesel engines quite distinctly. The submarine passed us by and went over to another raft about two miles away and we said, "It must be a Jap sub. just looking for any stray Japs in the water." The submarine stopped at the other raft and picked them up then she headed for us and my thoughts were, "Oh God – can it be true that she is going to pick us up!" She drew closer and I could see that they were a white crew, they sang out, "Who are you?" and we all yelled, "We are Australians!". We knew by their twang that they were Americans and it was sweet music to our ears. They threw us a rope and we tied it on to the rafts, we were too weak to get up on the submarine on our own and some of the sailors jumped in the sea and helped us up. When I got hold of that sub. I'll swear it was the tightest hold that I have ever had on anything in my life. When they pulled me on the deck I just flopped like a jelly fish, I must have used my last ounce of energy to climb aboard."

Cliff Farlow: "On the evening of the 4th day we heard the thunder in the water and we then saw a periscope coming up out of the water – it's a submarine – a bloody Jap sub. – they're not going to worry about us! But as it drew nearer and nearer it surfaced; at the time I thought it was thunder coming across the water – and then you saw the periscope coming, then it surfaced and blokes came out on the deck with machine guns and we thought we were going to be done over – then one of the blokes calls out, "They're Australians!" and two blokes jumped over the side and helped us and one crew was saying "For Chrissake hurry up – we gotta get down!". They picked the four of us up, we were the second lot to be

U.S.S. PAMPANITO rescues. Pic: U.S. National Archives

picked up – they knew there were other POWs about."

Bob Farrands: "The only time I thought I was not going to make it was Day 4. I didn't give a damn if I did go. The memory went back home to Ganmain while I was in the water – when I was a POW I dreamed every night of home – in the water I was just cursing and swearing, I was cursing the Japs. Occasionally I thought of the Mother and Father but I didn't dwell on it. I wasn't delirious with them – I was more delirious about water. I was absolutely buggered – I was craving for water. I would shut my eyes and dream I was back in Ganmain at Claude Smith's Cafe – I could see Claude standing by the soda fountain pouring a drink and I just couldn't reach. The water kept running, I kept reaching and just couldn't reach. I used to also dream of home – the old home with the verandah around the house and along one side the grape vines provided shade where Mum kept the water bag. No matter how I tried I couldn't reach that water bag! as soon as I closed my eyes the soda fountain and the full water bag would be there – dripping – dripping – cool water and I couldn't reach!

"I didn't believe it when they said they saw a mast – it was not until I heard the diesel motors – you could hear the beat of the engine then a rope came over and I grabbed hold of it and two blokes got my shoulders and pulled me in, they lifted me and then they lifted me up to the next one and they stood me up and they said, "Are you right mate?" and I said, "I'm as right as bloody rain now!" and they let me go and I went whack on my face!

"They started to wash me and apparently a recce plane was reported, I was rushed down the conning tower. The 'recce plane' turned out to be birds and whether they dived then or not I don't know but I was not washed until later down in the engine room.

"I was still conscious right through, I think I yapped all night because there were blokes about all night. The sailors did it in shifts, they did their Watch and they did a Watch with us and then they slept on the floor. They were asking us questions and I talked all night till someone said, "Shut up Bob!"

"In the beginning the blokes would say, "Well at least we're no longer POWs" and when the Jap ship came some blokes said, "I'm not going there, I'm through with them, I don't want them to pick me up" and other blokes would say, "Neither do I, neither do I – bugger them – we'll take our chance here." We thought the submarines would be back, we thought they would just sneak away a few hundred yards and then come back to have a look – but we didn't know it would be days and days before they got back. But that's what kept us going, the submarines were here once and they're sure to be still about here and we might be lucky to be picked up."

Reg Harris: "There was Sgt. Bill Cunneen and another bloke from Western Australia and he kept on saying, "Come on – I've got a kid back home, I want to get out of this." He was a great inspiration – "as long as we're afloat we're right!" he'd say. A few hours before we were picked up we found a whole piece of superstructure which we slid up on to our raft and we could all get up on it and sit up on it although we were down in the water to mid-chest. And then Bill Cunneen said, "I'm responsible for you men, hand me that bucket, there's a camp over behind that hill and I'11 go and get you a bucket of water." And we said, "Oh sit down Cunneen!" and poor old Bill sat down. Then later on he said, "I can hear a motor!" and we said, "You could see a bloody camp a while ago, shut up!" Then somebody else said, "I can hear a motor", and then gradually we could all hear it but we didn't want to build up our hopes; and then this huge monster seemed to come out of the water, I was almost blind but I could hear the motor but not able to see anything until it was practically on top of us. And here were these huge men standing on top, towering over us, and I thought, "God Almighty, the bloody Germans are here!" They all looked so clean and fair-haired, but they called out to us, "Who are you guys?" They knew of course because they'd already picked up some and we said, "We're Australians" and one of them said, "Why haven't you got a hat turned up at the side?!" They were kindness itself.

"This pick-up was what we had hung on for but we didn't know there was going to be so few of us. When the Yank was pulling the raft in I was the last one and I got caught in the exhaust from the submarine and it just washed the old raft out to sea again, I thought, "Christ – here we go – I'm gone again!" But he pulled it in and they helped me up the side of the submarine and I said, "I'm right I'm right I can walk" – and conked out like a bloody light!. They carried me down below and the first thing I remember is Miscamble saying, "We made it Harris we made it!"

Reg Stewart: "When we got on board my mate Bill Cunneen threw his arms around me and said, "Jungle! Jungle! you made it!" I could only hold him too and say, "Woolly Dog! Woolly Dog! Woolly Dog!" – the nickname he had been given when he had had his head out of a railway carriage window when the train was in the station and a boy, thinking it was a dog patted his mop of woolly black hair, then said, "Sorry – I thought it was a woolly dog!"

"We never drank any seawater but we seemed to be piddling all the time!"

Roy Cornford: "It was still hot and late that day we could hear the drone of an engine and we thought it was a plane, then we spotted this small black object and we thought it was a Jap corvette and it seemed to be going to the little black dots, 'rafts', so we started waving and eventually it came closer to us and we realised it was an American submarine. lt came over to our rafts and an American officer, Robert Bennett, dived into the sea with a rope and we were pulled over to the side of the submarine. I can remember holding my hands up and pleading with him not to grab my arms as they were all blistered with sun and oil and only skin and bones, I was pulled aboard and we shed our shorts and shirt and were amazed that we could wobbly walk on the deck of the submarine."

John Hocking: "On the 4th day there were only three of us left on the raft, one chap named Smith from South Australia, and we were using debris to paddle west to land which we found out later was some 150 miles away.

"I remember these two men because they were growling at me for not

U.S.S. PAMPANITO. Pic: U.S. National Archives

pulling my weight with the paddling because I was nodding off to sleep. I'm certain that had we not been rescued late in the day I would have drifted off into the darkness to never return. I was pretty well exhausted and had to be helped by the crew to board the submarine."

Bill McKitterick: "By Day 4 there were 7 of us from the 16 – we were in bad shape.

"Someone said they could hear a plane, maybe a message got out, some said they could feel a noise in the water – then another said they could see a mast, we were low in the water but we reckoned we could see about 20 miles. As we saw it it came closer, then it vanished and our hopes went with it, then it appeared again! From the level of the raft it looked like the QUEEN MARY – it was a wonderful sight. It was getting dark but we could see someone standing on the deck, we thought he was a German, but when they got closer someone called out, "Stay on your rafts" and two men jumped into the water and we were dragged in. My singlet was thrown away and I was dropped below."

Harold Martin: "The PAMPANITO approached us within shotgun range and we could see the crew standing on deck armed with a variety of weapons. We were shouting – one fellow put his fingers up 'V' for Victory. Later she turned around and came up within 30 yards of the raft."

Frank Jesse: "Most men were covered with sores due to being in the seawater and in the hot sun. We tried to huddle together during the cold nights, hallucinations affected many, imagining clouds to be rescue ships, some trying to paddle to the China Coast.

"On the evening of the fourth day we could not believe our eyes when the submarine appeared. At first the Americans could not determine who we were as we were covered with oil. I was pulled aboard by the submarine crew."

Claude Longey: "On the second night there were only 6 men on the back raft including my mate, and in the morning they were all gone, this continued day and night. There were only 9 men left when we saw what appeared to be a boat in the distance, it came towards us, we could not tell if it was a friendly boat, and then realised it was a submarine. It came closer and then turned and left us, we did not know if they were going to fire on us or what but they went away until they were hardly visible; they were picking up two's and small groups and then they turned and came straight back to us and they called to sit still they would pick us up – and we realised they were Americans. Two men jumped into the water and pulled the raft into the submarine, it was the PAMPANITO.

"Other men cut any clothes we had on off and put us down the conning tower, all black with oil out of the water. The sailors on board gave up their beds for us – black men from the oil among white sheets. Then the medical staff on board would only allow us two ozs. of fluid at a time. There were 92 men picked up by this submarine."

Reg Bullock and Jim Boulter had left the RAKUYO MARU together: "Jim told me, "I've got a daughter back home I haven't seen and I can't swim" and I said, “Never mind mate, you just do as I do and you’ll be alright”. They jumped together and were saved together. “Jim had a rough time spending a long time in the water without a hat”, remembered Reg Bullock, “we kept pouring water on him.”

Charlie Madden: “Day 4 we thought we heard a plane but the noise seemed to come from under us, then around us, then the sub about a few yards away, or it could have been our oil-caked eyes that we didn’t see it coming. It was just on dark.”

With Madden were Don McArdle and Harry Kinleyside.

* * * * * * * * * *

The submarine was the USS PAMPANITO which earlier in the day had rendezvoused with the USS SEALION to lay out a plan to search which would take them east to Luzon.

Paul Summers, the Skipper of PAMPANITO, recorded: “While patrolling on the surface on an easterly heading from Hainan Island in the South China Sea, Latitude 18°42'N., Longitude 114°00'E., the O.O.D. and bridge lookouts sighted a lifeboat and a large quantity of debris floating on the surface of a calm sea. This spot was a little to the north of where an enemy convoy had been intercepted and attacked by our wolf pack on the night of 11-12 September 1944. There was a possibility of the lifeboat being occupied so course was altered to go alongside, only to find it abandoned. At this time, 1610(I), a lookout reported that there were two rafts on the horizon with men on them. It was naturally believed that these would be Japanese, so small arms were broken out and preparations made for taking prisoners.

“On the approach to the first raft, which was a makeshift affair of hatch covers and timbers, it was noted that the fifteen men it contained were thickly covered with crude-oil and were clothed very scantily, though some had nondescript hats and a few wore the regulation Japanese soldier’s caps. They were waving frantically and all shouting at will so that no words could be distinguished, although one voice was finally heard to speak distinctly in English. While getting the raft alongside, orders were given to bring aboard the English speaking man, and by the time the first line was over the amazing announcement came to the bridge, “They are British and Australian prisoner-of-war shipwreck survivors.”

“All hands went into action immediately; those below decks sent up bales of rags and began preparing hot soup and tea in quantities; the Pharmacist’s mate assembled his gear for immediate treatment, and the rescue party commenced bringing the survivors aboard. The poor fellows were so frantic with joy at this unbelievable piece of good fortune that they began jumping from the raft and trying to clamber up the sides of the ship. Members of the rescue party dived over the side to make the raft fast, herded the survivors back onto the raft and aided them up to the ship’s deck. The weakened condition of these men, as well as their covering of slippery crude oil, made the actual recovery quite difficult. Some of them could help themselves, but the majority had to be lifted and dragged aboard bodily.

"The next problem was to clean some of the oil from their bodies and to treat their immediate needs before sending them below. While this job was being done the second raft was reached and the true bearings taken of three others within sight. The second raft contained more men who fortunately were comparatively free from oil, making the problem of bringing them aboard much easier.

"While heading for the next group, a small raft passed close aboard with its single occupant dead with part of the head gone (probably by a shark).

"Recovered third and fourth raft-loads of eleven emaciated ex-prisoners-of-war. Another small raft was sighted with one figure lying motionless on his back. He seemed to be still alive and when one of the ship's crew dived into the water with a line, he sat up startled and started to go over the side. The man in the water persuaded him to remain seated until he could be helped aboard. This man was almost blind and in a semi-conscious condition when brought aboard and remained unconscious almost continuously until he died the following evening.

"While the eleven men from the next raft were being brought aboard the after lookout reported "Three planes in formation astern". There were approximately fifty men topside at this time including bridge personnel and the rescue squad as well as many survivors who had as yet not been lowered down the hatch. Fortunately one of the planes was seen to flap its wings proving the formation to be large birds gliding in perfect order.

"This completed the rescue of all survivors in the immediate vicinity but a bearing had been taken on a raft now out of sight to the south, so the ship was headed in that direction at high speed. At 1810, two rafts were sighted ahead and soon thirteen more survivors were being rescued. While getting the men from the last of these two rafts the high periscope watch sighted another raft at 010°T, and also what appeared to be a ship's masts bearing 027°T, at the extreme range of vision. While headed toward the bearing of the raft, the ship was identified as a submarine that appeared to have a gun aft, making us very suspicious, since one of the survivors had stated that a German submarine was somewhere in this area and since it did not reply to an SJ radar challenge, we dived to periscope depth to investigate. After watching the submarine for a few minutes through the periscope and noting that it was practically dead in the water, decided that it must be the SEALION rescuing survivors, since we had sent a message to her earlier requesting that she come over and assist in rescue. So surfaced and resumed searching. It was almost completely dark by this time. A single man on a small raft was seen waving what appeared to be a white hat at the time, but later proved to be his 'bleached hand'. He was recovered and course was set for the last raft that had been sighted before diving. This raft was luckily located in the dark and another twelve men were rescued and stowed below, making a total of seventy three (73) survivors on board."

U.S.S. PAMPANITO.Pic: U.S. National Archives

Australian survivors rescued by submarine USS PAMPANITO.

Boulter, Pte. J.L.	VX.43376	2/2 MT.Regt.	South Melbourne, Vic.
Browne, Pte. J.F.M.	NX.50497	2/15 Fld.Regt.	Parramatta, NSW
Bullock, Pte. R.C.	QX. 9591	8 Div.Provost Coy.	Brisbane, Qld.
Chivars, Pte. H.C.	VX.26828	2/2 Pioneer Bn.	West Melbourne, Vic.
Cocking, Pte. A.J.	WX.16369	2/2 M.G. Bn.	Western Australia
Coombes, Pte. F.J.	NX. 2111	3 Res.M.T. Coy.	Sandringham, NSW
Cornford, Pte. R.	NX.44955	2/19 Bn.	Wollongong, NSW
Cunneen, Sgt. D.W.	VX.32993	4 A/Tk. Regt.	Nagambie, Vic.
Curran, Pte. M.W.	NX.37529	2/19 Bn.	Zetland, NSW
Farlow, Cpl. C.L.	NX.35756	2/19 Bn.	Hay, NSW
Farmer, Pte. F.L.	VX.60993	2/lO Ord.Wk.Shps.	Black Rock, Vic.
Farrands, Cpl. M.R.	NX.36050	2/19 Bn.	Ganmain, NSW
Flynn, Dvr. D.A.	SX.10228	2 Res.M.T. Coy.	Adelaide, S.A.
Gainger, Pte. R.J.	VX.61502	2/10 Ord.Wk.Shps.	Geelong West, Vic.
Gollin, Pte. R.G.	NX.44147	M.L.F.D.	Lismore, NSW
Harris, Gnr. R.J.	QX. 9275	2/10 R.A.E.	Brisbane, Qld.
Hart, Spr. R.H.	VX.23586	2/10 R.A.E.	Melbourne, Vic.
Hocking, Cpl. J.R.	VX.17768	2/2 Pioneer Bn.	Castlemaine, Vic.
Holcroft, Pte. F.	QX.23670	2/3 Ord.Stores Coy.	Brisbane, Qld.
Jesse, Sig. F.W.	VX.41958	2 Res.M.T. Coy.	Blackburn, Vic.
Kinleyside, Gnr. H.L.	VX.65127	4 A/Tk. Regt.	Mildura, Vic.
Lansdowne, Pte. J.H.	QX.13551	2/26 Bn.	Murwillumbah, NSW
Latham, Desp.Rdr. C.T.S.	NX.72262	3 M.T. Coy.	Merrylands, NSW
Longey, Pte. C.	TX. 4802	2/40 Bn.	Hobart, Tas.
Lynch, Pte. D.F.	QX.24156	2/2 Pioneer Bn.	Warwick, Qld.
Madden, Pte. C.W.	QX.22879	8 Div.H.Q.	Tweed Heads, NSW
Martin, Pte. H.D.	WX. 204	2/10 Ord.Wk.Shps.	Esperance, W.A.
Mawby, Pte. R.G.	VX. 2064	2/2 Pioneer Bn.	Murrumbeena, Vic.
McArdle, Cpl. D.	VX.36838	2/29 Bn.	Rushworth, Vic.
McKechnie, Bdr. C.	QX.14464	2/10 Fld.Regt.	Brisbane, Qld.
McKittrick, Pte. W.H.	NX.33414	2/12 Fld.Coy.RAE	Woollahra, NSW
Miscamble, Gnr. R.C.	QX.13804	2/10 Fld.Regt.	Brisbane, Qld.

Pascoe, Dvr. T.A.	WX. 7409	2/4 M.G. Bn.	Denmark, W.A.
Pickett, Sig. H.	WX. 9055	2/4 M.G. Bn.	Midland Junction, W.A
Renton, Pte. K.C.	VX.22728	2/2 Pioneer Bn.	Port Melbourne, Vic.
Smith, Sgt. J.O.	NX.32726	2/19 Bn.	North Bondi, NSW
Smith, Cpl. C.G.	SX.11294	4 M.l. Coy.	Goolwa, S.A.
Smith, Pte. P.	NX.35359	2/19 Bn.	Narrandera, NSW
Stewart, Gnr. R.S.	VX.31123	4 A/Tk. Regt.	Malvern, Vic.
Turner, Dvr. J.W.	SX.10112	2 Res.M.T.Coy.	Adelaide, S.A.
Vickers, Pte. J.A.	VX.59658	27 Bde. H.Q.	Melbourne, Vic.
Wall, Pte. R.J.	VX.58797	2 Res.M.T. Bn.	Hopetown, Vic.
Weigand, Spr. H.G.	NX.32373	2/12 R.A.E.	Katoomba, NSW
White, Pte. S.McL.		2/29 Bn.	Melbourne, Vic.
Williams, Cpl. K.	SX.11200	27 Bde.Army Ord.	Oak Bank, S.A.
Winter, Pte. A.D.	WX. 8110	2/4 M.G. Bn.	Redcliffe, W.A.
Winter, Pte. W.X.	WX.10373	2/4 M.G. Bn.	South Perth, W.A.

PAMPANITO reported later: "The general condition of the survivors when rescued was critical, with every man suffering from acute exhaustion, exposure, shock, starvation, dehydration and skin sores. About seventy percent of these men had drunk seawater, urine or blood during their four days on the rafts, and nearly all were covered with thick crude oil.

"As the survivors were brought aboard they were treated on deck as follows: the crude oil was wiped and then sponged off with diesel oil, and morphine was administered to those suffering from extreme shock. As soon as emergency cleaning and shock treatment were given, the men were lowered through the after battery hatch, given a cup of hot tea and a bowl of hot vegetable soup, after which each was given an eye irrigation followed by Butyn Sulfate and Boric Acid Ointment was applied to ease the irritation on the skin of each man's scrotum. This irritation being caused by the crude oil.

"Six of the more critical cases, who were given bunks in the after battery compartment, had their sores and ulcerations cleaned with Asechloramide in Triacetin 1:500 and dressed with Sulfathiasole Ointment 5%.

"About one quarter of the survivors were given sedatives of Phenobarbital or Sodium Amytal, depending upon each one's condition. Three men had rather severe cases of malaria, one of whom was in a state of delirium for four hours after being rescued. These men were given Quinine Hydrochloride in graduated doses, two men found to have severe Cellutitis infections were placed in bunks with parts elevated and dosed with Sulfadiazine with Sodium Bicarbonate at four hour intervals rather than the prescribed dose of 4 gm. of Sulfa, because of their condition. One man was found to have an injured back and a broken rib, but due to the acute tropical dermatitis infection which covered fifty percent of his body no strapping was done. This dermatitis infection was treated with Sulfathiasole Ointment covered with cotton dressings to make the man more comfortable in his bunk.

"By twelve hours after the rescue every man had received an examination and had had his worse sores cleaned with Azochloramide in Triacetin 1:500 and dressed with Sulfathiazole Ointment 5% or Sulfadiazine powder depending on each individual's condition. Upon questioning the men, it was found that during their two and half years of imprisonment all had had some degree of malaria; seventy percent had suffered from Pallagra or Beri Beri; fifty percent were affected by tropical dermatitis infections and all but three or four had Gingivitis or Vincents Angina. It was also learned that all had been exposed to Cholera, Dysentery, Typhus Fever, and other types of contagious diseases, so that although during their time on board no one showed any signs of having contracted any of these diseases, precautions were taken to keep isolated all cups, utensils, the head, etc. Within three hours after examination each survivor was receiving one cup of either water, tea with sugar and milk, cocoa or soup every hour for twenty four hours.

"The only casualty occurred the day following the rescue. This man died of acute exhaustion, exposure, shock, dehydration and possible internal haemorrhage. He had been in a state of delirium almost continuously since being brought aboard. Intravenous injections of Dextrose and saline solution were attempted, but without success due to the failure to locate a vein or even a drop of blood, the injections finally being given in the buttocks, but to no avail.

"From the second through the fourth day all but the six men who were critically ill were given baths, shampoos and shaves by members of the crew, while the six bed cases were bathed in their bunks. The officers and crew all donated clothing so that every survivor had under shirt and socks and most had shoes or sandals.

"The diet was gradually increased to include beef boullion, bread and butter, chicken broth and crackers, tomato consomme, egg-nog, canned fruit and finally soft-boil eggs and hash. Two multiple vitamin pills were given every fifteen hours, as well as a small amount of soft chocolate. Fruit juices, although given at first, were discontinued when they proved to be irritating.

"On the final days aboard, those men with the most aggravated eye conditions were given more frequent eye irrigations followed by Sulfathiazole Opthalmic ointment and all patients were given 1½ gr. of Atabrin."

When SEALION received PAMPANITO's request for assistance in the rescue of English and Australian prisoners-of-war, she immediately changed course and increased speed to head for the scene of the rescue.

Debris and wreckage were first sighted at 1750(I) beginning at Latitude 18-44 N, Longitude 114-09 E, extending south-westward to the horizon. A few minutes later SEALION passed through a heavy diesel oil slick and at 1820(I), the first of many dead bodies floated by. SEALION now was about 40 miles to the northwest of the torpedo attack made on a large convoy on the morning of 12 September. The periscope sheers of PAMPANITO were sighted bearing 225°T, indicating that the wreckage spread over an area at least ten miles square. The first group of living, shouting, beckoning survivors was sighted at 1831(I), an hour before sunset.

A rescue party consisting of three swimmers, a hauling out party, and a delivery and stripping party was organised for the rescue. By this time, several other rafts with survivors aboard and five or six lone men floating in life jackets had been sighted. The rescue became a race against darkness.

The first raft took a line at 1837(I) and the first survivor was lifted aboard at 1840(I). From then, until total darkness, the rescue work went on.

SEALION flooded down and rigged out the bow planes. Some survivors were hauled aboard on the forecastle, some amidships. Swimmers took lines to those too distant to reach from the deck or too weak to hold fast. The hauling out party lifted the oil-coated, water-soaked, half unconscious men to the deck, yanking them up by the life jackets, grabbing them under the arms, sliding and slipping the while endeavouring to keep their feet steady in the oily slime which remained on deck after the delivery party had raised the survivors from the deck. This party, after stripping them of their clothes, led or carried the exhausted survivors below.

Norm Nutley: "I had been alone for two days and on the fourth day I thought I heard a plane – my eyes were giving me agony, I tried to look at the sky but couldn't see anything. Then in the distance I thought I saw a motor boat and I thought my mates had reached shore and were out looking for us in a boat. I used a bamboo to try and row closer and then I recognised a submarine – didn't know whose but it was a chance of survival. It seemed to stop – start again and go further away. I remember thinking, "Geez things are not too good now" and I started to say farewells to my mother and two sisters. Then the submarine changed direction – came closer – so I left the plank and started swimming towards them. On the submarine one of the crew had called out "Man Overboard!" and one of the crew swam out and took me in on a line. When he dragged me aboard the submarine I remember saying to one of the crew, "Are you the bastards that sunk us?! "No Bud", he said, "we're here to save you – can you see the ladder?" but at that stage I collapsed.

Tony Clive: "On the fourth day I started to get tired, I was tired and gave myself another twelve or twentyfour hours at the most, people had been dropping off and you either conserved your own energy or helped the other and you both go.

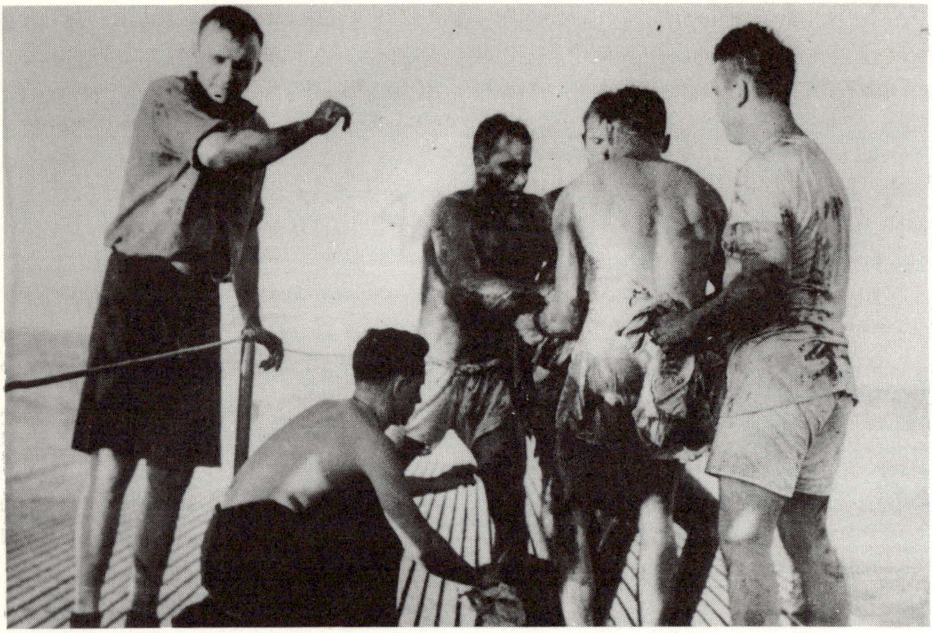

SEALION rescue party cleansing survivor.
Pic: U.S. National Archives

Survivors tied debris together for support.
Pic: U.S. National Archives

"As the day went on it started to get a bit rough and just on dusk I went up on the crest of a wave and I thought I saw something but I didn't say anything because they would think I was mad too – and I was not sure of anything at this stage. Then we went down the gully of a wave, came up, and it was still there and by this time it was getting closer and closer. I did not know what it was. Our hopes rose and I prayed – it felt like ages before it came close – and by that stage I had given up hope and I didn't care whether it was a Jap vessel or not – anything was better than where I was."

Norm Calvert: "The fourth morning our raft had been reduced to a Greek lad, George Mavrothalasitis, and myself. By mid morning George imagined he could see an island with water spurting up into the air and he decided to swim to it, I had no chance of stopping him, he swam for a short distance then disappeared into the sea. That afternoon I came across a young Englishman who was the sole survivor of another raft. We both took to the same raft and were still together when we were found, he was in pretty poor shape.

"The submarine sounded a bit like an aeroplane. I looked and saw the surfaced submarine circling us. We tried to use our hands to paddle towards it, but it kept moving away. Eventually the submarine, SEALION, pulled beside the raft and helped us aboard. The Yanks could not do enough for us, we were covered in oil, they cleaned us up although they had to cut all our hair off. I celebrated my 24th birthday aboard the submarine two days after being plucked from the raft."

Bob Collins: We drifted about 40 miles from the position of the sinking. Noel Day said, "You're a Navy bloke, what sort of ship is that?" It was the SEALION. Day was still in good condition and he swam to the submarine. Later, one of the American sailors said he had never heard any one swear like Day."

Les Bolger: "Bill Scarpella disappeared, I knew if I did not get picked up that day I would not be there the next day – I was hallucinating. I imagined a beautiful tropical green island, with beautiful girls there and I asked for a drink of water and they would not give any to me and I became quite abusive! I had lost my hat and I was very sunburned although the oil did protect us a lot but quite a lot got in my eyes.

"I thought of my people at home and that I would not see them again perhaps – every day I prayed in the water and offered up my prayers, I am a Catholic, and I prayed my final prayers, "Lord Have Mercy" every afternoon. Before I had left to go away to the war there was a Brown Nun, she was a friend of the family, and she gave me a medal, it shows St. Joseph holding up the Baby Jesus Christ, and she said, "This will bring you home", and I still have that medal.

"There were only four of us left on the raft when I was picked up, three English and myself."

For two hours SEALION manoeuvred in the cluttered water. As reported in her Log: "When darkness came, fiftyfour survivors had been rescued. How many of the thirteen hundred prisoners still lived among the bales and boxes cannot be estimated, but there were many. Even if daylight had lingered, only a very few

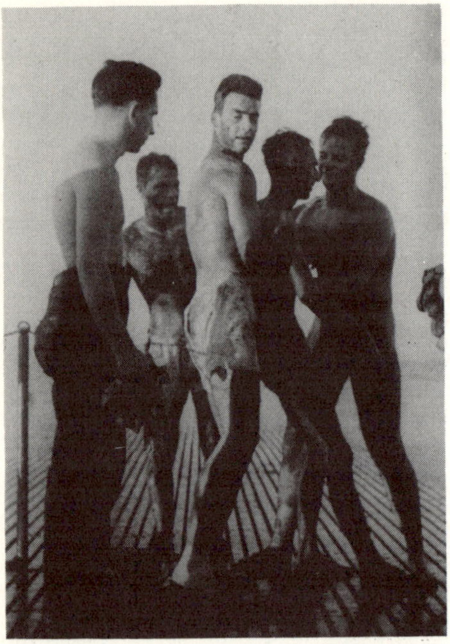

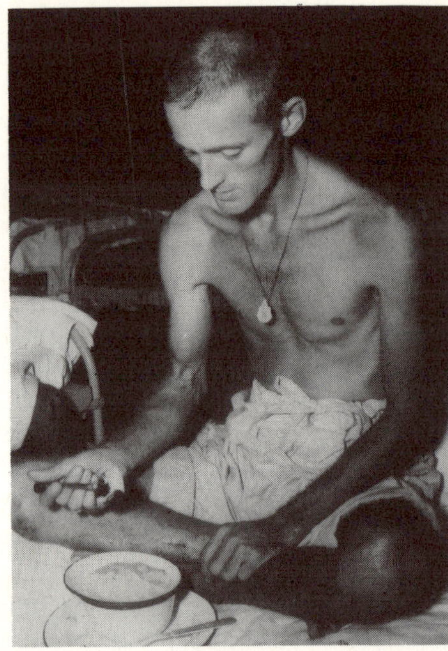

Left: Tony Clive being cleaned up. Norman Hunter on left. Pic: U.S. National Archives. Right: PERTH Seaman Bob Collins at Saipan. Pic: U.S. National Archives

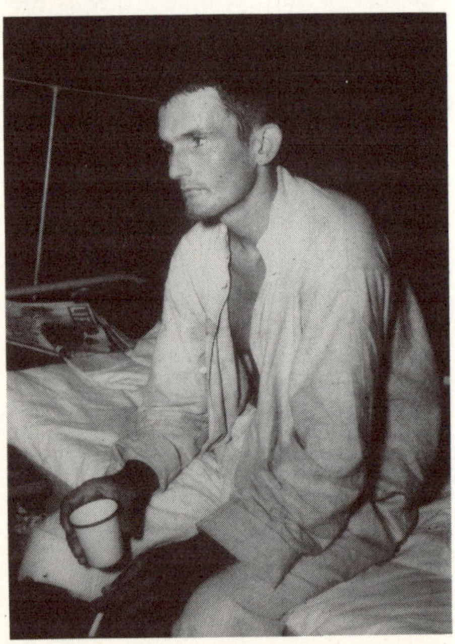

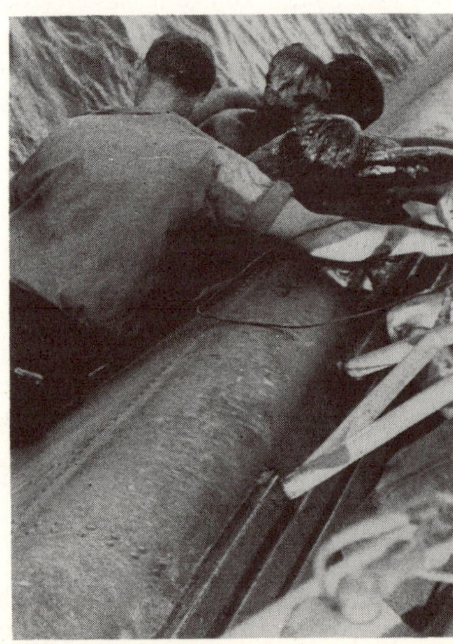

Left: Noel Day (RAAF) Saipan. Pic: U.S. National Archives
Right: A lone survivor approaching SEALION. Pic: U.S. National Archives

more could have been taken on board. The fortunate ones whom we had saved required nursing, care, medicine, and hospitalisation." With heavy heart SEALION turned east-ward and headed for Balintang Channel and Saipan at full speed.

The heartbreak on SEALION was nothing compared with the heartbreak the nearby survivors experienced when the submarine departed.

Eli Reich, Commander of SEALION wrote: "It was heart-breaking to leave so many dying men behind." The survivors have told how they hollered and called out "Over here!" only to see the submarine disappear and the thunder in the water was no longer heard.

Soon after, Reich broke radio silence and informed Pearl Harbour there were will many POWs alive. Admiral Lockwood then ordered the nearest submarines to continue the search, they were the "Eradicators", now comprising QUEENFISH and BARB. The third member of the pack, TUNNY, had been damaged and was forced to withdraw. Now heading for the rescue area they ran into a convoy of five ships – the POWs would have to wait – QUEENFISH opened the attack. BARB later manoeuvred, seeking a tanker – moving in closer an aircraft carrier was identified – Fluckey moved for an overlap to bring the tanker and carrier into line of fire – fired the bow torpedoes and tried to bring the stern tubes to bear when he was spotted by a destroyer. Fluckey dived and just missed being rammed, on the way down he heard two hits on the tanker and three on the carrier. Soon after they were depth charged. The BARB had sunk the 11,177 ton tanker AZUSA and the 20,000 ton carrier UNYO. It was believed this was the convoy the POWs had seen at Singapore.

The QUEENFISH and BARB arrived at the rescue area on September 17.

Neville Thams: "That day, I did see a submarine in the distance, but it was too far away to attract its attention. I had with me letters from home, a copy of Lt.Col. Nagatamo's "Work Cheerfully" speech, a small steel shaving mirror wrapped in a gas cape wallet, tucked inside my tunic and held in position by my lifejacket, or so I thought. Alas, requiring a mirror for signalling I found I had lost the wallet.

"When we were first torpedoed I had made up my mind that I hadn't endured, suffered and survived the hardships up to this time to suddenly despair. Even though in a hopeless situation, I believed I could last out two days – it would be tough going. Then at the end of the first two days, though very thirsty, hungry, covered in oil, I believed that I might manage another few days. That I did, but then it was a tremendous fight to keep hanging on. Almost alone in the sea, my English mate and I hang on we did, though chances of rescue were nil."

Norman Hunter: "There were two rescue parties on the SEALION, one by the conning tower and the other on the bow plane area: "Some of the rafts would drift towards us and I would swim out with a rope and they would be pulled in. They were mostly in small parties suffering from shock and didn't have much to say, they were just satisfied to stand and be washed down then they went below.

All the time we were thinking 'If a plane comes!!' we were not far from the China coast – we tried not to think about it.

"We had our general duties to carry out and slept wherever we could find space, with an additional 54 men on board we were really crowded. Occasionally you would go by the bunks and they would speak to you – a little more as we progressed towards Saipan riding a typhoon so everything was in turmoil.

"As men recovered they would be interrogated by the Captain."

Australian survivors rescued by submarine USS SEALION

Blake, Gnr. R.A.	VX.20802	4 A/Tk.Regt.	Mortlake, Vic.
Bolger, Gnr. L.J.	NX.56381	2/15 Fld.Regt.	Fairfield, NSW
Brown, Dvr. L.	SX. 8791	2 Res.M.T.Coy.	Orroroo, S.A.
Buerekner, Pte. E.F.	VX.23638	2/2 Pioneer Bn.	Tungimah, Vic.
Cage, Dvr. G.	SX. 8023	Ammn.Sub.Park	Adelaide, S.A.
Calvert, Pte. N.D.	QX.22922	2/29 Bn.	Nanango, Qld.
Clarkson, Pte. F.	VX.21783	2/2 Pioneer Bn.	Alexandria, Vic.
Clifford, Pte. V.	VX.20904	2/2 Pioneer Bn.	Richmond, Vic.
Clive, Cpl. A.A.	NX.32668	2/18 Bn.	Waverton, NSW
Deguara, Dvr. M.	QX.18570	3 M.T. Coy.	Mackay, Qld.
Downey, Pte. T.L.	VX.26308	2/29 Bn.	Traralgon, Vic.
Harris, Pte. J.L.	QX.18665	2/26 Bn.	Mackay, Qld.
Horsburgh, Spr. F.W.	VX.54298	2/10 Fld.Regt.	Kensington, Vic.
Johnson, Sig. T.P.	NX.58915	8 Div.Sigs.	Dungog, NSW
Kearney, Gnr. L.D.	WX.84276	2/4 M.G. Bn.	Mintaro, S.A.
Laws, Pte. R.E.	NX.18368	2/18 Bn.	East Sydney, NSW
Nutley, Gnr. N.A.	QX.17951	2/1O Fld.Regt.	Warrill View, Qld.
Ross, Dvr. J.M.	VX.24698	105 Gen.Tpt.Coy.	Glen Iris, Vic.
Sing, Pte. A.	WX.16424	2/4 M.G. Bn.	Northam, W.A.
Sprague, Pte. C.C.	VX.54602	2/2 Pioneer Bn.	Coburg, Vic.
R.A.N.			
Collins, A.B.R.	22177	HMAS PERTH	Newcastle, NSW
Houghton, A.B J.C.	23719	HMAS PERTH	Brisbane, Qld.
R.A.A.F.			
Day, LAC.Armourer, N.C.	35423	No.1 Recce. & Bomber Squadron	Byrock, NSW

SEALION later reported: "En route from the area to Saipan the after part of the ship beginning at the forward battery compartment except for the emergency spaces, was quarantined because all of the patients suffered from active or dormant malaria and perhaps from cholera, plague, dysentery, or other infectious diseases. Fortunately, none of the patients were so infected. The eight nurses were dosed with atebrine and adhered closely to regular antisepsis procedure. For five days these eight men and the Pharmacist's mate nursed the patients along. They bathed them, gave medication, and did a lot of dirty work cheerfully.

"The patients required so much care because they had been at hard labour for thirty months in Japanese prison camps in Malaya, Burma, and French Indo-China, where they existed on very dimished rations. As a result, they suffered from beri-beri, pellagra, malnutrition, infected scrotums, and general physical debilitation. All of this was aggravated by the effects of their long immersion and exposure after abandoning the RAKUYO MARU. They were a scrawny, scabrous lot of human beings, but, on SEALION's arrival in Saipan on 20 September 1944, the care given them by the nursing gang brought most of them around – only six of the fifty remaining survivors required stretchers."

DAY FIVE – SIX

U.S.S. QUEENFISH

Neville Thams wrote: "Day 4 found only four of us left. Late afternoon, we collected a former PERTH sailor alone on a raft, but we lost him through the night. On the 5th day we were quite alone. There were only 2 of us. We lost the others through the night. I was becoming semi-delirious and seemed to doze a lot. There had been virtually no conversation between us. What could we talk about? Our hopeless plight? That wouldn't do us much good. Our present position did not put us in the mood for conversation, it left us with our own thoughts. After all, we were only awaiting out our time.

"The sea was starting to toss our hatch cover about. Frequently I would fall off and had the problem of getting back on to the raft. Each time either of us fell off it would upset the buoyancy and most times the other would also fall off. Neither of us had much strength left and it was extremely difficult to climb back on the slippery raft. My eyes were covered in oil and I used a small piece of wood to scrape the oil from my eyelids. This was the day we saw a shark, it circled us for about 15 minutes, then it was gone. We were not unduly concerned, we were past the stage of worrying about death by shark attack or drowning."

Ray Wheeler: "Our numbers started to dwindle fast from the second day, with most seeming to drift off during the night. Drinking seawater or urine proved to be fatal to those who swallowed more than a mouthful over a protracted period. I lost my two mates on the third night, Walker (VX.63237) died quietly alongside me and Dart (VX.60684) peacefully in my arms.

"On the fourth morning I swam over to a raft that had more room and only two people on it, it was a bad move as both were drinking seawater and were quite delirious, I had to fight them off when they accused me of drinking their water so I returned to the main group. The swim took its toll and I fell off a raft and started to drift. Bancroft and Smith helped me onto their group of rafts and on the evening of that night we saw the first of the survivors being rescued by submarine, they were on the skyline a fair distance from us and although we hollered ourselves hoarse they failed to hear us or find us."

Arthur Bancroft: "The fourth day adrift on a one man raft in the broad expanse of the South China Sea commenced much the same as the previous days. The cold of the night was gradually replaced by the welcome warmth of the sun, the same sun we had cursed the day before because of the glaring heat it brought. We counted heads and were relieved to see that our party of six, all on individual rafts, was still intact.

"However, the new dawn heralded in prospects of a change in weather conditions with rain clouds gathering and the sea taking on a different hue and becoming ruffled. Before the day was over we were to drift through a heavy rain squall which provided us with much needed relief for our swollen and cracked lips. After nearly four days without food or water the rain was truly manna from heaven. We caught what rain we could in our mouths and managed to collect a small supply in an oil covered rice bucket which we had pulled from the sea the day before and kept just for this purpose.

"The spirit of our small group soared as we all felt that someone was looking after us. Although all we could see about us was open ocean without another living soul or object in sight there were unbeknown to us other survivors of the RAKUYO MARU within a few miles of us but at sea level we were unable to see them. Still we kept a watchful eye on the horizon, hopefully looking for signs of a source of rescue from the increasing prospects of succumbing from starvation, thirst and exposure to the elements; not that any of us really feared death at this particular moment as at least it would be a clean honorable one far away from the steaming jungles of Burma and Thailand where we had seen so many of our mates suffer and die in unbelievable squalor. Furthermore, we were at least free men at long last.

"Revived by the rain our confidence grew and I don't think we were completely surprised when late in the afternoon our ears caught the sound of powerful engines in the far distance. We knew that it was not the sound of aircraft, as we had heard and seen a lone aircraft in the sky the day before, so it just had to be craft different to what we had knowledge of before. Our thoughts turned to the likely source being diesel engines of a submarine on the surface, possibly recharging its batteries. If so, was it an American submarine although it could well be a Japanese submarine or even a German U-Boat, after all, we had heard of a German U-Boat in Singapore Harbour not that long ago. We hoped, of course, that should we be fortunate enough to be rescued it would be by Americans but there again we appreciated that beggars could not be choosers and we would accept a lift from the first one to come along.

"Eventually we sighted a vessel low down on the horizon and whilst the outline was at first difficult to recognise our earlier thinking was soon confirmed that it had to be a submarine. At first it seemed to be heading directly towards our group but then to our dismay it turned away. This unusual manoeuvring happened several times which lead us to believe that the submarine must be picking up other survivors of whose presence we were unaware.

"The submarine zig-zagged slowly towards us, dusk started closing in and we became concerned that the lookouts may miss seeing us in the gathering gloom. We balanced ourselves on our small rafts and waved our shirts and hollered to the best of our ability. As the submarine came closer our confidence of an early rescue grew stronger and stronger.

Suddenly, just as we felt certain that we had been sighted, the submarine turned away from us and we assumed other nearby survivors had been sighted and were being picked up. However, this was not to be so as the steady throb of the powerful diesel engines increased in intensity and the submarine quickly disappeared from sight against the darkening sky.

"Silence settled over our small group. All our energies had been fully expended over the past few hours. We must have all had our own secret thoughts and were silently praying that the Power that decreed that some of us should be spared would also take mercy on us.

"That night, huddled together in pairs for warmth with our rafts tied together to prevent them drifting apart, we encouraged each other that there must be other submarines in the area looking for survivors and that we were in good enough physical shape to last for several more days, if necessary.

"The next morning our spirits had been recharged with positive thoughts of what the new day would bring but we had to brace ourselves against a sudden change in weather conditions. This also helped us to overcome the disappointments of the previous day as we fought for survival in a rising sea which kept washing us off our rafts. We tied ourselves on as best we could and waited for a rescue we felt was not far away. That's when we wondered what the future would hold but we felt that if there was one around there must be others and that gave us confidence."

For those who witnessed the submarine picking up survivors and disappearing until there was no sound, despair set in for some, others, like Freddie Mills, heard someone from the submarine call out, 'Help is coming!"

Arthur Bancroft: "Next day we went back to the old routine of singing songs, telling stories and doing all that, we saw some rain coming towards us, the sea was starting to lift and the wind was starting to come up. We floated right down through a rain storm without getting one drop of water, it was raining on the left and raining on the right but we just drifted right through it but later the rain came and we caught in our hats and in our wooden rice bucket, we funnelled

Rescued after six days.
Pic: U.S. National Archives

Cleaning down before being placed down torpedo hatch.
Pic: U.S. National Archives

water from bits of life preservers and we ended up with about one third of a bucket of rainwater. It was a bit salty and a bit oily from the bucket but that kept us going until the next day.

"Next day the approaching typhoon was building up, we had a raft each and we tied the six of them together. As the waves got higher and the wind got more strength we had to tie ourselves on somehow because we knew if we got washed off we would never get back on again. When we suddenly heard another diesel engine we were so full of hope then that "This was it!"

"It was the USS QUEENFISH – she was trimmed down and we were being tossed around, the seas were quite horrific, at times we seemed to be looking down at the submarine and other times she was well up above. They threw ropes over and I grabbed one. Jack Bennett was in charge of rescue operations and he yelled out to me, "If you can hang on and let the others come through that one raft." We had to tie a rope around Ray Wheeler and they hauled him in first and then the others just came through the one raft while I hung on to the rope. They were hanging over with lifelines and helping them on board to the deck of the submarine because we were all capable of doing something. Some of the men picked up by the other submarines had been so weak and helpless the crew had to dive into the water to bring them back on board, Jack Bennett said even when the water was calm the men on QUEENFISH had been heaving lines out to people who just could not grab them, they just did not have the strength to hold on, so he thought we were in pretty good shape considering. I was the last one on so he grabbed me and pulled me aboard. He wrote that I landed on the raft and saluted him – I remember very clearly hopping on the foredeck of the submarine and looking up and the Captain was in the conning tower and I stood and saluted him and said, "Permission to come aboard Sir!" It was just a reflex thing that you did on coming aboard a ship. Jack Bennett still says I did it on the raft, I don't remember, in the emotion of the moment I could have been saluting everyone. (Years later, when Bancroft met Admiral Elliott Loughlin he told Bancroft he was moved by his action.)

"We learnt later the lookout saw us and reported we looked in good shape, so the Captain directed the boat to those who were not so active, so they left us till last.

"There were eight or ten fellows on deck so they took us down through the forward torpedo hatch and into the forward torpedo room which they set up as a Sick Bay. They soon found out I was an Australian sailor and not Army and they reckoned that was good enough for me to have a bunk down with the crew, so they took me down aft and laid me out on one of their bunks – covered in oil – and I remember looking up at the deckhead covered with naked girls – sailors would always have that – and they said, "Gee how long is it since you've eaten Digger?" and I said, "Oh six days I think", and they said, "Gee you must be hungry, what would you like to eat?" and I said, "Sausages!" – I'd been dreaming of sausages for two and a half years. So they went off and came back with a great big tin of sausages and they were just opening it up and the Pharmacist's Mate came along and says, "Hey! none of that!" and took it off me.

"The pin-ups made you feel life was worth living – we were just so amazed at the whole situation – nobody every dreamed of going on a submarine under those circumstances – and they had given me a sip of brandy which nearly burnt my throat out!"

George Hinchy: "On Day 6 Vic Cross said he saw a submarine with a white man on it and he said to stay on our rafts otherwise we could be rammed. The submarine came along and they threw an orange life jacket over with a ⅝" rope tied on it – I caught it with one finger and the next thing I was being hauled in to the deck like someone pulling a fish in – almost lost my finger. I was pulled in at the stern of the sub., she looked like a big whale, and a big sailor picked me up in his arms and put me down the after hatch. I was washed with alcohol to get rid of the oil and they were going to cut my hair and I remember saying, "Don't cut my hair and make me look like a Jap!" After that I blacked out. I kept my money belt with the Rising Sun badge all through."

Fred Mills: "We couldn't see anyone else the seas were rising and sometimes when we were up on a wave we would catch a brief glimpse of debris or maybe a raft. We were suffering from delirium, Harry Bunker said he could see something and someone said, "You old bugger you're seeing things!" Tempers were edgy, no one wanted to create false hopes.

"But the submarine was there – the message given by someone on the PAMPANITO had come true – we were being pulled towards the submarine and I gashed my head on the hull. I was covered in oil, and they put me on a bench on a lovely clean cream blanket. I woke the following day when they gave me a bath and removed the oil."

Phil Beilby: "By evening there only two of us left on the raft. Just before dark a rain squall came up so I took off my shorts, the only clothing I had, and made them into a trough and caught two mouthfuls of the most beautiful rainwater I have ever tasted. On the fourth day late morning I could hear engines in the distance but could not see anything because of the oil which had severely blurred my vision. We did not know at the time that two submarines, American, were rescuing people.

"We had drifted miles apart, there were rafts scattered for miles across the China Sea. I could still hear the sound of engines running so I grabbed a bamboo pole that was drifting nearby and fixed my shorts to the end of it and stood up on the unstable raft and waved the shorts for what seemed like hours. I was still waving as the sun went down and a big wave came and knocked me, bamboo pole and shorts, into the water. I managed to scramble back onto the raft but never saw my shorts again so I was in the 'raw' from then on.

"During that fourth day, a friend, Eddy Sullivan, was near us and was signalling in semaphore but failed to attract any attention. The next day was the fifth, which came and went without any sounds of engines, by this time my poor old

The oil saved many.
Pic: U.S. National Archives

Two more on debris.
Pic: U.S. National Archives

mate was very unwell and mentally wandering. I had a very good friend named Fred Annesley (WX.7905) and he was on a raft nearby, I called out to him and asked if he thought he could last much longer. He was quite a strong chap and he said he thought he could go a couple more days. However when morning came on the sixth day Fred and the raft were nowhere to be seen.

"The wind was rising and the sea very much rougher than we had previously experienced, little did I know a typhoon was on its way. By this time my raft mate was quite delirous and saying "I'm going down to my cabin to get some blankets", I had to pull him back several times. Things were looking pretty bad for us and I prayed several times that we might be rescued, even promised to live a better life in the future if we were wrenched from the deep.

"I think I was in a bit of a stupor by this time and about 2 p.m. I looked up and saw a submarine coming, roughly one to two hundred yards away. The shock of this very quickly brought me to my senses, I immediately jumped into the water and swam towards the submarine. Never expecting to see Americans, when I saw they were big men I thought they must be Germans. I called out to them and one yelled out, "Hang on buddy!" I then realised who they were. There was a strong wash coming from the submarine especially with the high waves and strong wind, so I floated on my back and paddled my way back to the raft, the sub. then did a big circle then came alongside us and pulled my mate and myself on board, the most wonderful experience one could possibly imagine.

"The submariners were the kindest people I have ever met, they gave up their bunks for us and slept wherever they could. They washed us down with solvent to remove the oil and filth that had accumulated on our skin.

"We had many seawater ulcers and skin chafed from under our arms by the life jacket as well as very bad sunburn. Harold Dixon, Pharmacist's Mate on QUEENFISH did wonders for our wounds and illnesses. When they pulled us out of the sea I asked them if they would look for Fred Annesley, they cruised around for some hours but no sign of Fred and his mate. I also asked about Jack Lovering (WX.11949) but no one had seen him.

"That night the sea was fairly boiling with the typhoon increasing in strength, so they decided to dive and escape from the surface turbulence. The submarine was then as steady as a rock.

"These wonderful people fed us with marvellous food, things we hadn't seen for years. They then gave us their own personal clothing, which was very acceptable seeing I was in my birthday suit. One of the crew named "Cowboy" Hendricks, even gave me his leather jacket which I prized for many a long day."

QUEENFISH reported in her Log details of the rescue:

17 September 1944

0108 (H) Received orders to proceed to search area towards which we were heading at time of contact. Set course 250°T, speed 17 knots.

0930 (H) Commenced searching in general designated area for survivors.
1200 (H) Changed course to 220°T.
1316 (H) Sighted two survivors on raft. As we closed them, could detect several other rafts in immediate vicinity. Commenced picking up survivors, taking on board the last of 18 recovered at 1545. By this time, the sea and wind began to pick up making the rescue work extremely arduous and hazardous. Only in a few cases were the weakened and emaciated survivors able to assist in their recovery and the officers and men on deck did yeoman service in lifting them bodily from the water. In one instance Ensign E.A. Desmond, Jr., USNR. plunged into the water to tow a raft back to the ship on which sat a survivor who was too weak to reach for a heaving line that had fallen at his feet. The performance of all hands was all that could be desired with particular praise for Lieut. J.E. Bennett, USN, Ens. E.A. Desmond, Jr., USNR, Reed, R.J., Cox, USNR, Nadeau, L.F., Jr., TM3c, USNR, Hendricks, O.B., QM1c, USN, and Milliren, T.E., S2c, USNR.
1545 (H) Continued search but saw only empty rafts with many lifeless bodies in the vicinity. Seas and wind increased.

18 September 1944
0000 (H) Set course to arrive at point designated for start of daylight search.
0232 (H) One survivor died having been in a complete coma since recovery from water.
1200 (H) Committed the body of the survivor to the deep. Weather had changed into a tropical disturbance with very high seas and near typhoon winds. Steered course 070°T at 2/3 speed making good 4 knots.
2325 (H) Second survivor died, never having regained consciousness since recovery from water.

19 September 1944
0139 (H) Changed course to 080°T.
0915 (H) Changed course to 090°T.
1028 (H) Committed body of second survivor to the deep.
1555 (H) Seas began to moderate. Changed speed to standard making good 9 to 10 knots."

QUEENFISH proceeded back to Saipan with her load of survivors passing Balintang Island on 20 September 1944. The weather was still hampering their progress and on 21 September her Log recorded:

21 September 1944
1930 (H) Wind and sea picking up slowing our speed by 4 knots. Began taking water in conning tower so slowed to standard, making good 10 knots.
2100 (H) Still taking water through conning tower hatch. Slowed to 150 rpm. making good 8 knots.

Survivors mingle with crew at Saipan.
Pic: U.S. National Archives

Cdr. Elliott Loughlin (centre)
Cdr. Swinburne (on right)
Pic: U.S. National Archives

2330 (H) Slowed to 2/3 speed.

22 September 1944

1530 (I) Wind and seas moderated to some extent. Changed speed to standard, making good 12 knots.

2130 (I) Changed speed to 17 knots.

23 September 1944

0900 (I) Sighted B-24 bomber (Aircraft#63) bearing 050°T, distant about 14 miles.

24 September 1944

0630 (I) Sighted USS SNOOK bearing 292°T, distant about 10 miles.

0705 (I) Sighted and passed on opposite course unidentified U.S. submarine.

1900 (I) Changed course to 090°T.

25 September 1944

0330 (K) Established radar communication with BARB.

0534 (K) Sighted DD USS CASE bearing 075°T, distant 7 miles. Proceeded on various courses at various speeds to Saipan escorted by CASE in company with SNOOK and BARB.

1030 (K) Moored to USS FULTON, Saipan Harbour. Transferred survivors to hospital, commenced taking on board fuel and torpedoes."

Australian Survivors rescued by USS QUEENFISH

Bancroft, A.B.A.	F. 3239	HMAS PERTH	Perth, W.A.
Beilby, Pte. P.J.	WX.12765	2/4 M.G. Bn.	Claremont, W.A.
Bowhay, Pte. S.B.	NX.52537	2/19 Bn.	Orange, NSW
Bunker, Pte. H.T.	WX. 9223	2/4 M.G. Bn.	Albany, W.A.
Cross, Pte. F.V.	WX. 7268	2/4 M.G. Bn.	Geraldton, W.A.
Hinchy, Dvr. G.F.	NX.31557	8 Div. H.Q.	Sydney, NSW
Lihou, Gnr. E.J.	QX. 9371	2/10 Fld.Arty.	Brisbane, Qld.
Mills, Gnr. F.C.	NX.32631	2/15 Fld.Regt.	Fairfield, NSW
Nunan, Pte. L.V.	NX.55450	Inf.Bde.,H.Q.	Menindee, NSW
Pearson, Dvr. E.A.	NX. 1208	3 Res.M.T. Coy.	Sydney. NSW
Smith, W.O. W.G.	QX. 4556	2/10 Fld. Arty.	Longreach, NSW
Wheeler, Pte. R.W.	VX.61409	2/10 Ord.Fld.W/Shps.	Melbourne, Vic.

DAY FIVE – SIX

U.S.S. BARB

Jack Flynn: "I had a little mate with me called Alby Meredith, an Air Force Corporal. I saw his throat moving one day and I said, "Alby you're not drinking seawater are you?" and he said, "No Jack, just rinsing my mouth out with it, it helps a lot." I knew he was drinking seawater and later on I saw him drifting away. I swam after him and just as I got to him he went down feet first with his arms outstretched.

"By the fourth day we were too weak to try and row so we just hung on to the raft and you could see rafts in the distance, little black dots here and there you would see as your raft lifted on the swell."

Ross Smith: "Day 4-6 – I was not religious but couldn't see death, I had no vision of it but I decided I was too young to die. While I had no idea how I was going to get out of it I kept telling myself I was too young to die.

"At this time there was only two of us left and there was no one else in sight. My mate was Cyril Hutchinson, he was becoming hard to get on with, perhaps I was also hard to get on with. We both disciplined ourselves not to drink seawater and for the next few days we were in the oil slick which gave our bodies some protection from the hot sun. Hutchinson said he saw a submarine. Hearing the diesel motors made so much noise after the quietness of the sea we thought the Japanese would also hear us. A line was thrown to us by one of the rescuing party but we couldn't stand up – I couldn't put the line on the raft. Someone secured us to the rope and we were taken aboard. It was a wonderful sensation. On board they cleaned us up and later cut all my oil matted hair off."

Jim Campbell: "When the day broke on the fifth morning, I was more dead than alive. I looked to see who and how many had survived. Six pairs of tortured eyes looked back at me. Their eyes said as clearly as words, "Who would be next?"

"Although we had almost given up all hope of rescue, we still retained our grip on the raft, more by instinct than by conscious effort. The other raft could not be seen now and a great feeling of loneliness added to our depression.

"Before the sun went down that evening three more died, demented and exhausted. As darkness closed in on us that fifth night, one more passed away, leaving Bernie Williams and myself on our raft.

"Bernie and I had been friends ever since the early days of 1940 when the 8th Division had been formed in Sydney. He was now in a bad way, being almost completely out of his mind from drinking seawater. I had resolutely refused to drink the seawater and my tongue was swollen, my lips cracked and my body practically dead. How I still hung on I cannot say, but I had to try desperately to keep my wits about me to enable me to watch over my mate Bernie.

"That night seemed to me to be eternal and try as I would to assist him, Bernie became worse. He repeatedly attacked me in his dementia and I had to fight for my life as well as his.

"The night was as black as ink and I tried frantically not to lose the raft and my mate, yet, despite my efforts, through sheer exhaustion I eventually lost the hopeless fight to keep him with me. My strength was utterly spent.

"I was now completely alone. The boards that had kept twenty men afloat were so small that they would not wholly support my single weight, I hung on by my chin and elbows – barely clinging to life.

"That sixth day was one of excruciating torture, my body was racked with an overwhelming numbness yet tired and aching where there was still feeling. The sun made my craving for water a searing agony.

"All day long I just drifted, I was alone in the vast and pitiless China Sea, countless miles from anywhere, yet I still refused to admit defeat. But that afternoon I acknowledged the inevitable and resigned myself to death which I felt was very near. I said goodbye to all my loved ones at home, my mother and father, brothers Tom and Leslie, and my sisters Veronica and Gladys.

"In thinking of my sweetheart, Jean, I drained a bitter draught to the very dregs. Through all the suffering her memory had kept me going. Now it was all but over. We had waited a long time to marry and now I had to say goodbye. My stinging eyes were stung again as tears came suddenly. Even though I had not drunk the seawater I began to suffer hallucination. I imagined all sorts of things – I could see slit trenches in the water and I only had to wait for a wave to recede for me to let the boards go and slide into them. I imagined a boat below me and waiting for the seas to abate before letting go and sliding down into the water and to the peace of death.

"These periods of delirium made it more and more difficult for me to resist the urge to let go. Towards evening, just when my resistance was about to

U.S.S. Barb

Pic: U.S. National Archives

collapse, I heard Jean's voice: "Hang on Jim, hang on!" It came clearly across the water and I struggled to keep my mummified hands on the boards.

"Then about an hour later, as the sun was setting, vision materialised 100 yards away. All my partly blinded eyes could see was a vessel of some sort and I tried desperately to make myself seen or heard. I must have been sighted – I was far too weak to call out. The submarine came closer and closer till it ranged right alongside me.

"I revived in an exquisitely comfortable bunk aboard the USS BARB. The first words I heard were, "Here, Bud, drink a little of this." I felt a cup against my swollen lips. His warning was in vain – I gripped the cup and his hand and did not let go until I had drunk the lot. I had never before tasted anything so beautiful as that first drink."

Jack Flynn: "I said to my mate, "Have a look over there" and he did and said, "It's a submarine." I had another look and said, "You're dotty, it's a destroyer" and we nearly had a stand-up fight about it. He won the day, sure enough it was a submarine. It was coming slowly towards us and on the foredeck we could see these big white blokes, then they started to back away from us. What a terrible feeling of despair. We thought they were Germans and were going to leave us. We found out later that what they were doing was to come up behind us otherwise the wind could have blown us on top of them, doing us more harm than good.

"When they were close enough, they threw out ropes with a loop in them to put over our heads and under our arms and they pulled us gently to the side of the submarine where the steps were. I made sure Murray Thompson had one on him, then away went the slouch hat. They had to handle us very carefully because wherever they touched us our skin came away in their hands.

"I remember being lowered down the conning tower and what a beautiful smell, coffee, cigarettes, and a lovely clean atmosphere. They had their mess tables made into beds with lovely clean sheets, it seemed a shame to put us on them. Suddenly I missed my rosary beads. There was one big sailor there, an Irish-American, who wanted to know what was the matter with me, I told him I had lost my rosary beads and up he went on top and found them. They had broken when I was on deck. He could see how grateful I was. While we were in the water with my beads round my neck the others said to me "You know how to pray Flynnie, say one for us!"

"The skipper of the submarine was Commander Fluckey. I was first to be questioned about what we had seen while in the water. This was done in what they called the Board Room, all the officers were there. I told them I had seen an aircraft carrier and its escort, I described it and the skipper said they had got them. When he had finished he knocked on the wall and a panel slid open. A big black head appeared in the opening and he said, "Good day", the skipper said, "Jackson – get Flynn a beer." I said, "No thanks, I don't drink". The skipper said, "What! an Aussie and you don't drink!" He was amazed." However Leo Cornelius accepted the offer and drank his beer on the spot.

Neville Thams: "Time was running out on the 6th day. Through the night I managed to catch a few raindrops, it was only a little. The sea was angry and keeping on the hatch cover was a real problem. We had not seen anyone for the past two days. My legs were covered with seawater sores. I was semi-delirious, imagining all the time if only I could make that big step of say 6 feet I would be safe. I would fall into the sea. Alas, it was only a dream. Our combined weight was too much and we were never on top of the water, always below the sea surface. Waves splashed over us, hitting me in the face. I can still feel the coolish water trickling down inside my tunic collar. It still makes me shudder. It was late in the afternoon of the 6th day when my mate spied a submarine heading in our direction. I waved my shorts, I had removed them about the 5th day, they were chafing me. And they became our flag if ever we had the opportunity to wave at something. I can still see the submarine, like some grey ghost, as it came our way, blowing out spray as it plowed through the waves. There was a sailor in blue with a white cap. When a rope was thrown I placed it under my armpits. I seemed to generate some unknown energy and was slowly hauled aboard. Another two hours, and I would have drowned. I remember saying, "Yanks!". Later, I learned that this was the United States Submarine BARB. My mate who was rescued with me, you know I don't even know his name. The attention given us by the officers, crew and the Pharmacist's Mate, William "Doc" Donnelly, was incredible. When roughly cleaned up, oil removed, I was tucked in a bunk. The rolling and shuddering of BARB while still on the surface searching for survivors, I was afraid the submarine might turn turtle."

Commander Fluckey, USS BARB, wrote of the rescued: "All were covered with a heavy coating of oil received when they drifted through an oil slick their second night on the rafts. This undoubtedly saved their lives. They were in the water or on their small wooden rafts for a period of five days before being picked up. This in addition to three years of prison life under the Japanese which included bashings, beatings, starvation (all survivors were 25-50 lbs. underweight) malaria, dysentery, pellagra, sores, ulcers, etc., and had left them in terrible physical condition. The at first dubious, then amazed, and finally hysterically thankful look on their faces, from the time they first sighted us approaching them, is one we shall never forget. Several of them were too weak to take the lines thrown them. These were rescued by the valiant efforts of Lt.Cdr. R.W. McNitt, Lt. J.G. Lanier, and Houston, C.S. MoMM2c, who dove in after them. Too much credit cannot be given to the crew for their superb performance and willing efforts in the production line we had formed from the deck party who picked them up, stripped them, and passed them on to the transportation gang to get them below, where they were received by the cleaners who removed the oil and grease, then on to the doctors and nurses for treatment, thence to the feeders, and finally to the sleepers who carried them off and tucked them in their bunks.

"The appreciation of the survivors was unbounded. Even those who couldn't talk expressed themselves tearfully through their glazed, oil-soaked eyes.

We regret there were no more, for we had found it possible, by taking over every square foot of space aboard ship, sleeping three to a torpedo rack, etc. to accommodate a hundred."

Australian Survivors rescued by USS BARB

Campbell, Pte. J.	NX.31161	Div. H.Q.	Blacktown, NSW
Cornelius, Pte. L.	VX.34456	2/2 Pioneer Bn.	Fairfield, Vic.
Flynn, Pte. J.J.	QX.19492	105 Gen.Tpt.Coy.	Norman Park, Qld.
Hampson, Sgt. R.D.	WX. 7123	2/4 M.G. Bn.	Perth, W.A.
Hutchinson, Pte. C.	QX.19201	2/26 Bn.	Merimbula, NSW
Munro, A.B. L.W.	S. 5186	HMAS PERTH	Byron Bay, NSW
New, Sig. H.R.	VX.53507	Signals	Blackburn, Vic.
Smith, Pte. R.	VX.28346	4 Res.M.T. Coy.	Prahran, Vic.
Thams, Pte. N.	QX.20997	2/10 Fld.Regt.	Southport, Qld.
Thompson, Pte. M.	SX. 8776	2 M.T. Coy.	Glossop, S.A.

Don Miller of Pittsburgh, U.S.A. and former crew member of USS BARB wrote: "The POWs were floating on ship wreckage, none in lifeboats, some were able to get all the way out of the water, but most just held on to the wreckage with their legs in the water.

"I remember the condition of the men as they came aboard, some of our crew jumped overboard to assist getting a line around them as they were too weak to help themselves. I took care of 'Darby' Munro, an Australian sailor from the cruiser PERTH. The men had been in the South China Sea for six days, had it not been for the oil from the tanker sunk at the same time the RAKUYO MARU sank I really don't think they could have lasted six days. The oil acted as a sun screen – when you tried to get the oil from their skin you felt the skin would come off too. Most were blind or had very little sight. All were covered with sores (most open). All had various kinds of tropical diseases. We cleaned them up as best we could without hurting them. They were given water, soup, and some spirits. As I recall, most had their clothes removed top-side before they were assisted down the ladder below. All were very weak and so thin – skin and bones.

"We would have been able to find more if the weather had not changed to a typhoon – no way could they have hung onto the wreckage. When I went on look-out topside I had to tie myself to the lookout platform or be washed overboard. The roughest sea I have ever experienced.

"We dove once from a plane contact, the rest of the five days the Australians and British were aboard were spent on the surface going at the fastest speed we could make with the rough sea to Saipan to get them better medical treatment.

"Everyone on board assisted in the cleaning up and feeding or whatever else they needed. The operation was a total crew effort, we were very lucky all fourteen of our guests made it to Saipan.

"Our Pharmacist Mate (Doctor) William E. Donnelly should be given credit for keeping them all alive. It seemed he never slept, was always either in the forward torpedo room or crews' quarters where we had our guests.

"For me, it was seeing how men could be so cruel to other men – something I will never forget. Of all the other things BARB did for the victory over Japan, this is the one I always have foremost in my mind. We had tears in our eyes as they left BARB at Saipan, with our Navy dungarees and white hats, some didn't fit too well but all but one walked off the gangway to the dock. One fellow still had a patch on his eye."

SAIPAN

The PAMPANITO and SEALION, racing for Saipan on September 18, were met by a destroyer, the USS CASE; it was the intention to transfer the survivors to the CASE however because of rising seas the trans-fer did not take place, instead, medical supplies and a doctor were taken aboard the submarines.

Despite the availability of the doctors, it was the Phamacists' Mate Maurie Demers on PAMPANITO and Roy Williams on SEALION, who continued to render care and constant attention to the survivors who remember with great emotion their outstanding devotion to them. The POWs said they did not want to be transferred, they wanted to stay with those who saved their lives. The officers were moved by the mens' expressions

PAMPANITO and SEALION arrived at Saipan on September 20 and moored alongside the tender, USS FULTON. After a feast of ice-cream and fruit they hadn't tasted for three years, the POWs were moved by barge to the 148 U.S. Military Hospital.

Charlie McKechnie: "We were taken to the American Army Hospital. We used to get into a lot of trouble with the American Army nurses, their rank was Lieutenant and our nurses' rank was Sister, and if you called the American nurses "Sister" you'd get a thick ear because they were thinking you were trying to get fresh with them and of course the only language we knew for an Army nurse was "Sister"!.

"We didn't know where Saipan was or how close it was to Japan, it was hard to realise there was no one going to yell at you. It was a complete change from one life to another without any intermediate break. I was in a daze and I

USS PAMPANITO Crew serves the survivors ice cream and fruit.
Pic: US National Archives

don't remember very much about that time."

Reg Harris: "I thought the American nursing sisters were the funniest people I'd ever encountered. One of them was always trying to dig a needle into me and she couldn't find any flesh to put it in. She said, "Goddam man – where is your flesh?!" I used to hold the skin up for her and she'd say, "Look away, look away" and I said, "No, it's alright, just pop it in there!". They thought we were mad and we probably were too. One night some Japs came down from the hills to steal the water and of course they opened fire on them with a machine gun. One bloke jumped out of bed and pulled his mattress off and hid under it. The Sister came along and she said, "What are you doing there guy?" and he said, "I'm not getting shot by those bastards now!"

Jack Flynn: "Before we landed at Saipan the BARB crew had a tarpaulin muster and gave us 75 dollars and so many cents each. We didn't see them again. They had to refuel, take on supplies and all and go to sea again, they were great to us, we will never forget their generosity and kindness.

"We were put into a big hospital under canvas there and put to bed, we were still in a pretty bad shape. During the night I couldn't sleep and a lovely blonde nurse (the first white woman we had seen for years) said to me, "What's the matter?" and I said, "I can't sleep". She gave me some sort of tablet and next thing I knew the sun was shining and all I could hear was Bing Crosby and The Andrews Sisters singing, "Lay That Pistol Down Babe". I didn't know where I was. They gave us an American dressing gown each, they were great, a deep red velvet, I felt like knocking it off!

"We didn't stay long there, but one night they had open-air movies, I was a bit frightened, I said to one Yank, "Don't you think you are a bit close to have bright lights?" and he said, "Don't matter where we are Bud, we gotta have our movies!"

The BARB and QUEENFISH battled the typhoon which raged for the next few days, some of the crew became ill but it did not affect the appetite of the survivors.

Arthur Bancroft: "After a couple of days they must have thought we could eat more food, so they started off baking a nice lot of fresh bread, they put that down in front of us and went away for butter and jam and things we had not seen for a couple of years. When they came back they said, "Where's the bread?" and we had eaten it all so they had to go and get some more but it was like eating cake to us. Then they started getting us on to solid food, there were a few who couldn't handle it for a while, but our group felt we were fairly fit considering. We were interrogated by the Captain, he wanted to know details of USS HOUSTON which was sunk with PERTH, because they had had no word of this, and he radioed it through to Saipan. They were very interested to know what sort of work we were doing, where we were working, and we could pinpoint the ammunition dumps in Saigon on the map for them because we were working around near the dumps. We could also pinpoint the camps on the railway line."

Survivors from BARB and QUEENFISH being taken ashore at Saipan.
Pic: US National Archives

Reg Stewart being assisted into barge
Pic: U.S. National Archives

George Hinchy: "After a few days I was able to move around, while at the toilet I noticed a mirror in the adjacent shower, I looked into it and didn't recognise myself! My face was covered in sores and growth – I was rather shocked."

On September 25 QUEENFISH and BARB moored alongside USS FULTON and transferred the survivors to barges for the transportation to the 148 General Hospital where they were anxious to find out who else had survived the sinking of the RAKUYO MARU.

The survivors were further interrogated by U.S. Navy Intelligence on every aspect of their observations during their travels from Saigon to Singapore – the ships they had seen, such as the SIBERIA MARU, at one time it was a hospital ship complete with appropriate markings, loaded with ammunition; then when they saw it at Singapore the Red Cross markings had been painted out. Many had sighted the big AWA MARU in Singapore with its bow badly damaged.

When the British Naval Representative with the U.S. Pacific Fleet arrived, he carried out further interrogations. The intelligence given by the survivors would have saved the lives of many hundreds of POWs still working along the Burma-Thailand Railway. All camps occupied by POWs were now known to the Allied Airforces – post-war pictures show the selective bombing of bridges with the nearby huts occupied by Prisoners untouched.

Captain Tufnell, R.N., singled out three men for Distinguished Conduct when the RAKUYO MARU was hit – Captain Arthur Sumner, Chief Petty Officer Vic Duncan and Able Seaman Petherbridge.

On 28 September 1944 the survivors boarded the American troop-ship ALCOA POLARIS and were taken to Guadalcanal in the Solomon Islands. There they remained for a few days at a U.S. Hospital awaiting transport to Australia. It appears the Australian Government at that time could not provide transport, consequently the Americans made a mine-layer, the MONADNUCK, available to take the survivors on the final leg of their journey home.

The Australian Army authorities sent Major Ray Steele, who had escaped from Borneo in 1943 and was now on special duties with MIS X, to interrogate the survivors, he boarded the ship en-route by way of a Jacob's ladder, and was pleased to meet up with some of his own Unit he had last seen in Singapore.

The 86 Australian (six were too ill to travel) survivors arrived at Brisbane on 18 October and were taken to.a Convalescent Hospital, Stewart House. Here they underwent further medical examination and were outfitted in Australian uniforms and interrogated again, finally given 90 days Leave they proceeded to their home States.

Elizabeth Duncan, wife of C.P.O. Vic Duncan, joined the W.R.A.N.S. after the loss of the HMAS PERTH was announced in March 1942 and Vic was posted missing. She was sent to Brisbane as a Signaller and, in the early hours sometime in October 1944, she took a message from Pearl Harbour; when it was de-coded it stated that four crew members of the PERTH had been recovered and would shortly arrive in Australia. When the survivors arrived in Brisbane arrangements

QUEENFISH Pharmacist's Mate Harold Dixon with his hand on Phil Beilby's shoulder. With others rescued by QUEENFISH. Pic: US National Archives

Survivors from New South Wales.Pic: US National Archives

Survivors from Victoria. Pic: US National Archives

Survivors from Queensland. Pic: US National Archives

Survivors from Western Australia. Pic: US National Archives

Survivors from South Australia. Pic: US National Archives

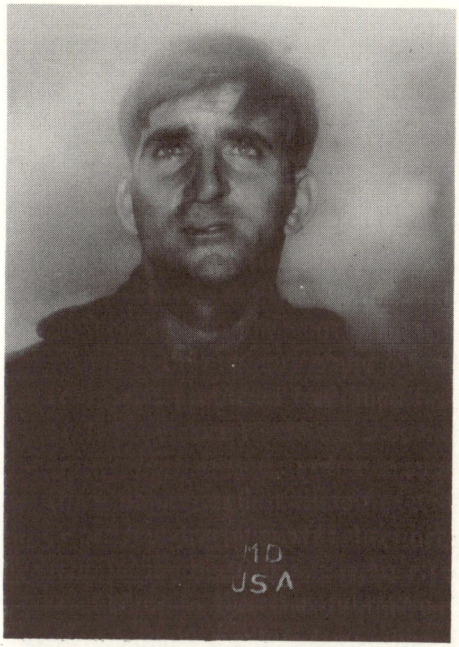

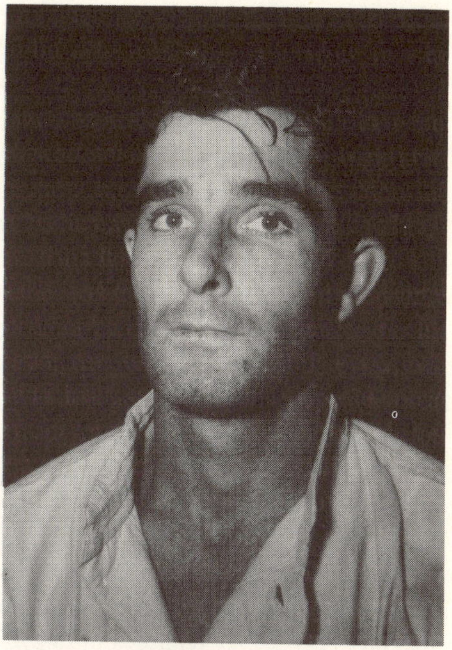

Left: Claude Longey – Tasmania. Pic: U.S. National Archives
Right: Bill Cunneen – Coleraine, Vic. Pic: U.S. National Archives

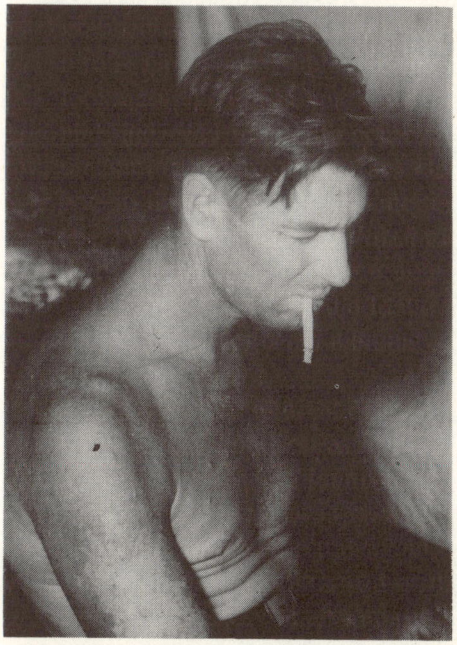

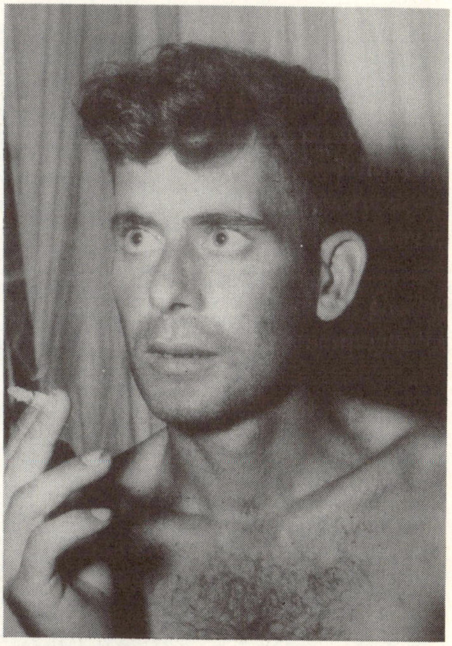

Left: Reg Bullock – Queensland. Pic: U.S. National Archives
Right: J.A. Vickers – Carlton, Vic. Pic: U.S. National Archives

were made for her to talk to Jack Houghton, he said he had seen Vic in a boat after the sinking, but advised her, "Don't build up your hopes."

Charlie McKechnie: "When we arrived at Brisbane we were interrogated and given uniforms. At this place there was a fellow involved with Red Cross work and knew my Mother who was always giving soldiers weekend accommodation. So he phoned her and asked if she could take a soldier for the weekend, "yes:", she said, "But he may stay a while", he said, "That's alright" my Mother replied – and then he said, "It's your son, he's come home!"

Cliff Farlow: "I was met in Sydney by my parents. Dad was one to purchase Lottery tickets – for special occasions – and couldn't help telling the girl at the window his son had returned from Malaya. She was very interested as her brother was in Malaya and asked him what Unit his son was in, did he know Ron Ryan – I was in a spot, I just couldn't withhold the truth so I told her Ron was drowned at sea. She was very shocked.

"We caught the South-West Mail at Central, next day we were delayed at Narrandera. Friends of my Mother's suggested they walk down and have a cup of tea; we arrived at the Australian Cafe (it was the only Cafe in town owned by an Australian) and a waitress took our order. She noticed my Unit colour patch and she said, "What are you doing here? Your Unit is in Malaya!" I replied, "That's right." "Well you shouldn't be here!" she said. Well, I tried to explain without giving too much information and then she said, "Did you know Ron Walkerdon?" Then I had to tell her he was killed in action and she just collapsed in a heap on

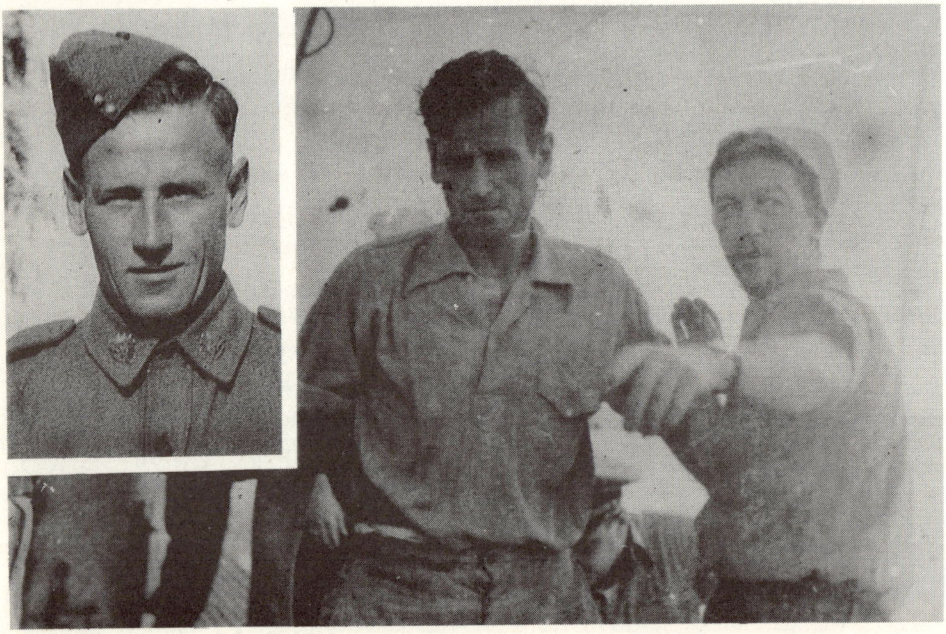

Reg Stewart being assisted by Pharmacist's Mate, Maurice Demers, USS PAMPANITO. Inset: Reg aged 17 years on Enlistment.
Pics: US National Archives and Dawn Stewart

the floor. it was a tough way for her to learn her husband had been killed.

"I arrived home to meet everyone and his dog on the Hay Railway Station, I was still bewildered – and that was the beginning of a 90 days' Leave."

Arthur Bancroft: "I had just arrived at Fremantle, still in U.S. Navy uniform, and while waiting there a lady kept looking at me and eventually she said, "Aren't you Arthur Bancroft?" "Yes Miss Tangney!" (later Senator Tangney), she had taught me at school. "Well!" she said, "what are you doing in a U.S. Navy uniform? I thought you were a prisoner of the Japanese!" Well I was I told her but I can't talk about it. At that time we were instructed not to talk about our rescue as Mr. Forde had not made his statement to Parliament."

Reg Stewart had lost his mother and sister when he was eight years old and remained with his father up to the time of his enlistment; his father, a horse-breaker, moved around the country and young Reg went with him, they were very close to one another. His father tried to stop him enlisting and joining his two older brothers because of his age, however he later relented. When Singapore fell Reg's father received a telegram advising him his son was "Reported Missing". No more news was heard of him until almost three years later when a telegram arrived advising, "Your son is safe in Allied hands – news to follow" but there was no more news despite repeated requests for information.

Reg arrived in Melbourne with his mates to a tumultuous welcome – but no one to meet Reg. He went home, there was no one there, he searched and found his father at the Armadale Hotel. Reg said, "My father almost collapsed – it was a highly emotional reunion in the hotel bar."

Word soon spread throughout the country a number of Australians had been rescued from a sunken Japanese transport by U.S. submarines. People travelled many miles to talk to these men who were still in a state of shock – so much had happened so quickly and they were not adjusted to cope with the large number of written enquiries from anxious relatives. They had been warned not to talk to the Press or to discuss past events with anyone. That was impossible – they were used to death and felt where they possessed positive information they should convey it to the families concerned and not keep them in suspense. However, there was one problem – they believed they were the only survivors and were not aware the Japanese rescued 82 Australians and 54 British.

The Australian Government, in consultation with British and United States Governments, decided a statement would have to be made, and on 17 November 1944, the Acting Prime Minister made a statement in the House of Representatives. This statement was released simultaneously in London and Washington and disclosed details of the harsh treatment the prisoners of war had received on the Burma-Thailand Railway.

He stated, in part: "When the line was completed in October, 1943, the prisoners of war who had constructed it were withdrawn through its southern terminus and were accommodated in Thailand. Some were transferred to Indo-China. It was from one party of these that a selection was made of the fittest for transfer to

First three survivors rescued arrive in Brisbane. From Left: Harold (Curly) Martin, Frank Farmer, Ken Williams.

Japan. The men recently rescued belonged to this group.

"By their dauntless courage and amazing endurance, the survivors from the Japanese transport have performed a great service. They have given an eye-witness account of the manner in which the Japanese treat their prisoners of war; they have managed to compile an almost complete list of their comrades who were shipped with them; and they have furnished long lists of names of Australians who have died mainly in Burma and Thailand, and of whose deaths the Japanese Government has not notified the Commonwealth.

"It is deeply regretted that, at this stage, it cannot be stated how many Australians have died. An early estimate places the death roll in Burma and Thailand at about 2,000 out of approximately 10,000 Australians. It is hoped that this estimate will prove too high, but unfortunately it may ultimately prove to be an understatement.

"The careful collation and checking of all this vast amount of information will take a considerable time, but all next-of-kin of men identified as casualties will be notified as soon as possible. Priority has been given to the preparation of the list of men not rescued from the sunken transport so that their next-of-kin may be informed. As to the fate of the 600 Australians not known to be rescued from the Japanese transport, it would appear that the chance of survival of any of them would depend upon their being able to reach land. That chance was very slender, but it is just possible that some may be alive. Only time can provide the answer.

Victorian Survivors looking better in Brisbane.

New South Wales survivors in Brisbane

"While all this work is receiving attention, relatives of Australian prisoners of war are especially asked to refrain from making any effort to contact or question the rescued men who have been returned to their homes. These men have been through harrowing experiences, have splendidly co-operated with service authorities during a lengthy interrogation and now richly deserve a peaceful and uninterrupted reunion with their families.

"It is felt that this information should be given to the public, even though the Government is profoundly aware of the anguish it will cause to the families of all Australians captured by the Japanese. It was considered that next-of-kin would wish to receive an authoritative statement of the facts.

"It should be understood that the foregoing description relates particularly to accommodation and conditions under which prisoners were worked in Burma and Thailand. When the men were withdrawn from the construction of the railway, their conditions were somewhat improved. The description, moreover, has no reference to camps in Hong Kong, Formosa, Occupied China, Korea and Japan, where it is believed present conditions may be relatively better, although still far below the standards we would desire.

"All the rescued men speak of the high courage shown by their comrades. Everywhere and in all circumstances, the Australians have maintained matchless morale. They have shown themselves undaunted in the face of death. The many who have survived privations and disease in the jungle have developed spiritual

Queensland group in Brisbane

and physical powers to triumph over adversity and over their captors. Let us look forward to the day of their release."

The statement alerted the public, the survivors were recognised by their Unit colour patch – an oval which had not been seen since 1941 – and in no time they were inundated with more letters from relatives.

Meanwhile back in Singapore the balance of the Japan party were boarding the big AWA MARU, pride of the Japanese Merchant Marine and often the target of U.S. submarines. "Blood" Bancroft's mates, Bill 'Buzzer' Bee and Val Savage had heard rumours of the sinking of the RAKUYO MARU and had no idea "Blood" was on his honeymoon back in Fremantle.

The AWA MARU hugged the coastline all the way to Japan, arriving there on 15 January 1945. On its next voyage, ostensibly to take relief supplies to southern regions for POWs – on 'safe passage' given by the U.S. Navy, it was sunk by USS QUEENFISH who never received the 'safe passage' message sent out by Pearl Harbour.

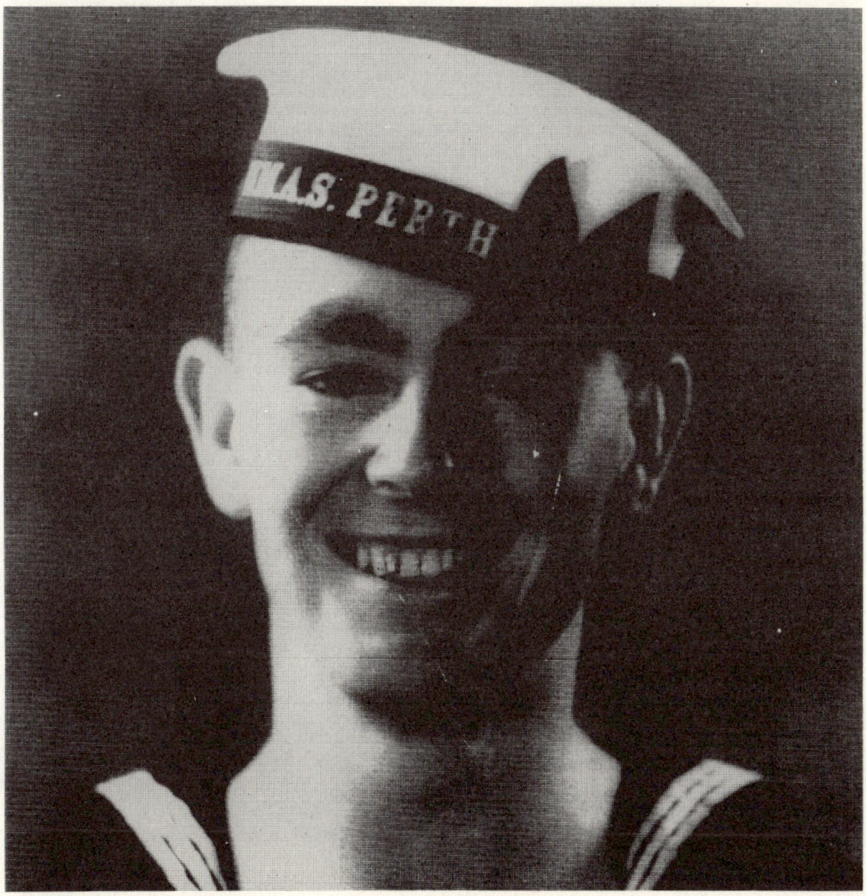

A.B. Arthur 'Blood' Bancroft.

Governor-General's Parade in Melbourne

Survivors attend Memorial Service at the Shrine, Melbourne. 15.02.45.

Left: Rear Admiral Eugene B. Fluckey, (USS BARB) sent this message: "To all you Aussies who did and took so much – my admiration." Pic: US Navy
Right: Lt.Cdr. Paul Summers – USS PAMPANITO

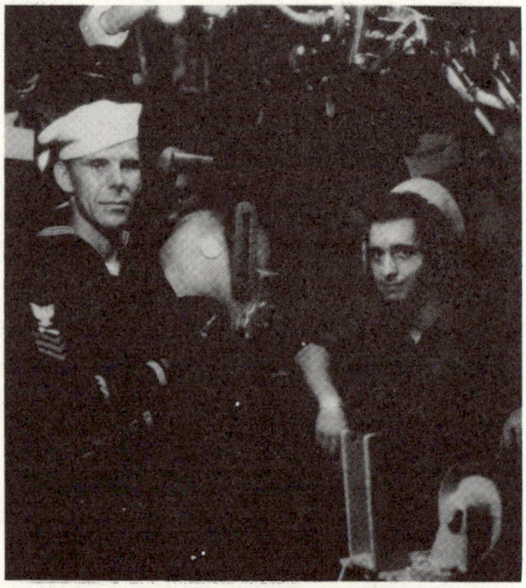

Left: Lt.Cdr. Eli Reich - USS SEALION which sank the RAKUYO MARU and rescued 54 survivors. Right: PAMPANITO Crewman Robert Bennett who participated in rescue and Paul Pappas who produced the cameras to record the events

JAPAN 1944-1945 – KAWASAKI

'Kitch' Loughnan: "We were treated far worse than ordinary human beings would treat the lowliest of animals. There was no attempt to give the pitifully sick cases, who were unable to move, any priority on disembarkation. We were sprayed and dipped in disinfectants like cattle. The Japanese stood by the side of the "bath" and pushed us under with a wooden pole. Many of the POWs were naked, some were clad only in a 'g' string improvised from the shirt sleeves of some more fortunate POWs, yet we were forced to march through the streets, in full view of the curious Japanese women and children, to some horse stables where we "staged" until night. Although almost everyone was suffering from either diarrhoea or dysentery we were not allowed to use or dig latrines before moving to the horse stables, we had to suffer further indignities by scratching holes in the dirt and relieving ourselves in full view of the Japanese women. It was the same at the horse stalls, except we were shielded from public gaze. After nightfall we were moved to a drill hall where we received our first meal since our disembarkation earlier in the day."

A total of 82 Australian survivors reached Moji, of these, 50 were selected to proceed to Kawasaki. The senior NCO in charge was Chief Petty Officer Vic Duncan, this party included eight seaman from HMAS PERTH and three R.A.A.F. personnel.

Twentynine Australians joined a large British group which was sent to Sakata on the west coast of Japan, the Medical Officer, Captain Rowland Richards, was with this group. The administration of the men was carried out by Sgt.Major Keith Martin, who also had the task of fronting the Japanese each day with the working parties.

Vic Duncan: "It was the following evening when fifty of us Australians were marched to the railway station. Keith Mills, a PERTH sailor, was too ill to walk and he pleaded with me not to be left behind and I piggy-backed him the 3/4 mile, he only weighed seven stone. In later times I was to wonder about fate and how he would have fared had I left him behind. I thought of it, too, when I had to sort out his body after a savage air raid in Tokyo.

"From the railway station I knew by the stars I was looking north across the Strait of Shomoneseki and when we travelled by train and arrived a couple of days later in the Tokyo area the question in my mind was "How had the train traversed the Strait?" Obviously, there must be an undersea tunnel which in fact there, connecting the two Islands.

"The camp in which we found ourselves was in the southeast of Tokyo and not too far from Tokyo Bay. The present occupants of the camp were British and American and they had been in Japan for a long time. We were issued with cotton blankets, working clothes of thin hessian-like materials, another pair of trousers and jacket of slightly thicker material to be used for dress occasions. Later, in the winter, I wore everything. The place was run by Sgt. Eno on Army lines with inspections to check on tidyness, blankets folded and piled with precision, etc., and punishment for the slightest misdemeanour.

"The report of the section details had to be given in Japanese to the inspecting Army man (usually Sgt. Eno) so it was an advantage to have some knowledge of Japanese.

"We thought it amusing that we were all subjected to a most thorough and extensive ability test that occupied many hours, however, it was even more amusing that irrespective of ability discovered we were all labourers!

"We were allocated to different sections of the Shiboura factory which was virtually on the edge of Tokyo Bay and about 2½ miles from our camp. It was an engineering factory in the general sense but I never saw a finished or completed article that could be recognised as such. Rather, they produced parts that went somewhere else. I found myself chiselling 'dogs' or 'burrs' off castings.

"The winter of 1944-1945 was the coldest ever known in Japan. We slept in two's and three's to try to keep warm. Getting to the factory through deep snow sometimes was a tiring experience for us in our half-starved condition. Feet were frozen all day, once when I dropped a heavy piece of steel on my foot it was some time before I felt a lovely warm glow that finally became a painful throbbing. After hobbling back to camp and removing my canvas footwear I discovered I had actually squashed my big toe and the blood had congealed in the shoe.

"Immediately after Christmas about 55 men, including me, were seriously ill with influenza or something similar, and fifteen died. I lay on my back for eight days and felt as though from neck to crutch was a cold marble slab. Luckily, for Christmas they had done something extremely rare, they had issued a portion of a Red Cross parcel and I had some powdered milk. it was the only thing I could get into my stomach, I couldn't look at anything else and I think it pulled me through. I must have looked very ill, for Laurie Luke squatted alongside of me looking almost tearful and with a catch in his voice said, "Gee, Vic, I never thought I'd see you like this." I remember saying, "Don't worry, Laurie, I'm too bloody mean to die, I'll be here when the Japs are getting their arses kick in."

"The air raids commenced about January 1945, one night when I believed it was too cold to get out of the blankets even though I could hear the bombers, there was a sudden flash and explosion, the blankets whipped almost off me amid a shower of broken glass from the windows. I jumped off the platform to the earthen floor and buckled at the knees as I was struck behind the neck by the feet of the man jumping from the deck above.

"Perhaps to absolve my conscience at being a prisoner, I carried out my own little acts of sabotage wherever possible. I gradually used up their store of cold chisels by blunting the cutting edges on the hardened vyce jaws, then grinding the chisel on the pretext of sharpening it but making sure I overheated its cutting edge thus destroying its hardness. However, one of the Japanese fitters discovered the surplus of useless chisels and angrily decided I had to make amends. He went to great trouble to demonstrate how the chisel should be heated in I had learned during my apprenticeship as a fitter and turner. With this knowledge I was able to harden the chisel in such a manner where the temper colours of straw to purple were correct but the end of the chisel shattered on impact. My most satisfying effort was the ruination of 200 steel plates which were not correctly annealed.

"Pat Major, a PERTH seaman, managed to leave a solid crowbar where, when the large guillotine operated, it cracked the casting of the main bearing. A worthy effort!

"One morning Pat discovered four fingers lying on the flat surface of the guillotine, obviously left there by one of the night shift who had had an accident. He collected them on a piece of newspaper and, poking them under the nose of the foreman, asked what should he do with them. The foreman almost vomited and in his haste to get away offered no suggestion, however, a couple of our chaps said, "Hey Pat, don't waste them, take them back to camp for the soup!"

"Our guards took great delight in running us to or from the factory so that some of the prisoners were completely exhausted and had to be helped by those able to do so. The guards would jump into the ranks and reign blows on anyone slipping back through the ranks due to tired

"My luck failed one morning when I practised dumb insolence to "Horseface" at the head of the column as I ignored his numerous requests to increase the pace. I had just repeated "Can't do" when I realised too late that his stave was inches from my head. I went down but thought I got straight up back on my feet. Frank McGovern told me I was "out to it" while "Horseface" kicked me in the body and head which accounted for the bruises and soreness and the bloody scab where the left lobe of my ear had nearly been severed.

"One day feeling lean mean and nasty as we shambled, staggered and were driven like cattle before the flailing staves of the "fu men" after our long day at work we were in no mood to enjoy the sight and sound of a few six year old boys on the side of the road looking healthy and happy and yelling exuberantly, "Captive!" Tommy Johnston's usual good nature must have been stretched to the limits for he said, "I could pick them up by the feet and bash their bloody brains out on the wall." I felt so tired that although I couldn't have done it myself, I could have watched and felt nothing.

"We were talking once about what we would do with the backpay the Government would owe us. Very quietly Tommy said, "I'd give every bloody penny they owe me to be safely out of this." My stubborn and frugal nature came to the fore as I said, "Bugger it, I've come this far, I'll see it out. I need that money to build a home." I was to think back on Tommy's foreboding later.

"Makiguchi was in charge of the section to which I had been allocated, he was a thoughtful, gentle, man in contrast to our Army and civilian guards. One day after the 3 pm radio propaganda, the younger Japanese tried to tell me of their "Victories" and that "Australia was starving", I told them the fighting was getting nearer and nearer to Japan and that Australia had countless millions of sheep, cattle and more wheat than they could eat. I knew enough Japanese to get my message across, although they said nothing their faces were sullen. Makiguchi's face had a sad smile as he nodded his head a little and said softly, "That's right."

"He asked me to make a key for a special lock he had, not wanting to reveal any skills I may have, even though I liked him, I said "Very difficult." He just smiled, tapped his head and said my head understood quite a lot. He told me the key was for his own use, so I discreetly cut, filed and produced a key for him, he tried it, smiled and quietly said, "Number One!".

"I remember vividly a day in March when two of us were taken outside of the factory, there still piles of dirty ice and snow lying about but the broken window panes were no longer festooned with sheets of ice hanging from them, the cold metal did not take the skin off one's fingers, I could feel I still had ten toes, and Japan's worse winter on record was behind us. I could feel the feeble sunlight on my face and just a little warmth through my hessian-like jacket and understood why primitive peoples had been sunworshippers. I said "Well Milton, we bloody well made it", and the whole 9 stone of me felt we were lining up for the last lap now that it was 1945.

"With the winter behind us, a few items of Red Cross clothing was given to the Dutch commandant, it was doled out on a lucky-draw system and I won a pair of socks. I was confident I would not be in Japan for another winter so I gave them to Makiguchi, he was very happy to accept them discreetly. Occasionally he would take me out of the building to help him to prize up the wooden floor blocks, they were set in tar and were a fire hazzard, so workers could take them away to burn at home. Being out of hearing of other Japanese we could converse on the war situation.

“About this time one of our Australians received a letter through the Red Cross, in it mention was made that a certain person had arrived home. Aware this person had been on the RAKUYO MARU, it was obvious he had been picked up by someone other than the Japanese.

“One of the Japanese approaching his 18th birthday would tell me “In four months I go into the Navy” etc. I told him that in two or three more months there wouldn’t be any Japanese Navy to go and he didn’t like that. When the time came for the young Japanese men to answer the call-up, all the other young people would stand in a circle around him with his “fried egg” head towel on his forehead and sing some stirring song. We took a sordid delight in calling out, “You’ll be bloody sorry!”

“Sometimes we had soldier guards as well as the civilian guards and there wasn’t much difference in how beastly they could be. One soldier we called “Napoleon” loved to show his skill at giving “flying mares” to POWs, these consisted of seizing one arm, throwing the body right over the shoulder and crashing it to the ground.

“Our “civvy” guards (fu men) thought up many ways of inflicting physical punishment including wide swinging “hay-makers” to the jaw or face, more frequently they used their wooden staves in savage jabs at all the soft and sensitive parts of the body or in descending, crashing blows to the head. On one occasion I felt the stave end in my neck muscle, rolled my shoulder to save my collarbone and sagged my knees so that the scrotum jab landed in the lower abdomen and lifted my underweight body into the man in line behind me. The broken skin on my back became abscessed and required lancing.this ‘fu man’, whose name was Watanabi, was particularly vicious. On one occasion Frank McGovern was able to raise a cheeky Irish grin as he gathered himself together after being ‘done over’ by this solidly built sadist.

“Young Rubberneck” was probably trying to ape the older “Rubberneck” in attacking prisoners in the factory but he wasn’t as skilful, I remember him attacking Laurie Luke over and over again until Laurie was buckling at the knees but trying to stay on his feet. My knuckles almost bled as I bit them in frustration knowing I was capable of killing this hateful bastard with my two hands.

“One afternoon he came into the toilet where the three squat-holes were occupied, he accused me of not working and ordered me into the only empty stall where the excreta was high and plenty. I told him “Piss off” after which I dodged his two short fist jabs at my mouth. The third jab drew blood and suddenly I had a fistful of the front of his tunic, I twisted it and stood him up on his toes off balance, resisted the urge to smash him on the brick wall then shot-putted him backwards out the door where he sprawled in the dirt. In less than ten seconds the toilet block was deserted and I had a comfortable ‘session’. Nobody wanted to be involved in the Jap “come-back”.

“As the adrenalin and rage subsided I felt apprehensive and fully expected I would be in real trouble when we mustered to go home, however I was not going to chicken out of the front line which had to number in Japanese and in which I usually fell in as my Japanese was good. I looked directly at "Young Rubberneck" and decided he was avoiding looking at me – anywhere else, but not at me. I decided he had been too ashamed to tell anybody for there was no follow-up, but a few days later as he checked the lines were "covered off" he gave me a light smack in the face as he passed by but he did not dally. All I had time to say in English was "I'll kill you you bastard when the time comes." I still marvel at how I got away with it.

"Onadero, the older 'fu man' we called "Rubberneck" was the prime bastard of them all. He would knock men down in a semi-conscious state then order the younger 'fu men' to throw a bucket of water over them; in freezing weather this was a good way of ensuring the men shivered for the rest of the day or caught a chill or pneumonia. Two Dutchmen he seemed to have a set on were like "punch-drunk" boxers after being worked over three times within a couple of weeks. One Dutch-Indonesian had to endure alternate lunges to the stomach and crashes to the head, the blood was streaming down his face from beneath the peak of his cap and we were forced to watch all this before being allowed to have our rice ration."

John Dwyer: "On one occasion while returning to camp from the factory where we worked as labourers, a Dutch POW known to us as "Dutchy" Voor-Jans, collapsed and fell to the ground and a china plate which he had hidden in his tunic dropped out.

"The escort guard we called "Rubberneck" noticed the incident and saw the plate. We continued marching for a hundred yards or so when we were halted by "Rubberneck", who gave the order from a distance in our rear. As we stood waiting for the next order we heard the unmistakeable sounds of a man moaning.

"Rubberneck" then rejoined us and ordered several POWs to walk back to Voor-Jans who was still lying on the roadway. They carried him back to the camp unconscious and he died shortly after we arrived back in camp.

"A Dutch medical officer examined Voor-Jans, there was a deep wound just above the bridge of his nose which had caused the fracture of the nose and lower forehead structure. An American medical orderly named Woods, later informed many POWs that he had witnessed "Rubberneck" pick up the plate and strike Voor-Jans across the forehead with its edge. Woods was brought before the Camp Commander, Lt. Tanaka, and his second-in-charge, Sgt. Eno, and asked if what he was alleged to have said was true, naturally Woods denied having made the statement knowing full well the consequences should he be foolish enough to do so. In spite of this denial it was obvious that someone had killed Voor-Jans with a heavy blow to the skull made by some fairly sharp instrument. We knew that "Rubberneck" had stayed with Voor-Jans when he had collapsed. In spite of these facts, the Dutch medical officer was forced to sign a certificate to the effect that Voor-Jans had died from pneumonia and beri-beri."

Vic Duncan: "There were times afterwards when they would joke among themselves, in my hearing, about Number 104 which was Voor-Jans' number, they frequently laughed about his death at the hands of "Rubberneck" as they walked beside our marching column on our way to the factory.

"Many a night I awoke and pondered the fate of "Rubberneck". I planned to continue in the Navy after the war, therefore at some time I would return to Tokyo Bay. I knew the approximate position of his home and planned I would waylay him in the dark and while I perpetrated atrocious butchery on him I would be reminding him he was to die slowly and painfully. But I was not to know that his home and most of Tokyo-Yokohama would be burned and blown away and that he would hang by the neck after the Tokyo War Trials. Now, so many years later, I look back remembering my intense hatred, anger and longing for vengeance against particular Japanese whose deeds caused our people to suffer indignities and death and I excuse myself by claiming righteous wrath. However, as I glared with hatred at "Rubberneck" one day as he walked past, my co-worker, Milton Elmore, from the U.S., said, "Goddam, Vic, He'll know what you're thinking, he'll kill both of us!" On one occasion I had the temerity to argue with "Rubberneck" as to my attempt to insulate my freezing feet from the cold concrete by standing on a piece of timber while working at the bench. I did lose the argument but all the punishment I received was a kick in the shins.

"Came the day when I asked Makiguchi how was Germany getting along in the war. He glanced carefully around before saying, "Yesterday, Germany finish." What an indescribable feeling surged through me as I realised we now on the last lap of our difficult obstacle course. Optimistically, I said to him, "In three months the war will be over."

Frank McGovern: "The first air raid was in March – recce planes came over in the afternoon, we had heavy winds then, these planes came over in the day and marked the area to be bombed, there must have been hundreds of those B29s. The raid was going for about an hour and probably getting closer, and they said, "Right, All men!" – they were going to evacuate the camp. We got all our bundles and got out into the compound and I thought it looked like a bloody great bushfire was going on. Down on each end of the street outside the camp they had watch-towers, as you know they are frightened of fire, there were water-tanks everywhere, but as we looked down the street there was a wall of fire, just rolling, roaring and consuming everything before it – then another bomb would drop and it would land and go whoooosh and the flames would spread out from it, we tried to crouch against a wall, the bomb would hit and fire would go everywhere. We got out of this narrow street to a fork in the road near an overhead bridge where there was a crowd of civilians. Sgt. Eno was leading our contingent with guards on each side and these civilians confronted us, you see in the glare of the fire the hate on their faces, they wanted to attack us. Sgt. Eno harangued them, they shook their fists, they wanted to get at us but out came his Samurai sword and he held it up, you could see the fire glinting on the sword, and he harangued them for another five minutes then he said "GO!" and they parted just like that. We went through and got out into open paddocks. The air raid went for about four hours. The following day we were taken back and there was nothing we could see over an area of I'd say about four square miles – all that was left was a few concrete buildings, telegraph posts – the rest was nothing."

Vic Duncan: "These gigantic fires lasted for about a week, more people died in them than were killed by the later atomic bombs. Makiguchi pointed to a middle-aged Japanese who had just arrived in the factory on a bike with a child strapped on his back. He looked absolutely exhausted physically and mentally. He had lost his wife and five children in the fire. We were now moved into the building in the factory itself and our sleep became more and more disturbed by air raids. We had lost everything, including blankets, and a further issue was found for us such as it was.

"The bombing continued and sometimes we would watch the action in the sky before smoke obscured the view. We could see amid the smoke of ack-ack bursts and searchlight beams the parachutes of airmen descending with what appeared to be tracer bullets trying to hit them. One American flyer landed in the canal behind our previous camp and was killed by irate local civilians.

"The night of 13-14 July 1945 was like any other. After midnight I woke up to the usual air raid and said to my mate Tommy Johnson, "I'm ducking out for a quick piss before the mob get out there." I had just left the latrine and I could hear the sound of debris landing very close. I suddenly felt myself crouching closer to the ground and as I dived into a depression between the toilet and our hut everything was blowing upwards and away, although I felt jarred and numb I knew that I had gone down further than I had gone up. I could feel timbers and other debris pinning me down but I managed to crawl forward and raise my head expecting to be looking at the wall of the building where I had been sleeping – in the reflected light from the sky I was looking into a huge crater. Our shelter had been completely blown away except for the two ends standing drunkenly about thirty yards apart. I realised that our hut had been built on top of an underground water reservoir, into which the dead and debris had landed, and I was on the edge of the crater.

"Japanese guards in great panic hounded us to move out and they ran us in great confusion. The factory had been badly hit, I found it difficult to recognise what had been the landmarks. We ran, but I found myself looking ahead for the next bit of slightest cover, even if it was only the raised gutter to partly protect my head in the event of bomb shrapnel as I frequently flattened against the earth as the deafening roar of the bombers and their loads created havoc and destruction on a vast scale. As we struggled to reach an area previously residential and now a wasteland which would be unlikely to be bombed again, I detected the smell of onions – some of the men had found a wrecked garden and made the most of it in spite of their fear.

"At the end of a two or three mile run, we rested in an area where nothing was left standing and waited for the raid to end. This took some hours, and it was daylight when we arrived back at the remains of our camp."

Frank McGovern: "The pattern bombing was getting closer day by day. This time it was for about an hour, I was sitting on a tatami mat and Keith Mills came along and said to me, "Mac, how about going up to the air raid shelter?" – these shelters were built up off the ground with a few sandbags, if you dug down any further than 2 ft. you got water – so I said, "What's the use Keith" and at that moment one came over and dropped a load and to me it sounded like a heap of bricks coming down. I rolled over on my stomach and the next minute up in the air – don't know how far – it was like slow motion – then down. Fortunately down feet first into the water in the crater the bomb had made, I could put my hands above my head and hold on to something when I came up. Next morning they found Keith's body in the crater, Pat Major and Tommy Johnson was killed."

Vic Duncan: "Frank McGovern had been blown sky high as he talked with Keith Mills, then he landed in the crater with his face just above water level and pinned there by a criss-cross of timbers and debris. I helped rescuing him from the crater where he had been held in great pain for six hours. Two of his lower spinal verterbrae had been fractured and he appeared to be paralysed from the waist down. He lay for two days on a stretcher with no treatment before being taken to hospital. About two weeks later when news got around about the murder of the two Dutch amputees Frank was advised to volunteer to return to camp 'fit for work'. The so-called "hospital" seemed a good place to get clear of so Frank tottered into line to go back to our camp.

"The task now was to collect the dead and injured who were in some cases pinned or buried in the debris. Having been virtually undressed and losing what footwear I had when the bomb blasted everything around me, I forced myself to remove shoes and trousers from a dead man but in this way I had clothes again.

"My worst fears were realised when Tommy Johnson's body was collected, he must have been directly over the blast, if not recognisable from his build, the tattoo of his wife's name, "Olive", on his forearm, told me all. The death of Tommy and the others, so suddenly and yet not so unexpectedly, was one of the telling blows I have remembered through all the years since.

"Sgt.-Major "Scotty" Heywood's body was found a couple of days later, it had been hurled upwards and over the high, saw-toothed factory roof. Two of the Dutchmen had their legs torn off and after successfully amputating and doctoring them, the Japanese medicos took into a room singly and, in spite of the presence of the American first-aid man, cut them in the groin artery and bled them to death.

"The bombing raids continued, the bombers were now accompanied by fighter aircraft who would strafe the area, the small hill nearby our camp seemed to be a landmark for the bombers and they would release their bombs and saturate the area between us and Tokyo Bay.

"Work in the factory had almost come to a standstill, some of us spent a lot of time carrying water in drums to the factory kitchen as many of the water pipes had been blown away. One time I passed a trolley of foodstuffs for the Japanese cookhouse and snatched a piece of cold pumpkin. As I swallowed it down hurriedly too late I realised it was practically frozen and it really gave me a pain in the stomach. I had found a 4 gal. can of whale oil and nearly every day I milked it with the aid of a 3/8" diameter steel rod, the viscosity of the oil allowed me to more than half fill a small tin the size of a breakfast cup I had, which was all I could "milk" daily, to be caught was unthinkable and punishment if caught even more so. My body must have really needed it for I could actually enjoy the oil. Prior to this I had dreams of being back in Australia and eating half a pound of butter straight out of the paper wrapper.

"As mid-August approached part of our daily chores was to carry water to the cookhouse and one of the Japanese girls indicated to me she would leave a rice ball for me in the nearby Japanese air-raid dugout every day. I couldn't believe my luck, for the few days that ended the war I would dive down the dugout, hastily gulp down the rice ball with bits of potato in it, then resurface. To be caught with it was a sure way of becoming a hospital case. Although the girl was probably sympathetic she did ask me if I was married and holding two of her fingers parallel indicating it was her and me. It definitely had a 'joining' meaning, which in my hungry and 'will-to-survive frame of mind didn't have much in its favour.

"There came a day when on arrival at the factory we didn't work, we were stuffed into a Japanese semi-dugout and the doors closed so that in the August heat we sweated and the air turned foul. This was puzzling as there were air raid alerts but no bombing. There was much conjecture and questioning – what was happening? Had there been a landing of the Americans on the Japanese homeland? When, at the end of the day, excited voices and activity could be heard outside I peered through the cracks in the door and could see not our our 'fu men' but soldiers increasing in number of our guards and they were fixing bayonets!

"We commenced our march back to camp but the Japanese people were no longer taking us for granted or ignoring us, they appeared to be having a fresh appraisal of us. When we were brought to a halt to await the passing of a train at a railway crossing, a woman approached one of the soldier guards. She was obviously distressed and upset, her eyes were red and swollen from crying and she was asking for the guard's permission to attack us, holding her hands up and clawed to show her intention. He dismissed her curtly.

"For months we had had little sleep or rest so that I slept deeply and was amazed to wake and find it was daylight – what had happened? – no air raid – I reached out and touched Frank McGovern on the shoulder, "Mac – the bloody war is over!"

"We did not return to the factory and after a day or two I joined other section leaders in the Jananese Administration building where we were informed that peace was being discussed but it would only come about on terms suitable to the Japanese. I felt and said this wasn't the true situation, this opinion was substantiated when the interpreter went on, to my surprise, to say, "We want you to know that we will never have communism in Japan, we will fight with the British and Americans against the Russians." I found myself laughing and saying, "Let's get home from this war before you start any others."

"Our old guards had vanished and the newcomers were unarmed and obviously going out of their way to avoid trouble. Our rations improved slightly and the rest from work was appreciated. A Swiss Red Cross man arrived and we heard of the atom bomb and its widespread death and destruction.

"I had decided, in spite of an Allied message that no Allies were ashore and to remain in our camps for safety reasons, to find my way to Tokyo Bay to try and see the Allied fleets I felt sure would be there. With a Japanese soldier to protect me from any attack, I made my way to the Bay where I was able to look at the vast armada of warships stretching as far as the eye could see. My attention became rivetted on the only survivor of PERTH's sister ships, the HOBART; she lay at anchor about five miles away and nearby a "County Class" cruiser was probably the SHROPSHIRE, which had replaced the CANBERRA as we had heard from our hidden radios back in 1942-1944. It was marvellous to see the Royal Australian Navy after all this time and it was ridiculous that two cruisers, dwarfed by numerous carriers, battleships and uncountable other men-of-war should assume such importance, but they did and I had to resist the urge to jump in a boat and get out there.

"I tramped around the Bay and came across a camp where the POWs had suffered fifty dead from bombing hits, some of the bodies were still missing, probably ploughed under by further bomb hits. As I walked in, a dark-haired, solid-looking Scot walked over and we shook hands, he glanced at my Japanese escort and asked if I wanted him "fixed up" but I assured him I had nothing against this member of our enemy and that I needed him to get back to camp. I eventually went on my way with a pack of foodstuffs that had been dropped into their camp by American aircraft, up to that time we had not received any drops.

"Guided by the P.O.W. on the roof of the camp, our first gift arrived in two 44 gallon drums welded together and full of 'goodies' but restrained by only one parachute. Luckily nobody was injured when the bulky object dropped and embedded itself in the dirt. After this six or seven parachutes, each supporting a wooden box, would drop in, sometimes a box would explode on impact and tins of "Spam" etc. would spin through the air. Only one man was injured, his arm was broken. There were about ninety men in camp but after a few days we had enough food to last us a year or so, we had countless toothbrushes and enough boots to equip a lot of centipedes.

"Some of the 'chutes overshot the camp and one was seen to go through a nearby Japanese dwelling. When we arrived we discovered the tragedy of a dying father and a distraught mother and children. We hastened to bring our camp doctor who said there was nothing he could do.

"Frank McGovern and I and others, fully appreciative of how the Japanese families had suffered in many ways, gave tinned food to the women and children in the surrounding area and they were so humble and grateful. They had known what it was to be severely rationed and restricted by Japan's Imperial Policy and it must have been an ordeal even if they had not had it as hard as we had. However, I could not convince myself to be friendly to the men folk. It was too soon for that.

"On instructions we were to be on the foreshore at a fixed place and time the following, we arrived at the appointed time and place and as the Yanks dropped the flap at the front of their barge and jumped on to the sacred soil of Japan, I remember saying, "You can have this bloody dung heap, we're going that way!" and pointing into Tokyo Bay.

"As we moved away from the land I watched Sgt. Eno standing on the wall, waving a small handkerchief in slow movements, sometimes dabbing a tear from a face that definitely showed emotion. My mind ranged through a few possible reasons for this behaviour but I came to no conclusion but one question – would I ever understand the Japanese mind?

"Ferried out to the Hospital ship BENEVOLENCE, we were undressed, disinfected, showered, dressed up like American sailors and some seriously ill people such as tuberculosis victims, segregated for special treatment. The kindness, concern and generosity accorded us was something I shall never forget. On the second night they found stretchers for us and I awoke to find that blankets had arrived and I had been covered and tucked in while I slept.

"Our next move was to the Royal Navy escort carrier SPEAKER, where the Naval lieutenant was taken aback when, instead of having a prefix like 'VX' or 'NX' etc., I gave '21589 RAN'. He said, "Where the bloody hell did you come from?" On being told "HMAS PERTH 1942", he had me escorted to the Chiefs' Mess where I was given my Chief's cap complete with badge and made very welcome.

The SPEAKER left Tokyo Bay with the first batch of ex-POWs, steaming up and down the rows of warships. We were assembled in an ordered group and as we passed the various ships they gave us a great welcome. It was a stirring occasion and I felt somewhat emotional, so did many others I am sure.

"When we steamed close to the two Australian cruisers, I mounted to the Bridge and the officer of the Watch was kind enough to send them my signal, "Greetings from men of HMAS PERTH, Vic Duncan, Frank McGovern, Sid Matson and Alf Thomas."

Captain D.N.C. Tufnell, Royal Navy representative attached to United States Pacific, arrived in Saipan soon after the USS PAMPANITO and USS SEALION arrived with the survivors of the RAKUYO MARU. At this time it was believed these men to be the only survivors.

At the conclusion of the interviews Capt. Tufnell reported in October 1944:

"Duncan, E.A.III. V.R.

"Practically every man who was interviewed had knowledge of Duncan. He apparently was very popular with all on board and it was due to his coolness and organisation that most of the personnel from No.2 Hatch managed to escape overboard when the ship was hit. Duncan took control of the situation and called the orders to the men. His coolness encouraged the men. With the hatch covers he prepared steps by means of which the men could escape quickly from the hatch. He distributed life-belts and advised the men in methods of going over the side and how to protect themselves against burning oil.

"Duncan was last seen returning to the ship on a raft. He was alone. It has not been possible to establish whether he did actually return. One Army man who returned to the ship saw Duncan aboard but he was unable to say whether that was after Duncan had returned on the raft or before Duncan took to the water.

"Reports to date indicate that Duncan remained on board until practically all other personnel had left."

In September 1945, Vic Duncan received this communication from the Admiralty:

"21 September 1945

"Sir,

"I am commanded by My Lords Commissioners of the Admiralty to inform you that they have learned with great pleasure that, on the advice of the First Lord, the King has been graciously pleased to award you the British Empire Medal for courage and devotion to duty in rescue work after the Japanese ship RAKUYO MARU, which was carrying Allied prisoners of war, had been torpedoed.

"This Award was published in the London Gazette Supplement of 11th September 1945.

Chief Petty Officer Vic Duncan

Released Prisoners of War at Yokohama Railway Station. L.to R.: Pte. George Carroll, Pte. JimKay, Cpl. Frank Lawrence, Pte. Jack White, Pte. Doug Mayers, Pte. Harold Ramsey, Pte. John Dwyer, Pte. Walter Williams, Pte. Bill Mayne and Driver Arthur Hunt. They were not only survivors from the sinking, the RAKUYO MARU on 12 September 1944 but also survived the B29 fire bombing raids. Pic: Australian War Memorial 19202

Group of Australian Servicemen return on HMS SPEAKER. Front L. to R. as marked: Frank McGovern, Syd Matson, CPO Duncan, Alf Thomas.

SINKING OF THE "MONTEVIDEO MARU"

As the QUEEN MARY sailed for Malaya in February 1942 carrying the 22 Brigade group of the 8 Division a Conference was being held in Singapore between the Australian Chiefs of Staff and Air Chief Brooke-Popham, British Commander in Chief Far East, to discuss the defence of northern Australia.

At this Conference it was decided the 23 Brigade of the 8 Division, comprising the three Battalions, 2/21, 2/22 and 2/40, would be detached to form the nucleus of those forces to be placed at isolated islands to the north of Australia – 2/40 Battalion "Sparrow Force" on Timor, 2/21 Battalion "Gull Force" on Ambon and 2/22 Battalion "Lark Force" on Rabaul.

The Chiefs of Staff would have been aware they had neither Naval or Air power to support these forces in the event of a sustained Japanese offensive and they would be ultimately sacrificed.

There seems there is no record they considered alternatives to placing battalion groups in this vulnerable location. No provisions were made for any sustained fighting, or consideration given to place specially trained Special Operations Forces equipped to infiltrate and land mine important Japanese objectives or to the insertion of hard hitting Commando groups to destroy supply dumps.

In the case of Rabaul, the Chiefs of Staff continued to reinforce Rabaul even after it had assessed their function was to "put up a jolly good show".

The relatives of the gallant men "Lark Force" endured more suffering than any other group in having to wait almost four years before the Acting Prime Minister announced in October 1945 those taken prisoner of war at Rabaul in

January 1942 were lost when a Japanese transport carrying them to Hainan was torpedoed by a U.S. submarine off Luzon on July 1, 1942, and there were no POW survivors.

The Australian Government sought information from the Japanese Government about the prisoners – they did not respond. It was not till the war ended and a special investigator, Major Williams, was appointed to proceed to Japan to interrogate the Chief of the Prisoner of War Information Bureau, Lt. Gen. Tamura, that it was established the Japanese received information of the loss of the POWs and Internees at their POW Information Bureau in 1943, and enquiries by the Australian Red Cross through the International Red Cross, failed to get any response from their Japanese counterparts. It appeared they stated because the ship carrying the POWs had not arrived in Japan they had no record of it.

The identity of the ship was not established until after the Japanese surrender when U.S. Navy teams researched Japanese Navy records on the identity of the ships sunk by U.S. submarines. At about the same time, Australian investigators were asking the Japanese the whereabouts of the prisoners and internees taken at Rabaul in January 1942.

During the early hours of 22 June 1942, the prisoners of war of the Malaguna Road Camp were awakened by Japanese guards. Here they separated the officers and divided the men in 'Kumis' of 50 men which were bundled off with their gear and later loaded on to the MONTEVIDEO MARU, a passenger cargo ship of 7267 tons. No doubt the Japanese, fearing an uprising on the ship, separated the officers who were later safely transferred to Japan together with 17 Australian nurses and a few civilians, on the NATUNO MARU.

It was not the practice of the Japanese to seek safe passage for transports carrying civilians or prisoners of war. In this case the ship was not escorted, instead, like many fast Allied transports, they relied on speed to out-run the submarines. However it seemed the top speed of the MONTEVIDEO MARU was somewhere around 17 to 18 knots, not sufficient to out-run a U.S. submarine.

The prisoners and civilians would have been crowded into the holds in less than humane conditions. Many of the men would have assessed, on boarding the ship, the possibility of taking her over and making a bold dash for New Guinea – this occurred when Australian POWs were loaded on other Japanese ships, they were still soldiers and would have considered all possibilities, finally deciding they had no hope ... On board the ship the Japanese said there were 853 prisoners and 205 civilians, the latter people who had played such an important role in the Administration of the Mandated Territories.

The U.S. Navy had no knowledge the ship was carrying the POWs, the only light seen on the ship was after it had been hit. It went down in six minutes. The submarine was the USS STURGEON, skippered by Lt.Cdr. Wright. who reported in his Log:

"30 June 1942: Patrolling northwest of Bojeador as before. Dove at dawn, surfaced at dusk. At 2216 sighted a darkened ship to southward. At first, due to bearing on which sighted, believed him to be on northerly course, but after a few minutes observation it was evident he was on a westerly course, and going at high speed. He quite evidently had stood out of Babuyan Channel, headed for Hainan. Put on all engines and worked up to full power, proceeding to westward in an attempt to get ahead of him. For an hour and a half we couldn't make a nickel. This fellow was really going, making at least 17 knots, and probably a bit more, as he appeared to be zig-zagging. At this time it looked a bit hopeless, but determined to hang on in the hope he would slow or change course toward us. His range at this time was estimated at around 18,000 yards. Sure enough, about midnight he slowed to about 12 knots. After that it was easy.

"1 July 1942: Proceeding to intercept target as before. Altered course to gain position ahead of him, and dove at 0146. When he got in periscope range, it could be seen that he was larger than first believed, also that his course was a little to the left of west, leaving us some 5,000 yards off the track. Was able to close some 1,000 yards of this, and then turned to fire stern tubes as:

i) Only three tubes available forward, and at this range and with large target four torpedo spread desirable.

ii) After tubes had 70D/ heads, while heads forward were small ones.

"At 0225 fired four torpedo spread, range 4,000 yards, from after tubes. At 0229 heard and observed explosion about 75-100 ft. abaft stack. At 0240 observed ship sink stern first. 0250 surfaced, proceeded to eastward, completing battery charge. Ship believed to be Rio de Janeiro Maru, or very similar type, although it is possible it was a larger ship, he was a big one. A few lights were observed on deck just after the explosion, but there was apparently no power available, and his bow was well up in the air in six minutes. Dove at dawn, No further contacts."

On 20 October 1945 Australian Authorities received a report from OSAKA SHOSEN KAISHA, the Owner of the MONTEVIDEO MARU which stated: "Concerning the Sinking of the MONTEVIDEO MARU:

1. Port of departure – Rabaul.
   Port of destination – Samah. (Hainan)
2. Time of the incident – 0300 hours, 1 July 1942.
3. Scene of the incident – About 60 miles northwest of-Bojeador Cape, Luzon Island.
4. Details of the incident:

The vessel in question, serving as a naval auxiliary, was transporting a considerable number of prisoners. At the time and place stated above she received on the starboard quarter two torpedoes from an enemy submarine. Numbers 4 and 5 holds were damaged and there was an explosion in Number 5 oil tank. Oil entered the engine room and the engines were stopped. Anti-flooding measures were taken but sufficient water entered to cause a list to starboard. The damaged holds filled rapidly and she settled further to starboard. In view of the imminent danger of sinking the captain gave the order to abandon ship.

"Although three life boats were lowered, all capsized and one was severely damaged. Several minutes after receiving the torpedoes the ship went down stern first. The boats were righted and boarded and although every effort was made to recover survivors, the number of missing was large. Since there was no longer any hope of finding the missing, the two boats left the area at 1000 hours, and reached the coast of Luzon near Bojeador Cape light in the evening of the next day, the 2nd. A camp was made there. The next day the area was reconnoitered and the use of a house in a nearby village was obtained. All personnel were able to rest there but it was very difficult to obtain food.

"The natives sent out immediately after the landing to contact the Japanese Army failed to return. Therefore on the next day, the 4th, it was decided that all personnel should set out overland toward Lavag, but about 0900 hours the party was attacked by enemy stragglers and natives. The party was absolutely defenseless, and although clubs and rocks were used for what they were worth, the majority of the personnel was either dead or missing after the attack. The personnel who were admitted to the field hospital by 25 July were a party of eighteen under Quartermaster 3rd Class Katsuishhi, Shozo, who made their way from Bubon to Lavag, suffering frequent enemy attacks on the way. Some were wounded and all suffered greatly from hunger, exhauston, but to unbelievable fortitude all survived the trip. One died in the hospital later."

Major Williams reported: "Lt.Gen. Tamura and his staff professed complete frankness and co-operation, but evasions and deceptions continued to be indulged in when frankness appeared inexpedient. In this connection, attention is invited to the following:

"It will be recalled that the Prisoner of War Information Bureau received from the Navy Department full details of the casualties on 6 January 1943, but never transmitted that information. There is ample documentary evidence that the Bureau informed International Red Cross and others on several occasions that it did not have the information.

"In reply to my written inquiry as to why the information was not released, Lt.Gen. Tamura, under date 13 October gave the following explanation:

"However, rolls of such persons given in that letter were 'written in 'Kana' (Japanese character spelling) and were not usable as material for immediate advice. At that time we centered our attention first to advise to the opponent countries living war prisoners ..."

"I informed Lt.Gen. Tamura that such excuses were in direct conflict with the advices that had been given to the International Red Cross and others, and that I could not accept them as the truth. After I had made my views entirely clear, Lt.Gen. Tamura stated that he would correct his memorandum, which he thereupon asked me to return. I informed him that I could not return, but that I would await a correction.

"The draft of a second memorandum was thereupon produced, but in view of my criticism of the misinformation contained therein, it was abandoned.

Finally, under date of 4th November 1945, Lt.Gen. Tamura has provided a signed memorandum reading as follows:

"Information of the loss of 1053 Prisoners of War and Civilian internees on SS MONTEVIDEO MARU has not been forwarded to the Australian Authorities. This is a sheer dereliction on the part of this Bureau to have failed to advise the Australian Government of the subject in question. This Bureau sincerely expresses its deep regret and hereby tenders profound apology.

"The originals of the above 3 memoranda are attached for information.

"We were informed for the first time by the letter dated January 6, 1943, from the Japanese Navy Ministery of the fact that Australian surrenderers at Rabaul were disastered on board the MONTEVIDEO MARU. However, rolls of such persons given in that letter were written in 'Kana' (Japanese character spelling) and were not usable as material for immediate advice. At that time we centered our attention, first to advise the opponent countries living war prisoners who had been taken to regular camps and also those who were in the hands of our operating forces and were not yet taken to regular POW camps. Nevertheless, this task was hindered by facing extremely difficulty in investigating the actual state of war prisoners owing to vastness of war operational area and to frequent transfers of war prisoners in large scale. And, such difficulties were being doubled by restraint of traffic and communication, which were steadily growing worse with the progress of warfare. Consequently by the termination of war we were not able to complete our information even on the living war prisoners.

"With regard to the subject in question we tried incessantly to carry on the preparatory work for advice, but we were in the situation that the volume of our office work in general was always exceeding our office capacity, which was constantly curbed by the general trend of war. Hence, we could not complete the report on the subject before the war ended. However, in accordance with our duty to reply all inquiries made relative to war prisoners we have, upon receiving inquiries on Rabaul war prisoners and civilians, made all possible investigations within our reach and made efforts to reply them in every instance, although, very much to our regret that such replies were not completed by the termination of war.

(Signed) H. TAMURA
Lt.General

13 October 1945."

Despite the evidence of the sinking of the MONTEVIDEO MARU, rumour circulated that the POWs never left Rabaul, that they were taken out into the jungle and massacred.

Exhaustive investigations were made of these claims and no evidence was ever found to give these claims any credence.

It is known where the Japanese endeavoured to cover up atrocities, such as at Sandakan, much evidence was found. Personal items such as watches were later discovered on Japanese, Australian shoulder badges were found among charred remains and even documents, clothing, paybooks which had been buried, were discovered. No such evidence was ever found on the island of New Britain or anywhere else to support such a claim.

The relatives of the men of "Lark Force" endured more suffering than any other group in having to wait so long, they had feared the worst earlier in 1943 when letters arrived in Australia from other POWs held by the Japanese but there was no news of "Lark Force" personnel.

The blame for the tragedy lay squarely with the Japanese Imperial General Headquarters in not seeking safe passage for ships carrying Allied POWs and internees. Some thousands of U.S. POWs were also lost at sea in unmarked ships – the prisoners were battened down in the holds and when some of them broke free they were machine-gunned.

Left: L/Cpl. Kevin Geyer. NX.47935. "Elberta" Tenterfield, NSW. Pic: Mr. H.S. Inglis, Tenterfield, NSW. Right: Gnr. George Thornton. NX.55060. Sydney, NSW Pic: Mr. C.O. (Bill) Harry, 2/22 Assn.

Left: Colin Maxwell Brooker. VX.41522 Dunolly, Vic. Pic: Mr. C.O. (Bill) Harry, 2/22 Assn. Right: Sgt. Arthur Gullidge. VX.37499 Bandmaster 2/22 Regimental Band. Pic: Mr. C.O. (Bill) Harry, 2/22 Assn.

Left: Sgt. R.L. (Dick) Spunner VX.23667 A top lifesaver and highly talented amateur boxer whose youthful experience belied these skills. He was goaded into a fight by a Japanese Sergeant who felt sure he would be an easy mark Spunner flattened him and was rewarded with a first and only beer in a Japanese Sergeants Mess. Pic: Mr. C.O. (Bill) Harry, 2/22 Assn.

Right: Cpl. Frank Pascoe. VX.28754. His daughter Suzanne was born August 1941. Pic: Mr. C.O. (Bill) Harry, 2/22 Assn.

Left: Cpl. Walter Thomas Cracknell. NX.32378 Goondiwindi, NSW. Pic: Mrs. K.K. Sands. Right: Cpl. E.T. (Ted) Bosse. VX.19621. Pic. Mr. C.O. (Bill) Harry, 2/22 Assn.

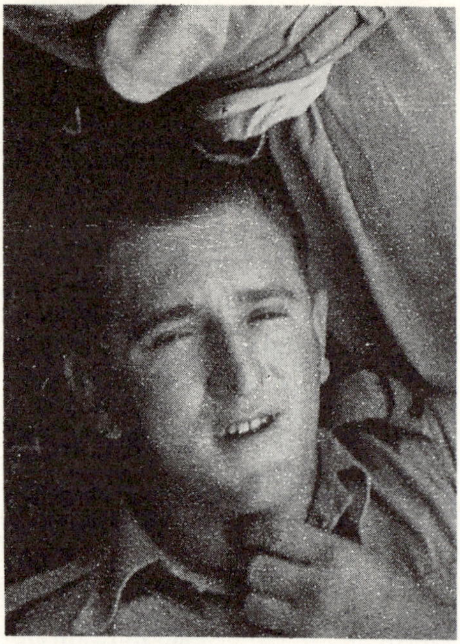

Left: Pte. Andrew Craig Baird. Pic: Sister, Mrs. Leo Cornelius.
Right: Pte. Ray Nugent, 2/22 Bn. Pic: Mr. C.O. (Bill) Harry, 2/22 Assn.

Left: L/Cpl. W.A.G. Smith, 2/22 Bn. Pic: Mr. C.O. (Bill) Harry, 2/22 Assn.

HONOUR ROLL - MONTEVIDEO MARU

Abbott, Gnr. C.J.	NX. 52416	4 A/Tk.Regt.		01.07.42	39
Abbott, Pte. W.V.	VX. 36790	2/22 Bn.	East Geelong, Vic.	01.07.42	29
Ackland, Pte. M.A.	VX. 47645	2/22 Bn.	Geelong, Vic.	01.07.42	39
Adams, Pte. A.W.	VX. 23998	2/22 Bn.	Yarraville, Vic.	01.07.42	26
Ainsbury, Pte. D.R.	QX. 10930	1 Indep.Coy	Maryborough, Qld.	01.07.42	19
Alcock, Gnr. T.M.	NX.191470	A/A.& Mil.Lndg. Crft. Def.(Rabaul) RAA	Candelo, NSW	01.07.42	19
Alexander, Gnr. R.H.	NX.191471	A/A.& Mil.Lndg.Crft. Def.(Rabaul) RAA	Bega, NSW	01.07.42	21
Allatt, Sgt. C.E.	VX. 37021	2/22 Bn.	Sandringham, Vic.	01.07.42	29
Allen, Pte. Alfred	VX. 24385	2/22 Bn.	Malvern, Vic.	01.07.42	31
Allen, Cpl. J.P.L.	QX. 64943	HQ.New Guin.Area	Ashgrove, Qld.	01.07.42	20
Allsop, Rfn. K.C.	NGX. 464	N.G.Vol.Rifles	NeutralBay, NSW	01.07.42	32
Anderson, Gnr. R.G.	TX. 5218	Hvy.Bty. RAA	Launceston, Tas.	01.07.42	19
Andrew, Pte. Basil	VX. 34318	1 Indep.Coy.	Orbost, Vic.	01.07.42	26
Andrew, L/Cpl. H.E.	VX. 26890	2/22 Bn.	Echuca, Vic.	01.07.42	30
Angwin, Pte. E.A.	VX. 46936	2/22 Bn.		01.07.42	37
Apsey, Pte. W.G.	VX. 46493	2/22 Bn.	Gardenvale, Vic.	01.07.42	23
Armstrong, S/Sgt. William	VX.129416	Hvy.Bty. RAA	West Coburg, Vic.	01.07.42	38
Armstrong, Pte. W.E.	WX. 9761	1 Indep. Coy.	Maylands, W.A.	01.07.42	28
Arnold, Pte. D.M.	VX. 24227	2/22 Bn.	Minhamite, Vic.	01.07.42	23
Arrow, Gnr. E.J.	NX.191455 A	/A. & Mil.Lndg Crft. Def.(Rabaul) RAA	Tichborne, NSW	01.07.42	20
Arthur, Pte. J.R.	VX. 42088	2/22 Bn.		01.07.42	31
Ashley, Gnr. I.E.G.	VX.129354	Hvy.Bty. RAA		01.07.42	23
Attwood, Pte. F.J.	NX. 69687	1 Indep. Coy,	Casino, NSW	01.07.42	28
Austine, Pte. A.H.	VX. 13397	2/22 Bn.	North Clyde, Vic.	01.07.42	33
Baird, L/Cpl. A.C.	VX. 24605	2/22 Bn.	Toorak, Vic.	01.07.42	30
Baird, Gnr. I.J.	VX. 25515	4 A/Tk. Regt.	Wellington, N2	01.07.42	24
Baldwin, Pte. Robert	VX. 41231	2/22 Bn.	North Fitzroy, Vic.	01.07.42	32
Bapty, Sgt. Lance	NX.191432	Hvy.Bty. RAA	Sandy Bay, Tas.	01.07.42	23
Barber, Sgt. J.A.	VX. 41564	2/22 Bn.	Beaumaris, Vic.	01.07.42	34
Barker, Pte. E.B.	VX. 28659	2/22 Bn.	Donald, Vic.	01.07.42	29
Barnett, Gnr. T.J.	QX. 64919	Hvy.Bty. RAA	Windsor, Qld.	01.07.42	21
Barraclough, Gnr. A.K.	NX.191480 A	A/A.& Mil.Lndg. Crft. Def.(Rabaul)RAA	Kensington, NSW	01.07.42	20
Barrett, Pte. R.W.	NX. 20493	1 Indep. Coy.	Mayiield, NSW	01.07.42	22
Barrett, Pte. Ronald	VX. 23987	2/22 Bn.	Maidstone, Vic.	01.07.42	21
Barry, Gnr. A.N.	VX. 48429	4 A/Tk.Regt.	Chelsea, Vic.	01.07.42	24
Bartels, Gnr. T.G.	TX.	4368 Hvy.Bty. RAA	Lwr. Langley, Tas.	01.07.42	23
Barton, Pte. A.W.	VX. 23146	2/22 Bn.	Coburg, Vic.	01.07.42	29
Batchler, Sigmn. A.J.	TX. 16308	Ftrss.Sigs.	New Town, Tas.	01.07.42	21
Baxter, L/Cpl. R.H.	VX. 25760	2/22 Bn.	Nth Balwyn, Vic.	01.07.42	24
Bayly, Pte. L.J.	VX. 23614	2/22 Bn.	Richmond, Vic.	01.07.42	35
Beames, Pte. Robert	VX. 33887	2/22 Bn.	Terang, Vic.	01.07.42	37
Beckett, Rfn. H.J.	NGX.465	New Guin.Vol.Rifles	Chatswood, NSW	01.07.42	
Beecroft, Pte. R.J.	VX. 35550	2/22 Bn.	Fairiield, Vic.	01.07.42	23
Begg, Pte. R.W.	VX. 47276	2/22 Bn.	Pakenham Upper Vic.	01.07.42	27
Belcher, Cpl. T.S.	VX. 23827	2/22 Bn.	East Brunswick Vic.	01.07.42	23
Bell, Gnr. D.L.	VX.129353	Hvy.Bty. RAA	Potts Point, NSW	01.07.42	32
Bennett, Pte. F.C.G.	VX. 21580	2/22 Bn.		01.07.42	38
Bennett, Pte. R.J.	VX. 24153	2/22 Bn.	Fitzroy, Vic.	01.07.42	25
Benson, W.0.2. C.R.	VX. 24155	2/22 Bn.	Coleraine, Vic.	01.07.42	44
Benzley, Pte. W.E.	VX. 22879	2/22 Bn.		01.07.42	36
Bernaldo, Cpl. J.C.	VX.129399	Ftrss.Engrs.	Windsor, Vic.	01.07.42	20
Bernstein, Pte. Harry	VX. 28109	2/22 Bn.	Lwr. Clapton, UK	01.07.42	41
Berwick, Gnr. K.M.	NX. 30466	4 A/Tk.Regt.	Goulburn, NSW	01.07.42	24
Berwick, L/Cpl. N.W.	VX. 30069	2/22 Bn.	Mooee Ponds, Vic.	01.07.42	21
Bethune, Pte. C.F.	VX. 48411	2/22 Bn.	Armidale, Vic.	01.07.42	25

Beuthin, Pte. E.F.	VX. 31719	2/22 Bn.	South Yarra, Vic.	01.07.42	32
Bexton, Pte. Victor	NX. 56324	1 Indep.Coy.	Willoughby, NSW	01.07.42	24
Biden, Gnr. Peter	NX.191444	A/A.& Mil.Lndg.Crft. Def.(Rabaul)RAA	Willoughby, NSW	01.07.42	23
Bierton, Pte. H.S.	VX. 23965	2/22 Bn.	Footscray, Vic.	01.07.42	34
Bignell, Pte. C.E.	NGX. 200	2/22 Bn.	Manly, NSW	01.07.42	22
Bird, Cpl. R.A.	NGX. 500	New Guin.Vol.Rfls.	Sandgate, Qld.	01.07.42	34
Birkin, Pte. Frederick	VX. 32484	2/22 Bn.	Carwarp, Vic.	01.07.42	25
Bischoff, Rin. C.R.	NGX. 461	New Guin.Vol.Rfls.	Potts Point, NSW	01.07.42	18
Bjorklof, Gnr. H.R.G.	NX. 55339	4 A/Tk. Regt.	Sherwood, Qld.	01.07.42	36
Bleasby, Pte. C.W.	VX. 50213	1 Indep.Coy.	Richmond, Vic.	01.07.42	21
Blennerhassett, Pte. D.A.	VX. 23502	2/22 Bn.	Kew, Vic.	01.07.42	27
Boisen, L/Cpl. L.A.	VX. 38738	2/22 Bn.	Richmond, Vic.	01.07.42	23
Bollman, Cpl. A.F.	QX. 64940	AAOC	Toowong, Qld.	01.07.42	23
Booth, Spr. Cyril	VX.129363	Ftrss.Engrs.	South Yarra, Vic.	01.07.42	24
Bosse, L/Cpl. E.T.	VX. 19621	2/22 Bn.	Hughesdale, Vic.	01.07.42	25
Boswell, Gnr. C.A.	VX.129393	Hvy.Bty., RAA	Yarraville, Vic.	01.07.42	23
Boyd, L/Cpl. C.W.	VX. 29988	1 Indep.Coy.	Somerville, Vic.	01.07.42	23
Boyle, Pte. J.M.	VX. 24202	2/22 Bn.	Carlton, Vic.	01.07.42	28
Boyle, L/Sgt. P.R.	NX. 65450	4 A/Tk.Regt.	Wee Waa, NSW	01.07.42	25
Bradbury, Pte. J.F.	VX. 34278	2/22 Bn.	San Remo, Vic.	01.07.42	25
Brain, Cpl. R.M.	NGX. 502	New Guin.Vol.Rfls.	Thornton, Vic.	01.07.42	39
Broadbent, Pte. Frederick	VX. 24734	2/22 Bn.	Leongatha, Vic.	01.07.42	29
Broadbent, Pte. G.L.	VX. 23970	2/22 Bn.	North Fitzroy, Vic.	01.07.42	23
Brock, Pte. A.B.	VX. 24496	2/22 Bn.	Richmond, Vic.	01.07.42	24
Bromilow, Pte. R.H.	VX. 48425	1 Indep.Coy.	GeelongWest, Vic.	01.07.42	26
Brooker, L/Cpl. C.M.	VX. 41522	2/22 Bn.	Essendon, Vic.	01.07.42	23
Brough, L/Cpl. J.J.	VX. 30830	2/22 Bn.	Werneth, Vic.	01.07.42	35
Brown, L/Cpl. C.A.C.	VX. 25915	2/22 Bn.	South Yarra, Vic.	01.07.42	32
Brown, Pte. E.J.	WX. 10624	1 Indep.Coy.	Cranbrook, W.A.	01.07.42	19
Brown, Spr. John	QX. 64926	Ftrss.Engrs.	Wyreema, Qld.	01.07.42	20
Brown, Pte. K.G.	VX. 44440	2/22 Bn.	Northcote, Vic.	01.07.42	26
Brown, Sgt. K.W.	VX. 46519	2/22 Bn.	Flinders, Vic.	01.07.42	22
Brown, Gnr. L.M.	VX.129377	Hvy.Bty., RAA	Ivanhoe, Vic.	01.07.42	21
Brown, Pte. L.R.	VX. 37163	2/22 Bn.	Seymour, Vic.	01.07.42	23
Brown, Gnr. Max	NX. 37550	4 A/Tk.Regt.	Homebush, NSW	01.07.42	22
Brown, Pte. Victor	VX. 46516	2/22 Bn.	Moorabbin, Vic.	01.07.42	23
Brown, Pte. W.R.	VX. 23855	2/22 Bn.	Brunswick, Vic.	01.07.42	23
Brown-Bishop, Pte. Ronald	QX. 12632	1 Indep.Coy.	Hamilton, NSW	01.07.42	23
Browne, Pte. P.T.L.	NX. 68349	1 Indep.Coy.	Balgowlah, NSW	01.07.42	27
Bryen, Rfn. F.C.	NGX 491	New Guin.Vol.Rfls.	Bondi, NSW	01.07.42	31
Bullinaria, Gnr. T.L.	NX. 19855	4 A/Tk.Regt.	Elizabeth Bay, NSW	01.07.42	23
Burdett, Sgt. C.R.	QX. 64912	AAOC	Bardon, Qld.	01.07.42	22
Burgess, Pte. E.L.	NX. 26478	8 Div. Sup. Coy. AASC	North Sydney, NSW	01.07.42	35
Burgess, Gnr. J.B.	NX. 34493	4 A/Tk.Regt.	Bondi, NSW	01.07.42	29
Burgoyne, Pte. I.D.	VX. 37386	2/22 Bn.	Surrey Hills, Vic.	01.07.42	23
Burns, Cpl. R.C.	VX. 29566	2/22 Bn.	Benalla, Vic.	01.07.42	29
Burrell, Pte. D.C.	VX. 50405	1 Indep.Coy.	Merbein, Vic.	01.07.42	22
Burrowes, Sgt. Robert	VX.129397	Ftrss.Engrs.	Middle Park, Vic.	01.07.42	24
Burton, Pte. J.A.F.	VX. 46522	2/22 Bn.	Garden Vale, Vic.	01.07.42	26
Butler, Pte. E.J.	QX. 64932	AASC	Berat, Qld.	01.07.42	25
Byrne, Pte. P.J.	NX. 26672	1 Indep.Coy.	Fairfield, NSW	01.07.42	23
Cairns, Pte. R.F.	VX. 37500	2/22 Bn.	North Brunswick. Vic.	01.07.42	23
Callaghan, Pte. N.R.	NX. 52913	8 Div. Sup. Coy. AASC	Randwick, NSW	01.07.42	28
Cameron, Pte. J.A.E.	VX. 26803	2/22 Bn.	Fife, Scotland	01.07.42	31
Cameron, Pte. S.A.	VX. 26283	2/22 Bn.	Double Bay, NSW	01.07.42	23
Cameron, Pte. W.J.	VX. 32771	2/22 Bn.	Lilydale, Vic.	01.07.42	30
Carr, L/Sgt. Albert	VX. 29724	1 Indep.Coy.	Coburg, Vic.	01.07.42	39
Carr, Gnr. J.E.	TX. 4362	Hvy.Bty.RAA	East Melbourne, Vic.	01.07.42	20
Carter, Pte. E.G.	VX. 37824	2/22 Bn.	Kaniva, Vic.	01.07.42	23
Carter, Pte. F.J.	VX. 24160	2/22 Bn.	Balmoral, Vic.	01.07.42	28

Carter, Pte. J.T.	NX. 68061	1 Indep.Coy.	Barraba, NSW	01.07.42	26
Carter, Gnr. N.F.W.	NX.191475	A/A. & Mil. Lndg. Crft. Def. (Rabaul) RAA	Concord, NSW	01.07.42	20
Casey, Gnr. K.P.	QX. 64921	Hvy.Bty., RAA	Newmarket, Qld.	01.07.42	21
Chalmers, Cpl. Francis	VX. 48400	2/22 Bn.	East Malvern, Vic.	01.07.42	24
Champ, L/Sgt. P.L. (MID)	VX. 16103	2/22 Bn.	Toorak, Vic.	01.07.42	22
Cheney, Cpl. G.A.	VX. 24076	2/22 Bn.	Ballarat, Vic.	01.07.42	24
Chenhall, Spr. D.W.	VX.129400	Ftrss.Engrs.	Traralgon, Vic.	01.07.42	22
Chisholm, Pte. R.J.	VX. 26380	2/22 Bn.	Brunswick, Vic.	01.07.42	38
Clarke, Pte. C.W.	VX. 43466	2/22 Bn.	Albert Park, Vic.	01.07.42	24
Clarke, L/Sgt. R.J.	VX. 23989	2/22 Bn.	Footscray, Vic.	01.07.42	42
Clay, Gnr. M.A.	VX.129376	Hvy.Bty. RAA	West Preston, Vic.	01.07.42	23
Claydon, Gnr. C.E.	VX.129360	Hvy.Bty. RAA	Yea, Vic.	01.07.42	39
Cobden, Pte. A.C.	VX. 28761	2/22 Bn.	Beaufort, Vic.	01.07.42	32
Cock, Cpl. A.J.	VX. 47528	2/22 Bn.	Tullamarine, Vic.	01.07.42	25
Cocking, Pte. F.R.	VX. 46831	2/22 Bn.	Amphitheatre, Vic.	01.07.42	30
Cocksedge, Pte. A.A.	VX. 27904	2/22 Bn.	Won Wron, Vic.	01.07.42	31
Codd, Sgt. R.A.	SX. 11442	Hvy.Bty. RAA	North Unley, S.A.	01.07.42	27
Cody, L/Cpl. T.L.	VX. 44632	2/22 Bn.	Coleraine, Vic.	01.07.42	24
Cogan, Gnr. T.E.J.	VX. 43247	4 A/Tk. Regt.	North Perth, W.A.	01.07.42	23
Coles, Pte. C.J.	VX. 35750	2/22 Bn.	North Geelong, Vic.	01.07.42	23
Collins, Pte. H.J.	VX. 23628	2/22 Bn.	Yackandandah, Vic.	01.07.42	27
Collins, Gnr. L.H.	VX. 44844	4 A/Tk. Regt.	Ascot Vale, Vic.	01.07.42	25
Connop, Pte. T.R.	VX. 22066	2/22 Bn.	Prahran, Vic.	01.07.42	42
Connor, Gnr. R.E.	VX. 40019	4 A/Tk. Regt.		01.07.42	48
Cook, Gnr. Colin	NX.191446	A/A. & Mil. Lndg. Crft. Def.(Rabaul)	Randwick, NSW	01.07.42	19
Cook, Pte. E.H.	NX. 69680	1 Indep.Coy.	Sth.Yardley,Birm.UK	01.07.42	22
Cooper, Cpl. A.L.E.	VX. 23857	2/22 Bn.	South Melbourne, Vic.	01.07.42	24
Cooper, Gnr. A.C.	NX.191469	A/A. & Mil. Lndg. Crft. Def. (Rabaul) RAA	Bega, NSW	01.07.42	19
Cooper, Pte. E.N.	VX. 28340	2/22 Bn.	Rainbow, Vic.	01.07.42	30
Cooper, Bdr. W.L.	VX. 33388	4 A/Tk. Regt.	Surrey Hills, Vic.	01.07.42	41
Core, Cpl. R.M.	SX. 38279	Ftrss.Engrs.	Firle, S.A.	01.07.42	22
Corley, Pte. Kevin	QX. 64922	HQ New Guin. Area	Stanthorpe, Qld.	01.07.42	27
Cornelious, Pte. S.R.A.	VX. 30103	2/22 Bn.	South Morang, Vic.	01.07.42	21
Cortous, Pte. J.D.	VX. 47637	2/22 Bn.	Geelong, Vic.	01.07.42	23
Coulthard, Pte. C.E.	VX. 40231	2/22 Bn.	Yarram, Vic.	01.07.42	30
Cox, Bdr. H.E.	NX. 33037	4 A/Tk. Regt.	Denistone East, NSW	01.07.42	37
Cracknell, Cpl. W.T.	NX. 32378	1 Indep.Coy.	Chatswood, NSW	01.07.42	29
Craddock, Pte. H.L.	VX. 24078	2/22 Bn.	Colac, Vic.	01.07.42	33
Cramling, Pte. W.H.	VX. 29190	2/22 Bn.		01.07.42	29
Crawford, Bdr. A.J.	TX. 4360	Hvy.Bty. RAA	Hobart, Tas.	01.07.42	21
Crawiord, Gnr. H.M.	TX. 4364	Hvy.Bty. RAA	Hobart, Tas.	01.07.42	21
Crichton, Gnr. Thomas	VX. 25507	4 A/Tk.Regt.	Leitchville, Vic.	01.07.42	20
Crombie, Gnr. P.C.	VX. 25551	4 A/Tk.Regt.	Stanhope, Vic.	01.07.42	22
Crosbie, Pte. J.B.	QX. 64914	Canteen Service		01.07.42	48
Cross, Pte. P.J.	VX. 18439	2/22 Bn.	Bendigo, Vic.	01.07.42	33
Crozier, Sgt. R.V.	VX.129398	Ftrss.Engrs.	Caulfield, Vic.	01.07.42	21
Cumberland, Pte. R.G.	VX. 24802	2/22 Bn.	St.Kilda, Vic.	01.07.42	34
Cummins, Gnr. E.F.	VX.129379	Hvy.Bty. RAA	Glen Iris, Vic.	01.07.42	26
Curphey, Sgt. D.T.	VX. 30278	2/22 Bn.	Hawthorn, Vic.	01.07.42	25
Curry, Pte. William	VX. 24206	2/22 Bn.	Sebastopol, Vic.	01.07.42	38
Curtis, Cpl. N.E.H.	VX. 42144	2/22 Bn.	Wangaratta, Vic.	01.07.42	26
Curtis, Pte. R.G.	NX. 66279	1 Indep.Coy.	Goulburn, NSW	01.07.42	24
Dale, Gnr. R.A.	VX.129374	Hvy.Bty. RAA	Essendan North, Vic.	01.07.42	23
Dallimore, Pte. R.J.	VX. 15423	2/22 Bn.		01.07.42	37
Dalton, Bdr. F.P.	VX.129336	Hvy.Bty. RAA	Warrnambool	01.07.42	26
Dalton, Pte. G.C.	VX. 24211	2/22 Bn.	East Brunswick, Vic.	01.07.42	22
Dalziel, L/Cpl. R.V.	VX. 24094	2/22 Bn.	North Geelong, Vic.	01.07.42	36
Dargin, L/Bdr. B.C.	NX. 59242	4 A/lk.Regt.	Sydney, NSW	01.07.42	27

Davidson, Cpl. G.T.	VX.129411	Ftrss.Sigs.	Bairnsdale, Vic.	01.07.42	25
Davis, Pte. A.L.C.	VX. 35679	1 Indep.Coy.	Waratah, Tas.	01.07.42	21
Day, Pte. J.W.	NX. 53100	1 Indep.Coy.	Perth, W.A.	01.07.42	26
Deacon, Rfn. L.A.	NGX. 505	New Guin. Vol. Rlfs.	Marybrough, Qld	01.07.42	27
Deakin, Cpl. A.H.	QX. 64937	AAOC	New Farm, Qld.	01.07.42	28
Deakin, Pte. C.H.	VX. 26707	2/22 Bn.	Heidelberg, Vic.	01.07.42	21
Dennis, L/Cpl. W.E.R.	WX. 8167	1 Indep.Coy.	Claremont, W.A.	01.07.42	29
Densley, Pte. G.R.	WX. 9936	1 Indep.Coy.	Kalamunda, W.A.	01.07.42	25
Denton, Gnr. A.R.	NX.191456	A/A. & Mil. Lndg. Crft. Def. (Rabaul) RAA	Chatswood, NSW	01.07.42	18
Denyer, Pte. A.T.J.	VX. 38402	2/22 Bn.	Surrey Hills, Vic.	01.07.42	37
Deppeler, Cpl. C.P.	VX. 46521	2/22 Bn.	Beech Forest, Vic.	01.07.42	23
Dickenson, Pte. George	VX. 27624	2/22 Bn.	Richmond, Vic.	01.07.42	41
Dinon, Bdr. P.V.P.	TX. 4377	Hvy.Bty. RAA	Orford, Tas.	01.07.42	22
Dobson, Pte. Frederick	VX. 26660	2/22 Bn.		01.07.42	36
Dockwray, Pte. E.T.E.	VX. 22943	2/22 Bn.	Oakleigh, Vic.	01.07.42	32
Domeney, Cpl. R.E.	TX. 4408	Ftrss.Engrs.	Flower Pot, Tas.	01.07.42	26
Donegan, W.0.2. J.F.	SX. 38277	Ftrss.Engrs.	Essendon, Vic.	01.07.42	24
Dowling, L/Bdr. P.G.	SX. 11419	Hvy.Bty. RAA	Black Forest, S.A.	01.07.42	24
Drane, Pte. Francis	VX. 31242	2/22 Bn.		01.07.42	32
Draper, S/Sgt. W.J.	VX. 46463	2/22 Bn.	Murrumbeena, Vic.	01.07.42	27
Drayton, Pte. E.J.	VX. 44935	2/22 Bn.	Geelong, Vic.	01.07.42	25
Drever, Pte. A.H.	VX. 37801	2/22 Bn.	Carlton, Vic.	01.07.42	26
Drew, Pte. K.R.	VX. 37496	2/22 Bn.	Northcote, Vic.	01.07.42	20
Duggan, L/Cpl. H.T.	VX. 21225	2/22 Bn.	Coburg, Vic.	01.07.42	25
Dunnett, Gnr. M.C.	NX. 55300	4 A/Tk. Regt.	Coolah, NSW	01.07.42	26
Dwyer, Sigmn. R.E.	QX. 17983	8 Div. Sigs. attached 1 Indep. Coy.	Mount Morgan, Qld.	01.07.42	21
Ead, Pte. H.J.	VX. 47259	2/22 Bn.	Amherst, Vic.	01.07.42	41
Earle, Pte. R.M.	VX. 35581	2/22 Bn.	Launching Place Vic.	01.07.42	42
Ebbels, Pte. F.C.	VX. 22852	2/22 Bn.	Olinda, Vic.	01.07.42	28
Ede, Pte. E.T.	QX. 64930	HQ. New Guin. Area	Shorncliffe, Qld.	01.07.42	32
Edelsten, Gnr. Ivor	VX.129339	Hvy.Bty. RAA	St. Arnaud, Vic.	01.07.42	31
Edgecumbe, Pte. H.J.	VX. 33067	2/22 Bn.	Shepparton, Vic.	01.07.42	28
Edwards, Cpl. M.R.	SX. 38278	Ftrss.Engrs.	Mitcham, S.A.	01.07.42	25
Edwards, Pte. W.E.	VX. 23953	2/22 Bn.	Alexandra, Vic.	01.07.42	25
Ekblade, Pte. W.G.	NGX. 198	2/22 Bn.	Sydney, NSW	01.07.42	26
Ellen, L/Cpl. Ernest	VX. 28619	2/22 Bn.	St. Arnaud, Vic.	01.07.42	26
Elliott, Pte. R.K.	VX. 30227	2/22 Bn.	Wangaratta, Vic.	01.07.42	23
Ellis, Pte. W.A.	VX. 26375	2/22 Bn.	Northcote, Vic.	01.07.42	34
Elstead, Pte. J.G.	VX. 44954	2/22 Bn.	North Geelong, Vic.	01.07.42	32
Enston, Pte. Ronald	VX. 23764	2/22 Bn.		01.07.42	25
Ettershank, Pte. Moore	VX. 26452	2/22 Bn.	Coburg, Vic.	01.07.42	29
Evans, Gnr. D.R.	SX. 11421	Hvy.Bty. RAA	Murray Bridge, S.A.	01.07.42	19
Evans, Pte. E.J.	VX. 38401	2/22 Bn.	Heathcote, Vic.	01.07.42	40
Evans, Gnr. J.N.	NX.191472	AA.&Mil.Lndg. Crft. Def. (Rabaul) RAA	Manly, NSW	01.07.42	18
Evans, Pte. L.C.	NX. 53002	1 Indep.Coy.	Elizabeth Bay, NSW	01.07.42	28
Evans, Gnr. O.A.	NX.191464	Hvy.Bty. RAA	Cessnock, NSW	01.07.42	19
Evans, Sgt. W.J.	NGX. 471	New Guin.Vol Rfls.	Port Moresby, N.Guin.	01.07.42	31
Everingham, Pte. W.L.	NX. 58628	1 Indep.Coy.	Narromine, NSW	01.07.42	23
Excell, Gnr. E.T. (i)	NX. 51008	4 A/Tk. Regt.	Maylands, W.A.	01.07.42	34
Fagan, L/Cpl. W.J.	QX. 14023	1 Indep.Coy.	Lutwyche, Qld.	01.07.42	28
Fahey, Gnr. John	QX. 64920	Hvy.Bty. RAA	Windsor, Qld.	01.07.42	21
Fairchild, L/Cpl. R.L.	VX. 29751	2/22 Bn.	South Melbourne, Vic.	01.07.42	28
Fairweather, Pte. J.R.	VX. 23752	2/22 Bn.	Northcote, Vic.	01.07.42	30
Ferguson, Pte. A.F.	VX. 22932	2/22 Bn.	East Melbourne, Vic.	01.07.42	38
Fernandez, Pte.Albert	NX. 19620	2/10Fd.Amb.	Sydney, NSW	01.07.42	43

(i) Served as Munro, Gnr. E.T.

Fidler, Cpl. D.J.	VX.129412	Ftrss.Sigs.	Northcote, Vic.	01.07.42	26
Finch, Gnr. A.T.	NX. 72185	4 A/Tk.Regt.	Auburn, NSW	01.07.42	23
Findlay, Spr. D.D.	SX. 38283	Ftrss.Engrs.	Rosewater Gdns, S.A.	01.07.42	21
Firmstone, Pte. E.D.	VX. 23936	2/22 Bn.	Ashfield, NSW	01.07.42	30
Fisher, Spr. A.K.	VX.129341	Ftrss.Engrs.	Geelong West, Vic.	01.07.42	22
Fisher, Pte. E.A.	VX. 31792	2/22 Bn.	Moolap, Vic.	01.07.42	29
Fitzgerald, Pte. E.A.	VX. 24224	2/22 Bn.		01.07.42	23
Fitzgerald, Gnr. J.B.	TX. 4367	Hvy.Bty. RAA	Hobart, Tas.	01.07.42	20
Flood, Pte. W.E.	QX. 8467	1 Indep.Coy.	Nth Rockhampton, Qld.	01.07.42	25
Florance, Sgt. V.A.	NGX. 508	New Guin.Vol. Rfls.	Gordon, NSW	01.07.42	
Forbes, Pte. R.G.	VX. 24123	2/22 Bn.	Geelong, Vic.	01.07.42	26
Foster, Pte. A.J.	NX. 69365	2/22 Bn.	Wellington City, N2	01.07.42	33
Fox, Pte. A.R.J.	VX. 46697	2/22 Bn.	SouthYarra, Vic.	01.07.42	22
Franks, Pte. A.B.	NX. 47288	1 Indep.Coy.	Gundy, NSW	01.07.42	23
Fraser, Pte. R.A.	NX. 68894	1 Indep.Coy.	Mascot, NSW	01.07.42	21
Freeman, Gnr. Ronald	NX. 53296	4 A/Tk. Regt.	Punchbowl, NSW	01.07.42	27
Freeman, Bdr. W.A.	NX. 54320	4 A/Tk. Regt.	Punchbowl, NSW	01.07.42	30
Fry, Pte. A.R.	VX. 37635	2/22 Bn.	South Yarra, Vic.	01.07.42	24
Fuller, Cpl. H.D.	VX. 41149	2/22 Bn.	Albert Park, Vic.	01.07.42	24
Fuller, Pte. R.A.	VX. 42507	2/22 Bn.	Tocumwal, NSW	01.07.42	29
Gadsen, Pte. C.T.	VX. 44167	2/22 Bn.	Windsor, Vic.	01.07.42	33
Gair, L/Cpl. N.R.	VX. 28693	2/22 Bn.	Oakleigh, Vic.	01.07.42	25
Garden, Pte. Thomas	VX. 26337	2/22 Bn.		01.07.42	42
Garnett, Bdr. K.J.E.	TX. 4385	Hvy.Bty. RAA	Bellerive, Tas.	01.07.42	23
Gault, L/Cpl. W.J.	VX. 22475	2/22 Bn.	East Brunswick, Vic.	01.07.42	32
Geldard, Rfn. G.A.	NGX. 511	New Guin.Vol. Rfls.	New Farm, Qld.	01.07.42	24
Genat, Pte. B.P.	VX. 44110	2/22 Bn.	Nullawarre, Vic.	01.07.42	22
George, Pte. A.J.	NX. 41372	1 Indep.Coy.	Glen Innes, NSW	01.07.42	22
Gerard, Pte. H.C.	QX. 64935	AAOC	Sth Townsville, Qld.	01.07.42	22
Geyer, L/Cpl. K.V.	NX. 47935	1 Indep.Coy.	Tenterfield, NSW	01.07.42	24
Ghiggioli, L/Cpl. E.K.	NX. 36559	1 Indep.Coy.	Mangoplah, NSW	01.07.42	23
Gibson, Pte. Harry	VX. 23917	2/22 Bn.	Coburg, Vic.	01.07.42	33
Gilchrist, Sgt. B.Mcl.	NX.191442	A/A. & Mil. Lndg. Crft. Def. (Rabaul) RAA	Chatswood, NSW	01.07.42	21
Gilding, Gnr. D.R.	NX. 67539	4 A/Tk. Regt.	Strathfield, NSW	01.07.42	23
Giles, Pte. W.C.	VX. 28640	2/22 Bn.	St. Arnaud, Vic.	01.07.42	24
Gilfillan, Gnr. D.F.	NX. 57187	4 A/Tk. Regt.	Lindfield, NSW	01.07.42	38
Gittins, Pte. Frederick	VX. 42242	2/22 Bn.		01.07.42	39
Glasson, Pte. R.C.	NX. 53322	1 Indep.Coy.	Kings Cross, NSW	01.07.42	31
Godfrey, Pte. T.G.	VX. 51750	1 Indep.Coy.	Ballarat, Vic.	01.07.42	19
Goodwin, L/Sgt. Harry	VX. 24079	2/22 Bn.	Queenscliffe, Vic.	01.07.42	30
Goodwyn, Rfn. H.R.	NGX. 472	New Guin.Vol. Rfls.	Jandowae, Qld.	01.07.42	39
Gordon, Gnr. Thomas	NX.191459	A/A.&Mil.Lndg.Crft. Def. (Rabaul) RAA	West Hartlepool Co. Durham, UK.	01.07.42	35
Grady, Pte. H.W.	VX. 30015	2/22 Bn.	Sth Brunswick, Vic.	01.07.42	23
Gratton, Sgt. K.W.	SX. 11445	R.A.A.	Seacliff, S.A.	01.07.42	23
Graycon, Gnr. Ronald	NX.191461	A/A.&Mil.Lndg.Crft. Def. (Rabaul) RAA	Willoughby, NSW	01.07.42	19
Green, Sgt. Ernest	NX.191434	A/A.&Mil.Lndg.Crft. Def. (Rabaul) RAA	St. Ives, NSW	01.07.42	26
Gregory, Gnr. Norman	VX. 25934	4 A/Tk. Regt.		01.07.42	23
Gribble, Pte. E.W.	VX. 48011	2/22 Bn.	Sth Ballarat, Vic.	01.07.42	23
Griffin, L/Cpl. G.M.	VX. 45089	2/22 Bn.	Heywood, Vic.	01.07.42	27
Griffiths, Pte. F.T.	VX. 37889	2/22 Bn.	Womboota, NSW	01.07.42	23
Griffiths, Pte. Kevin	VX. 37778	2/22 Bn.		01.07.42	23
Grimshaw, Gnr. R.V.	NX. 52704	4 A/Tk. Regt.		01.07.42	23
Grinlington, L/Cpl. W.G.	VX. 26939	2/22 Bn.	Glen Iris, Vic.	01.07.42	23
Groat, Pte. J.G.	VX. 23647	2/22 Bn.	Devenish, Vic.	01.07.42	28
Crundy, Gnr. M.C.	TX. 4446	Hvy.Bty., RAA	Hobart, Tas.	01.07.42	21
Guffie, Pte. E.R.	VX. 37432	2/22 Bn.	Albert Park, Vic.	01.07.42	36
Gullidge, Sgt. W.A.	VX. 37499	2/22 Bn.		01.07.42	33

Gulliiord, Pte. H.A.	NX. 51811	1 Indep.Coy.	Chatswood, NSW	01.07.42	25
Gumley, Gnr. Darald	NX.191473	A/A.&Mil.Lndg.Crft. Def. (Rabaul) RAA	Bangalow, NSW	01.07.42	19
Guy, Gnr. R.H.	NX. 55433	4 A/Tk. Regt.		01.07.42	38
Hains, Pte. F.R.	VX. 38306	2/22 Bn.	Beaufort, Vic.	01.07.42	28
Haisman, Pte, L.W.	VX. 40823	2/22 Bn.	Rochester, Vic.	01.07.42	26
Halliday, Cpl. R.K.	SX. 38280	Ftrss.Engrs.	Hyde Park, S.A.	01.07.42	23
Hanchett, Pte. R.A.	VX. 38740	2/22 Bn.	Camperdown, Vic.	01.07.42	30
Hancock, Pte. A.V.	VX. 36946	2/22 Bn.	Lancefield, Vic.	01.07.42	28
Hanigan, Pte. B.K.	VX. 25260	2/22 Bn.	Albert Park, Vic.	01.07.42	23
Hannah, Cpl. Geoffrey	VX.129410	Ftrss.Engrs.	Camberwell, Vic.	01.07.42	27
Hannah, Sgt. R.B.	VX. 37681	2/22 Bn.		01.07.42	24
Hannay, Sgt. J.D.	NX. 26379	1 Indep.Coy.	Lindfield, NSW	01.07.42	24
Hanning, Pte. R.A.T.	VX. 44232	2/22 Bn.	Koriella, Vic.	01.07.42	22
Hannon, Gnr. W.A.	NX.191462	A/A.&Mil.Lndg.Crft. Def. (Rabaul) RAA	Marrickville, NSW	01.07.42	18
Hansford, Pte. E.J.	VX. 36926	2/22 Bn.	West Footscray, Vic.	01.07.42	27
Hanson, Pte. H.R.	VX. 38476	2/22 Bn.	Northcote, Vic.	01.07.42	41
Harcourt, Pte. R.T.	VX. 19987	2/22 Bn.	South Melbourne, Vic.	01.07.42	41
Hardy, Gnr. K.M.	TX. 4402	Hvy.Bty., RAA	Moonah, Tas.	01.07.42	20
Hardy, Pte. R.A.	VX. 24164	2/22 Bn.	Portland, Vic.	01.07.42	22
Harling, Cpl. J.A.N.	VX. 43922	2/22 Bn.	Auburn, Vic.	01.07.42	35
Harman, Cpl. R.A.	VX. 36997	1 Indep.Coy.	Hawthorn East, Vic.	01.07.42	23
Harrington, Gnr. G.C.	NX.191465	A/A.&Mil.Lndg.Crft. Def. (Rabaul) RAA	Hornsby, NSW	01.07.42	22
Harris, L/Cp1. H.J.	VX. 28985	2/22 Bn.	Ringwood, Vic.	01.07.42	33
Harrison, Pte. Robert	QX. 1877	1 Indep.Coy.	Speers Point, NSW	01.07.42	22
Hartigan, L/Bdr. B.R.	NX.191448	A/A.&Mil.Lndg.Crft. Def. (Rabaul) RAA	Townsville, Qld.	01.07.42	19
Hartley, Pte. T.E.	VX. 44999	2/22 Bn.	Airey's Inlet, Vic.	01.07.42	21
Harvey, W.0.2. C.R.	SX. 2676	1 Indep.Coy.	Salisbury, S.A.	01.07.42	33
Harvey, Pte. H.D.	VX. 37492	2/22 Bn.	Brunswick, Vic.	01.07.42	32
Haslam, Cpl. Frederick	NGX. 493	New Guin.Vol. Rfls.	New Farm, Qld.	01.07.42	40
Hatcher, Gnr. l.L.O.	VX.129348	Hvy.Bty., RAA	MiddleBrighton, Vic.	01.07.42	20
Hawkins, Pte. A.W.	NX. 68309	19 Spec Dental Unit	Matraville, NSW	01.07.42	40
Hayes, Pte. J.W.	VX. 23568	2/22 Bn.	Hamilton, Vic.	01.07.42	24
Haywood, Gnr. C.C.G.	SX. 11446	R.A.A.	Sth.Melbourne, Vic.	01.07.42	19
Heeley, Spr. George	VX.129352	Ftrss.Engrs.	St. Kilda, Vic.	01.07.42	36
Heffer, Pte. D.G.	VX. 37308	2/22 Bn.	Murrabit, Vic.	01.07.42	38
Hellman, Pte. R.E.	NX. 55152	1 Indep.Coy.	Ashfield, NSW	01.07.42	22
Henderson, Pte. J.J.W.	VX. 19568	2/22 Bn.	Bairnsdale, Vic.	01.07.42	29
Henderson, Pte. Thomas	VX. 37502	2/22 Bn.	Ferntree Gully, Vic.	01.07.42	25
Hennessy, Sigmn. T.S.	VX.129364	Ftrss.Sigs.	East Prahran, Vic.	01.07.42	19
Henry, Pte. J.K.	NX. 68641	1 Indep.Coy.	Abbotsford Point, NSW	01.07.42	22
Henson, Pte. C.F.	WX. 9744	1 Indep.Coy.	Mt. Lawley, W.A.	01.07.42	29
Hepburn, Pte. G.W.	NX. 30767	8 Div. Sup. Coy. AASC	Narrandera, NSW	01.07.42	25
Heriot, Bdr. F.J.	NX.191485	A/A.&Mil.Lndg.Crft. Def. (Rabaul) RAA	Longueville, NSW	01.07.42	24
Herron, Gnr. A.H.	VX.129349	Hvy.Bty., RAA	Fitzroy, Vic.	01.07.42	20
Hertwig, Pte. A.M.	VX. 48458	2/22 Bn.	North Geelong, Vic.	01.07.42	25
Hibbs, Pte. B.H.	VX. 40700	2/22 Bn.	Yarram, Vic.	01.07.42	39
Hickey, Pte. H.J.	VX. 24156	2/22 Bn.	Digby, Vic.	01.07.42	39
Hicks, Cpl. C.F.	VX. 47899	2/22 Bn.	Ballarat, Vic.	01.07.42	41
Higgins, Bdr. D.K.I.	SX. 11426	Hvy.Btn., RAA	Millswood, S.A.	01.07.42	27
Highland, Pte. Charles	QX. 15058	1 Indep.Coy.	Bundaberg, Qld.	01.07.42	31
Hill, Gnr. A.D.	VX. 32136	4 A/Tk. Regt.	Red Cliffs, Vic.	01.07.42	38
Hill, Pte. A.R.	VX. 21429	2/22 Bn.	Frankston, Vic.	01.07.42	36
Hoare, L/Cpl. M.A.E.	VX. 35707	2/22 Bn.	The Rock, NSW	01.07.42	31
Hoare, Pte. R.A.	VX. 45205	2/22 Bn.	Newport, Vic.	01.07.42	28
Hobbs, Cpl. Harry	SX. 2773	1 Indep. Coy.	Murray Bridge, S.A.	01.07.42	24
Hodder, L/Cpl. M.T.	VX. 38737	2/22 Bn.	Ballarat, Vic.	01.07.42	23

Hodges, Gnr. L.A.	QX. 64933	Hvy.Bty.,RAA	Laidley, Qld.	01.07.42	31
Hogan, Pte. A.J.	NX. 66115	1 Indep.Coy.	Bankstown, NSW	01.07.42	23
Holmes, Pte. R.H.	VX. 23935	2/22 Bn.		01.07.42	37
Hopkins, Rfn. E.R.	NGX. 473	New Guin. Vol. Rfls.		01.07.42	39
Hopkins, Pte. F.E.	NX. 54986	1 Indep. Coy.	Rockdale, NSW	01.07.42	27
Hottes, L/Cpl. E.S.	NX. 41382	1 Indep. Coy.	Glen Innes, NSW	01.07.42	34
Houghton, Cpl. A.H.	VX. 47283	2/22 Bn.	Warrnambool, Vic.	01.07.42	27
Houghton, Rfn. C.W.B.	NGX. 510	New Guin. Vol. Rfls.	Cremorne, NSW	01.07.42	35
Howard, Pte. J.L.	VX. 46854	2/22 Bn.	Leongatha, Vic.	01.07.42	32
Howell, Sgt. A.Mcl.	SX. 11424	Hvy. Bty., RAA	Bannockburn, Vic.	01.07.42	31
Howlett, Pte. W.L.	VX. 24179	2/22 Bn.	Dergholm, Vic.	01.07.42	23
Hoye, Pte. M.T.	VX. 28632	2/22 Bn.	St. Arnaud, Vic.	01.07.42	34
Hudson, Cpl. L.A.	NX. 25197	2/10Fd. Amb.	Kensington, NSW	01.07.42	33
Hughes, Pte. F.R.	VX. 34527	1 Indep. Coy.	Maryborough, Vic.	01.07.42	28
Hulett, Pte. L.A.	VX. 25911	2/22 Bn.	Brighton, Vic.	01.07.42	30
Hyatt, Pte. J.R.	NX. 41342	1 Indep. Coy.	Glen Innes, NSW	01.07.42	24
I'Anson, Pte. Donald	VX. 32466	2/22 Bn.	Edithvale, Vic.	01.07.42	27
Ingold, Pte. S.A.	QX. 64931	AAOC	Hendra, Qld.	01.07.42	21
Ireland, Gnr. K.H.	NX.191486	Hvy.Bty.,RAA	West Maitland, NSW	01.07.42	17
Irvine, Pte. F.A.	QX. 10308	1 Indep. Coy.	Manly, Qld.	01.07.42	22
Izard, Sgt. J.F.	VX. 32509	4 A/Tk. Regt.	Merbein South, Vic.	01.07.42	32
Jackson, Cpl. Colin	QX. 12940	1 Indep.Coy.	Gympie, Qld.	01.07.42	24
Jackson, Pte. F.L.	VX. 29405	2/22 Bn.	Preston, Vic.	01.07.42	43
Jackson, Pte. W.T.	VX. 25049	2/22 Bn.	Manchester, UK	01.07.42	30
James, Gnr. J.R.	VX.129370	Hvy.Bty.,RAA	Collingwood, Vic.	01.07.42	22
Jarrett, Pte. J.L.	NX. 69971	1 Indep. Coy.	Parramatta, NSW	01.07.42	21
Jeffery, Pte. J.W.	VX. 29427	2/22 Bn.	Preston, Vic.	01.07.42	39
Jeffress, Spr. C.H.	VX.129407	Ftrss.Engrs.	Caulfield, Vic.	01.07.42	25
Jeffrey, L/Sgt. H.S. (MID)	VX. 25734	2/22 Bn.	Burwood, Vic.	01.07.42	25
Jeffreys, Gnr. A.C.	TX. 4365	Hvy. Bty., RAA	South Yarra, Vic.	01.07.42	20
Job, S/Sgt. S.R.	VX.129351	Canteen Service	Glenelg, S.A.	01.07.42	52
Jobe, L/Cpl. H.A.	VX. 44847	2/22 Bn.	Melbourne, Vic.	01.07.42	28
Johns, Gnr. William	NX.191435	Hvy. Bty., RAA	Shortland, NSW	01.07.42	20
Johnson, Rfn. A.A.	NGX. 462	New Guin.Vol.Rfls.	Brisbane, Qld.	01.07.42	18
Johnson, L/Cpl. J.H.	VX. 23546	2/22 Bn.	Clifton Hill,Vic.	01.07.42	37
Johnston, Rfn. Lineker	NGX. 513	New Guin. Vol. Rfls.	Brighton, Vic.	01.07.42	28
Joiner, Pte. R.J.	VX. 23640	2/22 Bn.	Yea, Vic.	01.07.42	29
Jones, Cpl. J.T.	VX.129402	Ftrss.Engrs.	Kew, Vic.	01.07.42	39
Jones, Gnr. L.B.	VX.129359	Hvy.Bty.,RAA	East Brunswick Vic.	01.07.42	27
Jones, Pte. R.A.	VX. 22948	2/22 Bn.	Lavender Bay, NSW	01.07.42	26
Jones, Pte. W.A.	VX. 38713	2/22 Bn.	London, England	01.07.42	40
Jordon, Bdr. E.H.	TX. 4381	Hvy.Bty., RAA	New Town, Tas.	01.07.42	21
Judd, Pte. Lester	VX. 37843	2/22 Bn.	Swan Hill, Vic.	01.07.42	23
Kahle, Pte. H.G.	VX. 47669	2/22 Bn.	Sth Geelong, Vic.	01.07.42	22
Kavanagh, Gnr. J.L.	VX.129383	Hvy.Bty., RAA	Leongatha, Vic.	01.07.42	20
Keid, Cpl. N.L.	QX. 64902	AAOC	Toowong, Qld.	01.07.42	31
Kelly, Pte. B.G.	NX. 47922	1 Indep.Coy.	South Grafton, NSW	01.07.42	22
Kelly, Cpl. C.H.	QX. 64925	AAOC	Wilston, Qld.	01.07.42	27
Kelly, W.O. J.F.	882	R.A.A.F.	Morningside, Qld.	01.07.42	37
Kelly, Sgt. R.L. (MID)	VX. 33979	2/22 Bn.	St Kilda, Vic.	01.07.42	42
Kennedy, Pte. J.L.	VX. 30571	2/22 Bn.	Essendon, Vic.	01.07.42	22
Kennedy, L/Cpl. K.J.	VX. 43946	2/22 Bn.	Burwood, Vic.	01.07.42	37
Kennedy, Pte. Norris	VX. 23834	2/22 Bn.	Newtown, Vic.	01.07.42	22
Kerr, Gnr. J.S.	NX. 50859	4 A/Tk. Regt.	Newtown, NSW	01.07.42	44
Ketels, Pte. Frederick	VX. 21621	2/22 Bn.	Leongatha, Vic.	01.07.42	28
Kimber, Pte. Thomas	VX. 23265	2/22 Bn.		01.07.42	38
Kingston, Gnr. R.H.	QX. 64916	HQ. A.A. Bty., RAA	Annerley, Qld.	01.07.42	19
Kirk, Sgt, B,.l,	TX. 4359	Hvy.Bty., RAA	Hobart, Tas.	01.07.42	23
Kirkpatrick, L/Cpl, F.G.	VX. 30813	2/22 Bn.	Ballarat, Vic.	01.07.42	25

Kitchen, L/Cpl, Stanley	VX. 47027	2/22 Bn.		01.07.42	24
Krake, Bdr. E.F.	VX. 32513	4 A/Tk. Regt.	Merbein, Vic.	01.07.42	29
Ladner, Pte. W.F.	VX. 24105	2/22 Bn.	Ballarat, Vic.	01.07.42	41
Laird, Cpl. D.A.	NX. 33602	1 Indep. Coy.	Guildford, NSW	01.07.42	22
Lake, Gnr. G.J.	VX. 33950	4 A/Tk. Regt.	Kerang, Vic.	01.07.42	24
Lambert, L/Cpl. L.A.	NX. 66033	1 Indep. Coy.	Haberfield, NSW	01.07.42	30
Lamble, Sgt. G.R.	VX. 34959	1 Indep. Coy.		01.07.42	29
Lamborn, Pte. W.G.	NX. 13400	1 Indep. Coy.	Coolongolook, NSW	01.07.42	24
Lambton, Pte. Lawrence	VX. 25979	2/22 Bn.	Caulfield, Vic.	01.07.42	21
Lambton, Pte. Richard	VX. 38273	2/22 Bn.	Caulfield, Vic.	01.07.42	23
Langdon, Pte. R.M.	NX. 35227	2/10 Fd.Amb.		01.07.42	22
Langlands, L/Cpl. R.W.	VX. 44864	2/22 Bn.	Parkdale, Vic.	01.07.42	23
Lanham, Pte. G.W.	VX. 26758	2/22 Bn.	Albury, NSW	01.07.42	28
Laurisch, Pte. A.W. (ii)	VX. 36488	2/22 Bn.	Mount Hawthorn, W.A.	01.07.42	26
Ledger, Rin. W.A.	NGX. 474	New Guin. Vol. Rfls.	North Bondi, NSW	01.07.42	24
Leeder, Sgt. H.C.	VX. 37669	2/22 Bn.	Merbein South, Vic.	01.07.42	25
Lees, Bdr. G.A.	VX.129346	R.A.A.	Black Rock, Vic.	01.07.42	23
Lees, Pte. Raymond	VX. 44688	1 Indep.Coy.		01.07.42	19
Leighton, Pte. R.F.	VX. 24557	2/22 Bn.	Boronia, Vic.	01.07.42	27
Lett, Pte. S.A.	VX. 23101	2/22 Bn.	Bairnsdale, Vic.	01.07.42	27
Lewins, Pte. Stephen	VX. 37017	2/22 Bn.	West Preston, Vic.	01.07.42	35
Lewis, Gnr. A.H.J.	TX. 4363	Hvy.Bty., RAA	Hobart, Tas.	01.07.42	26
Limbert, Pte. F.G.	VX. 26548	2/22 Bn.		01.07.42	23
Linnell, Pte. E.G.	VX. 24415	2/22 Bn.	Sandringham, Vic.	01.07.42	27
Little, Pte. D.J.	NX. 30647	1 Indep.Coy.	Tingha, NSW	01.07.42	24
Lloyd, Pte. I.L.B.	VX. 27730	2/22 Bn.	Murrumbeena, Vic.	01.07.42	36
Locantro, Gnr. Robert	VX.129369	Hvy.Bty.,RAA	Moonee Ponds, Vic.	01.07.42	18
Lock, Pte. Edwin	VX. 27639	2/22 Bn.	St.Kilda, Vic.	01.07.42	12
Logan, L/Cpl. A.J.	VX. 25889	2/22 Bn.	Ashburton, Vic.	01.07.42	33
Lord, Sgt. F.H.	NX. 31037	8 Div. Sup. Coy.AASC	Yass, NSW	01.07.42	32
Lovell, Gnr. L.L.	TX. 4448	Hvy.Bty.,RAA	Huon, Tas.	01.07.42	22
Lovett, Spr. N.J.	QX. 64927	Ftrss.Engrs.	Stanthorpe, Qld.	01.07.42	20
Lowe, Pte. W.J.	NX. 65718	1 Indep.Coy.	Manly, NSW	01.07.42	29
Lumby, Cpl. G.C.	VX. 29635	2/22 Bn.	Monea, Vic.	01.07.42	33
Lyons, Gnr. L.J.	NX. 60128	4 A/Tk. Regt.	Junee, NSW	01.07.42	32
Lyons, Pte. M.S.	VX. 33432	1 Indep. Coy.	Richmond, Vic.	01.07.42	25
Lyons, Pte. V.A.	VX. 38403	2/22 Bn.	Echuca, Vic.	01.07.42	27
McAdam, Pte. C.J.	VX. 23147	2/22 Bn.	Moonee Ponds, Vic.	01.07.42	35
MacAdam, L/Cpl. E.G.	NGX. 503	New Guin.Vol.Rfls.	Woolwich, NSW	01.07.42	43
McAliece, Cpl. C.G.	VX. 34459	1 Indep.Coy.	Cheltenham, Vic.	01.07.42	25
McArthur, Pte. Donald	VX. 44284	2/22 Bn.	Terang, Vic.	01.07.42	27
McAuliffe, Gnr. M.J.	QX. 64924	Hvy.Bty.,RAA	Bardon, Qld.	01.07.42	19
McCaffrey, W.0.2. Frederick	SX. 38789	Hvy.Bty.,RAA	Port Adelaide, S.A.	01.07.42	43
McCallum, Gnr. H.D.	VX.129415	Hvy.Bty.,RAA	Hampton Park, Vic.	01.07.42	20
McCarthy, Cpl. I.L.	VX. 46438	2/22 Bn.	Essendon, Vic.	01.07.42	33
McClelland, L/Cpl. H.G.	VX. 22935	2/22 Bn.	Kensington, NSW	01.07.42	33
McColl, Pte. A.S.	VX. 32715	2/22 Bn.	Mansfield, Vic.	01.07.42	22
McCutchan, Pte. T.A.	VX. 24404	2/22 Bn.	Sandringham, Vic.	01.07.42	37
McDiarmid, Pte. Anthony	NX. 31697	1 Indep.Coy.	Altarnum, Cornwall,UK	01.07.42	23
McDougall, Pte. Duncan	VX. 23298	1 Indep.Coy.	Williamstown,Vic.	01.07.42	29
McEachran, Pte. H.H.	VX. 30854	2/22 Bn.	Dimboola, Vic.	01.07.42	37
McEwan, Sgt. W.F.	NGX. 476	New Guin.Vol.Rfls.	Darlinghurst, NSW	01.07.42	49
McGavin, W.0.2. F.W.	QX. 64939	AAOC	Enoggera, Qld.	01.07.42	31
McGinnisken, Pte. A.T.	VX. 24184	2/22 Bn.	Horsham, Vic.	01.07.42	24
McGowan, S/Sgt. James	QX. 64913	AAOC	Yeronga, Qld.	01.07.42	40
MacGowan, Sgt. M.H.	VX. 14699	2/22 Bn.	Tecoma, Vic.	01.07.42	26
McGowan, Pte. T.H.	VX. 22959	2/22 Bn.	Preston, Vic.	01.07.42	37
McGregor, Pte. Sydney	VX. 24433	2/22 Bn.	McKinnon, Vic.	01.07.42	41

(ii) Served as Owen, Pte. A.J.

McInnes, Gnr. F.T.	VX.129356	Hvy.Bty., RAA		01.07.42	22
McIntosh, Pte. G.R.	VX. 14758	2/22 Bn.		01.07.42	34
McIntosh, Gnr. K.R.J.	VX.129413	Hvy.Bty., RAA	West Brunswick, Vic.	01.07.42	20
McKenna, Pte. A.T.	VX. 29179	2/22 Bn.	Orbost, Vic.	01.07.42	39
McKenzie, Gnr. A.B.	NX.191458	A/A.&Mil.Lndg.Crft. Def.(Rabaul) RAA	Mudgee, NSW	01.07.42	27
McKenzie, Pte. Maxwell	VX. 40227	2/22 Bn.		01.07.42	28
McKenzie, Pte. M.C.	VX. 24186	2/22 Bn.	Portland, Vic.	01.07.42	33
McKeown, Pte. G.S.	NX. 53992	1 Indep.Coy.	Narrabeen Nth., NSW	01.07.42	27
McKeown, Pte. J.S.	NX. 69443	1 Indep.Coy.	Narrabeen Nth., NSW	01.07.42	25
McKernan, L/Cpl. Charles	VX. 23914	2/22 Bn.	Black Rock, Vic.	01.07.42	30
McKinlay, Cpl. Augustine	VX. 21184	2/22 Bn.	Toorak, Vic.	01.07.42	42
Mackinnon, Pte. R.C.	VX. 36103	2/22 Bn.	Thornbury, Vic.	01.07.42	26
McLean, L/Cpl. C.A.E.	VX. 27189	2/22 Bn.	Coburg, Vic.	01.07.42	40
Maclean, Sgt. C.I.	NGX. 475	New Guin.Vol.Rfls.	Warrawee, NSW	01.07.42	36
McLean, Cpl. C.J.	VX. 24172	2/22 Bn.	Edenhope, Vic.	01.07.42	23
McLean, L/Cpl. L.D.	VX. 24190	2/22 Bn.	Sth. Geelong, Vic.	01.07.42	25
McLean, Gnr. L.J.	VX.129382	Hvy.Bty.,RAA	Richmond, Vic.	01.07.42	20
McLellan, W.0.2. H.E. (MID)	VX. 23892	2/22 Bn.	West Brunswick, Vic.	01.07.42	42
MacLennan, Pte. R.J.	VX. 21265	2/22 Bn.	South Yarra, Vic.	01.07.42	34
McLennan, Pte. W.A.	VX. 23813	2/22 Bn.	St.Kilda, Vic.	01.07.42	34
McMahon, Pte. J.W.	VX. 28468	2/22 Bn.	Hanwood, NSW	01.07.42	25
McMinn, Pte. R.D.	VX. 24104	2/22 Bn.	Apollo Bay, Vic.	01.07.42	37
McNally, Sgt. P.W.	VX. 46458	2/22 Bn.	Middle Park, Vic.	01.07.42	28
McNamara, Pte. J.J.	VX. 29194	2/22 Bn.	Albury, NSW	01.07.42	27
McNamara, L/Cpl. S.W.	NX. 30512	1 Indep.Coy.	Toobeah, Qld.	01.07.42	23
McPherson, Pte. M.A.A.	VX. 39656	2/22 Bn.	Hobart, Tas.	01.07.42	19
McShane, Gnr. G.J.	TX. 4383	Hvy.Bty.,RAA	Hobart, Tas.	01.07.42	20
Mahaffy, Pte. Gerald	VX. 24242	2/22 Bn.		01.07.42	37
Maher, Pte. Charles	VX. 36821	2/22 Bn.	Tatura, Vic.	01.07.42	40
Mahony, Pte. P.F.	VX. 37761	2/22 Bn.	Hawthorn, Vic.	01.07.42	40
Malcolm, Gnr. A.L.	VX.129358	Hvy.Bty.,RAA	Prahran, Vic.	01.07.42	21
Mann, Sgt. E.C.	VX.129404	Ftrss.Engrs.	Geelong, Vic	01.07.42	23
Mansfield, Pte. K.J.	WX. 9748	1 Indep.Coy.	Palmyra, W.A.	01.07.42	22
Mansley, Pte. F.W.	NX. 60075	8 Div.Sup.Coy.AASC	Randwick, NSW	01.07.42	24
Manyon, Gnr. J.A.	NX. 72162	4 A/Tk.Regt.	Hurstville, NSW	01.07.42	22
Marshall, Pte. E.G.	VX. 47705	2/22 Bn.	Footscray, Vic.	01.07.42	24
Martin, Gnr. L.E.	VX.129381	Hvy.Bty.,RAA	Cheltenham, Vic.	01.07.42	20
Mason, Pte. W.R.	VX. 26748	2/22 Bn	Wangaratta, Vic.	01.07.42	40
Mathieson, Pte. A.V.	VX. 43006	2/22 Bn.	Box Hill, Vic.	01.07.42	31
Matthews, L/Bdr. G.F.	SX. 11449	R.A.A.	Stepney, S.A.	01.07.42	20
Matthews, Pte. W.M.	VX. 23933	2/22 Bn.	Coburg, Vic.	01.07.42	19
May, Pte. Albert	VX. 30504	2/22 Bn.	Carlton, Vic.	01.07.42	35
Meddings, Pte. F.R.	VX. 27254	2/22 Bn.	Geelong, Vic.	01.07.42	22
Meldrum, Pte. A.C.	VX. 29726	2/22 Bn.	Huntly, ABD., Scot.	01.07.42	38
Melling, L/Cpl. William	VX. 38226	2/22 Bn.	Forrest, Vic.	01.07.42	31
Melville, Pte. W.R.	VX. 23748	2/22 Bn.	St.Kilda, Vic.	01.07.42	38
Metcalfe, L/Cpl. J.E.	VX. 20913	1 Indep.Coy.	Bright, Vic.	01.07.42	27
Meyer, Pte. J.E.	VX. 24132	2/22 Bn.	Geelong, Vic.	01.07.42	28
Meyers, Pte. L.E.	VX. 23994	2/22 Bn.	Footscray, Vic.	01.07.42	30
Millard, Gnr. W.J.	NX. 55037	4 A/Tk.Regt.	Fremantle, W.A.	01.07.42	28
Miller, Gnr. A.C.P.	VX.129372	Hvy.Bty.,RAA	Hawthorn, Vic.	01.07.42	21
Miller, Pte. F.K.	VX. 23372	2/22 Bn.	Thornbury, Vic.	01.07.42	36
Miller, Pte. H.W.	NX. 67436	1 Indep.Coy.	Neutral Bay, NSW	01.07.42	38
Millican, Pte. V.E.	VX. 13046	2/22 Bn.	North Fitzroy, Vic.	01.07.42	22
Mills, Gnr. Jack	SX. 11448	Hvy.Bty.,RAA	Whyalla, S.A.	01.07.42	23
Mills, Pte. R.G.	VX. 23962	2/22 Bn.		01.07.42	24
Mitchell, Pte. A.E	VX. 29553	2/22 Bn.	Tallangatta, Vic.	01.07.42	23
Mitchell, Pte. Allan	VX. 37825	2/22 Bn.	Hopetoun, Vic.	01.07.42	25
Mitchell, Cpl. K.R.	NX. 68224	19Spec.Dental Unit	Guildford, NSW	01.07.42	19
Mitchell, Pte. M.E.	VX. 23756	2/22 Bn.	Nth. Melbourne, Vic.	01.07.42	40
Mitchelson, Pte. William	VX. 26115	2/22 Bn.	Malvern, Vic.	01.07.42	37

Mitchem, Pte. P.H.	VX. 46495	2/22 Bn.	Hastings, Vic.	01.07.42	21
Moffat, Pte. A.E.	NX. 58485	1 Indep.Coy.	Annandale, NSW	01.07.42	29
Mooney, Pte. Hamilton	VX. 30009	2/22 Bn.		01.07.42	42
Mooney, Pte. H.C.	VX. 28778	2/22 Bn.	Coburg, Vic.	01.07.42	22
Moore, Rfn. C.H.G.	NGX. 506	New Guin.Vol.Rfls.	Perth, W.A.	01.07.42	32
Moore, Pte. Dudley	VX. 48357	2/22 Bn.	Greta South, Vic.	01.07.42	31
Moore, S/Sgt. E.H.	NX. 68225	19Spec. Dental Unit	Bondi Beach, NSW	01.07.42	35
Moore, Gnr. F.F.	VX.129340	Hvy.Bty.,RAA	Yarraville, Vic.	01.07.42	25
Moorehead, Pte. H.C.	VX. 48850	2/22 Bn.	Bentleigh, Vic.	01.07.42	22
Moran, W.O.2. R.L.H.	VX. 40323	2/22 Bn.	Melbourne, Vic.	01.07.42	41
Morcom, S/Sgt. D.R.	VX.129335	Ftrss.Sigs.	Elwood, Vic.	01.07.42	22
Morell, Pte. J.F.	NGX. 466	1 Indep.Coy.	Randwick, NSW	01.07.42	23
Morgan, Pte. H.S.	VX. 48036	2/22 Bn.	Ballarat, Vic.	01.07.42	33
Morgan, Cpl. H.W. (MID)	VX. 40805	2/22 Bn.	Fairfield, Vic.	01.07.42	27
Morris, Sgt. Oliver (MID)	VX. 30759	2/22 Bn.		01.07.42	42
Morrison, Gnr. C.J.	NX. 54424	4 A/Tk.Regt.	Brookvale, NSW	01.07.42	27
Morton, Pte. G.J.	VX. 36881	2/22 Bn.		01.07.42	24
Morton, Pte. W.E.	NX. 65604	1 Indep.Coy.	Strathfield, NSW	01.07.42	30
Moss, Pte. Lewis	VX. 26651	2/22 Bn.	Preston, Vic.	01.07.42	35
Mottershead, Spr. F.T.	VX.129403	Ftrss.Engrs.	Northcote, Vic.	01.07.42	20
Mountford, W.0.2. F.A.	QX. 64901	Ftrss.Engrs.	Enoggera, Qld.	01.07.42	36
Mundy, Gnr. R.A.	TX. 4356	Hvy.Bty.,RAA	Nubeena, Tas.	01.07.42	20
Munro, L/Cpl. J.C.	NX. 65623	1 Indep.Coy.	Unley Parl, S.A.	01.07.42	34
Murphy, Gnr. J.J.	NX.191478	A/A.&Mil.Lndg.Crft. Def.(Rabaul)RAA	Marrickville, NSW	01.07.42	20
Murphy, Gnr. W.J.J.	NX. 53516	4 A/Tk.Regt.	North Ipswich, Qld.	01.07.42	23
Murray, Bdr. A.K.	VX. 31458	4 A/Tk.Regt.	Alexandra, Vic.	01.07.42	25
Murray, Pte. E.G.	VX. 34563	2/22 Bn.	Walwa, Vic.	01.07.42	39
Murray, Spr. M.J.	SX. 38282	Ftrss.Engrs.	Rosewater Garndens, SA	01.07.42	23
Murray, Pte. N.J.	VX. 35780	1 Indep.Coy.	Kew, Vic.	01.07.42	34
Naylor, Pte. M.R.	VX. 23721	2/22 Bn.	Oakleigh, Vic.	01.07.42	37
Neil, Cpl. J.M.	QX. 64909	HQ. New Guin. Area	Greenslopes, Qld.	01.07.42	20
Nelson, Pte. J.A.	VX. 22863	2/22 Bn.	Thornbury, Vic.	01.07.42	27
Newman, Pte. H.G.	VX. 24138	2/22 Bn.	Apollo Bay, Vic.	01.07.42	32
Newman, Gnr. K.A.	TX. 4399	Hvy.Bty.,RAA	West Hobart, Tas.	01.07.42	27
Newton, L/Cpl. E.J.	VX. 21625	2/22 Bn.	Binginwarri, Vic.	01.07.42	30
Newton, Pte. T.E.	NX. 33388	8 Div. Sup. Coy. AASC	Narrabeen, NSW	01.07.42	29
Nicholls, L/Cpl. J.W.	VX. 50047	2/22 Bn.	Springhurst, Vic.	01.07.42	25
Nicholson, Pte. S.L.	NX. 66807	1 Indep.Coy.	Merrylands, Nsw	01.07.42	21
Nisbet, Pte. Donald	VX. 21363	2/22 Bn.	Boronia, Vic.	01.07.42	24
Nixon, Cpl. S.W.	VX. 21364	2/22 Bn.	St.Kilda, Vic.	01.07.42	36
Nolan, Pte. Charles	WX. 10520	1 Indep.Coy.	VictoriaPark, W.A.	01.07.42	23
Noonan, Cpl. A.P.	SX. 6384	1 Indep.Coy.	Georgetown, S.A.	01.07.42	28
Norgrove, Gnr. Glynn	VX. 25769	4 A/Tk.Regt.	Hawthorn, Vic.	01.07.42	19
Norris, Cpl. L.A. (iii)	VX. 23719	2/22 Bn.	Sunbury, Vic.	01.07.42	37
Norton, Pte. R.E.G.	VX. 48165	1 Indep.Coy.	East Ringwood, Vic.	01.07.42	23
Nugent, L/Cpl. R.S.	VX. 29537	2/22 Bn.	Walwa. Vic	01.07.42	27
O'Brien, Pte. J.M.	VX. 23921	2/22 Bn.	Sth. Brunswick, Vic.	01.07.42	30
O'Brien, Pte. L.J.	VX. 37429	2/22 Bn.	Kew, Vic.	01.07.42	29
O'Connor, Gnr. H.V.	NX.191439	Hvy.Bty.,RAA	Weston, NSW	01.07.42	24
Oliver, Gnr. A.R.	VX.129378	Hvy.Bty.,RAA		01.07.42	20
Olney, Pte. W.J.	VX. 30074	2/22 Bn.	Warburton, Vic.	01.07.42	25
Olsen, Pte. C.J.	QX. 14904	1 Indep.Coy.	Tuchekoi, Qld.	01.07.42	22
O'Neil, Cpl. B.R.D.	VX. 19523	2/22 Bn.	Box Hill, Vic.	01.07.42	20
O'Neill, Pte. A.W. (MID)	VX. 28900	2/22 Bn.	Kew, Vic.	01.07.42	33
O'Shea, Gnr. J.W.	NX.191445	A/A.&Mil.Lndg.Crft. Def.(Rabaul) RAA	Bondi, NSW	01.07.42	21

(iii) Served as Elliott, Cpl. J.W.

Padey, Sgt. Stanley	VX. 21748	2/22 Bn.	Yarraville, Vic.	01.07.42	26
Paine, Pte. R.L.	SX. 10876	1 Indep.Coy.	Bridgewater, S.A.	01.07.42	29
Palmer, Pte. K.W.	VX. 42093	2/22 Bn.	Moonee Ponds, Vic.	01.07.42	22
Pannell, Cpl. H.J.	VX. 37513	2/22 Bn.	Camberwell, Vic.	01.07.42	38
Parker, L/Bdr. Arthur	NX.191449	A/A.&Mil.Lndg.Crft. Def.(Rabaul) RAA	Darlinghurst, NSW	01.07.42	19
Parker, Pte. J.A.	VX. 22890	2/22 Bn.	North Carlton, Vic.	01.07.42	22
Parker, Pte. S.R.	VX. 37491	2/22 Bn.	West Brunswick, Vic.	01.07.42	23
Parkin, Gnr. R.G.	VX.129375	Hvy.Bty., RAA		01.07.42	25
Parsons, Pte. J.H.	VX. 30375	2/22 Bn.		01.07.42	36
Pascoe, L/Cpl. F.W.	VX. 28754	2/22 Bn.	Surrey Hills, Vic.	01.07.42	25
Paton, Bdr. M.G.	TX. 4392	Hvy.Bty.,RAA	Battery Point, Tas.	01.07.42	25
Patterson, Pte. B.G.	NX. 36777	1 Indep.Coy.	Wagga Wagga, NSW	01.07.42	22
Patterson, Pte. D.S.	VX. 24110	2/22 Bn.	Geelong East, Vic.	01.07.42	32
Patterson, Sgt. W.S.	VX. 20713	1 Indep.Coy.	Casterton, Vic.	01.07.42	31
Pattinson, Gnr. Allen	VX. 32561	4 A/Tk. Regt.	Murchison, Vic.	01.07.42	34
Pattle, Pte. L.J.	VX. 29127	2/22 Bn.	Sth. Melbourne, Vic.	01.07.42	23
Peachey, Pte. D.J.	VX. 23893	2/22 Bn.	Coburg, Vic.	01.07.42	24
Pearce, Pte. J.N.	NX. 27364	1 Indep.Coy.	Leichhardt NSW	01.07.42	25
Pearce, Gnr. J.H.	TX. 4393	Hvy.Bty., RAA	Lindisfarne, Tas.	01.07.42	19
Pedder, L/Cpl. Leonard	VX. 23410	2/22 Bn.	Fitzroy, Vic.	01.07.42	36
Peel, Cpl. D.C.	VX. 24072	2/22 Bn.	Drysdale, Vic.	01.07.42	30
Peel, Gnr. E.H.	VX. 44227	4 A/Tk. Regt.	Jindivick, Vic.	01.07.42	33
Pemble, Pte. N.T.F.	NX. 55192	1 Indep.Coy.		01.07.42	22
Peplow, L/Cpl. W.J.	VX. 35842	2/22 Bn.	Pine Lodge Sth., Vic.	01.07.42	23
Perkins, Gnr. L.J.	NX. 51739	4 A/Tk. Regt.	Surry Hills, NSW	01.07.42	31
Perryman, Gnr. J.E.	VX.129347	Hvy.Bty., RAA	Merbein, Vic.	01.07.42	23
Peters, Spr. G.E.	VX.129365	Ftrss.Engrs.	Mitiamo, Vic.	01.07.42	34
Peters, Sgt. H.J.F.	NX.191443	A/A.&Mil.Lndg.Crft. Def.(Rabaul) RAA	Sydney, NSW	01.07.42	22
Peters, Pte. H.E.	VX. 46523	2/22 Bn.	Fitzroy, Vic.	01.07.42	22
Petersen, Pte. H.J.	QX. 7985	1 Indep.Coy.	Harvey Ck., Qld.	01.07.42	23
Phillips, L/Bdr. D.E.	TX. 4366	Hvy.Bty., RAA	Sorell, Tas.	01.07.42	20
Phillpott, Rfn. W.H.	NGX. 477	New Guin.Vol.Rfls.	Elizabeth Bay, NSW	01.07.42	35
Philp, Pte. E.C.	VX. 26656	2/22 Bn.	Glen Iris, Vic.	01.07.42	22
Philpott, Sgt. A.E.	VX. 50161	1 Indep.Coy.	Geelong, Vic.	01.07.42	29
Picken, L/Cpl. L.R.	TX. 4419	Ftrss.Engrs.	Hobart, Tas.	01.07.42	23
Pickford, Pte. W.J.	NX. 57238	1 Indep.Coy.	Newtown, NSW	01.07.42	21
Pitt, Cpl. Arthur	VX. 43971	2/22 Bn.	Mornington, Vic.	01.07.42	35
Plummer, S/Sgt. H.O.	NGX. 478	New Guin.Vol.Rfls.	Castle Hill, NSW	01.07.42	40
Pollock, Cpl. F.M.	VX. 51076	1 Indep.Coy.	East Prahran, Vic.	01.07.42	21
Porter, Gnr. Henry	VX.129343	Hvy.Bty., RAA	Maidstone, Vic.	01.07.42	19
Potter, Pte. Roy	VX. 25166	1 Indep.Coy.	Thornbury, Vic.	01.07.42	24
Powell, Pte. I.C.	VX. 29302	2/22 Bn.	Turriff, Vic.	01.07.42	26
Power, Cpl. F.R.	QX. 64928	AAOC	Newstead, Qld.	01.07.42	22
Price, Pte. D.K.	VX. 23926	2/22 Bn.		01.07.42	24
Price, L/Bdr. J.W.	SX. 11430	Hvy.Bty., RAA	Plympton, S.A.	01.07.42	28
Price, L/Cpl. T.V.	SX. 38284	Ftrss.Sigs.	Hyde Park, S.A.	01.07.42	29
Pring, Bdr. C.H.	NX. 26728	4 A/Tk. Regt.	Darling Point, NSW	01.07.42	22
Purves, Cpl. T.A.	VX. 28166	2/22 Bn.	Glenhuntly, Vic.	01.07.42	33
Quinn, Pte. Laurence	VX. 43012	2/22 Bn.		01.07.42	41
Radford, Pte. Ernest	VX. 46496	2/22 Bn.	Dromana, Vic.	01.07.42	38
Rae, Pte. F.M.	NX. 36268	1 Indep.Coy.	Bendigo, Vic.	01.07.42	29
Ramsay, Bdr. J.L.	TX. 4384	Hvy.Bty., RAA	New Town, Tas.	01.07.42	30
Ramsay, Cpl. K.M.	NX. 25468	1 Indep.Coy.	Bellevue Hill, NSW	01.07.42	27
Rankin, Rin. D.J.	NGX. 509	New Guin.Vol.Rfls.	Cremorne, NSW	01.07.42	42
Ravenhill, Pte. Stanley	VX. 26605	2/22 Bn.	Thornbury, Vic.	01.07.42	35
Rawlings, Spr. W.M.	VX.129366	Ftrss.Engrs.		01.07.42	36
Reed, Cpl. G.B.	VX. 20657	1 Indep.Coy.	Bungowannah, NSW	01.07.42	31
Reeve, Cpl. S.J.G.	NX. 46731	1 Indep.Coy.	Raymond Tce., NSW	01.07.42	22

Regan, Gnr. C.A.	NX.191476	A/A.&Mil.Lndg.Crft. Def.(Rabaul) RAA	Hurstville, NSW	01.07.42	19
Reichelt, Sgt. John	VX. 21640	2/22 Bn.	Caulfield, Vic.	01.07.42	25
Reid, Pte. H.J.	VX. 30852	2/22 Bn.	Ballarat, Vic.	01.07.42	32
Render, Pte. David	VX. 32916	2/22 Bn.	Sth. Yarra, Vic.	01.07.42	27
Render, Spr. J.M.	VX.129387	Ftrss.Engrs.	Frankston, Vic.	01.07.42	34
Rentle, Pte. C.D.	VX. 25779	2/22 Bn.	Hawthorn, Vic.	01.07.42	31
Reynalds, Pte. C.V.	VX. 30789	2/22 Bn.	East Brunswick, Vic.	01.07.42	29
Reynard, Cpl. J.S.	VX.129337	Ftrss.Engrs.	Queenscliff, Vic.	01.07.42	21
Reynolds, Rfn. W.R.	NGX. 480	New Guin.Vol.Rfls.	Cremorne, NSW	01.07.42	21
Richards, Bdr. E.S.	TX. 4380	Hvy.Bty., RAA	Sorell, Tas.	01.07.42	26
Riedell, Pte. L.G.	VX. 47467	1 Indep.Coy.	Tongala, Vic.	01.07.42	21
Robb, Gnr. R.P.	NX.191433	Hvy.Bty., RAA	Rozelle, NSW	01.07.42	25
Roberts, Sgt. R.S.	SX. 2804	1 Indep.Coy.	Nth.Walkerville, S.A.	01.07.42	27
Roberts, Pte. S.L.	NX. 69464	1 Indep.Coy.		01.07.42	24
Robertson, Cpl. J.S.	VX. 37497	2/22 Bn.	Preston, Vic.	01.07.42	25
Robins, Pte. N.C.	VX. 47692	2/22 Bn.	Clifton Hill,Vic.	01.07.42	25
Robinson, Pte. C.G.	VX. 28880	2/22 Bn.	East Malvern	01.07.42	24
Robinson, Bdr. E.R.	VX. 32331	4 A/Tk. Regt.	Dimboola, Vic.	01.07.42	22
Rodgers, L/Cpl. R.G.	VX. 23908	2/22 Bn.	North Carlton, Vic.	01.07.42	38
Rodway, Cpl. J.L.	TX. 4413	Ftrss.Engrs.	Sandy Bay, Tas.	01.07.42	22
Rosewarne, Gnr. C.W.	VX.129395	Hvy.Bty., RAA	Footscray, Vic.	01.07.42	25
Ross, Rfn. H.J.	NGX. 481	New Guin.Vol.Rfls.	Artarmon, NSW	01.07.42	
Ross, L/Cpl. R.E.	VX. 48415	2/22 Bn.	Shepparton, Vic.	01.07.42	25
Rossiter, Pte. A.D.	VX. 26017	2/22 Bn.	Chatham, Vic.	01.07.42	23
Rowe, Gnr. C.T.	VX.129394	Hvy.Bty., RAA	Williamstown, Vic.	01.07.42	23
Rowland, Pte. L.E.	VX. 24175	2/22 Bn.	Portland, Vic.	01.07.42	41
Russell, Pte. K.G.	VX. 30014	2/22 Bn.	Newport, Vic.	01.07.42	27
Russell, Cpl. R.W.	VX. 26518	2/22 Bn.	MooneePonds, Vic.	01.07.42	21
Ryan, Gnr. A.W.	NX. 28194	4 A/Tk. Regt.	North Sydney, NSW	01.07.42	29
Ryan, Sgt. F.W.	NGX. 501	New Guinn.Vol.Rfls.	Malvern, S.A.	01.07.42	42
Ryan, Pte. G.E.	VX. 28580	2/22 Bn.	Moonee Ponds, Vic.	01.07.42	32
Ryan, Gnr. R.J.	NX. 54527	4 A/Tk. Regt.	Glenbrook. NSW	01.07.42	36
Sadler, Cpl. F.H.	NX. 68342	1 Indep.Coy.	Dubbo, NSW	01.07.42	36
Salway, Gnr. P.J.	NX.191468	A/A.&Mil.Lndg.Crft. Def.(Rabaul)RAA	Bega, NSW	01.07.42	19
Sampson, Pte. K.J.	VX. 35106	1 Indep.Coy.	East Malvern, Vic.	01.07.42	22
Samuels, Sgt. A.A.	QX. 64911	AAOC	HollanndPark, Qld.	01.07.42	22
Sangster, S/Sgt. Thomas	VX. 43436	2/22 Bn.	Leongatha, Vic.	01.07.42	42
Sargeant, Pte. A.J.	VX. 24120	2/22 Bn.	Pomberneit, Vic.	01.07.42	29
Sauer, Pte. C.A.	WX 211	1 Indep.Coy.	Kalgoorlie, W.A.	01.07.42	23
Saunders, Rfn. L.C.	NGX. 482	New Guin.Vol.Rlfs.	Roseville, NSW	01.07.42	
Sawyer, Pte. Horace	VX. 25013	2/22 Bn.	Wonthaggi, Vic.	01.07.42	42
Schiffmann, Pte. H.F.	NX. 40995	1 Indep.Coy.	Tenterfield, NSW	01.07.42	38
Schilling, L/Cpl. V.G.	VX. 41250	2/22 Bn.	Warracknabeal. Vic.	01.07.42	24
Scott, Pte. E.C.	VX. 38551	2/22 Bn.	Gymbowen, Vic.	01.07.42	23
Scriven, Sigmn. A.C.	SX. 38286	Ftrss.Sigs.	Kelmscott, S.A.	01.07.42	25
Seach, Pte. L.J.	VX. 38851	2/22 Bn.	Brighton, Vic.	01.07.42	41
Seamark, Gnr. J.C.	NX.191481	A/A.&Mil.Lndg.Crft. Def.(Rabaul) RAA	Macksville, NSW	01.07.42	19
Searcy, Pte. M.R.	SX. 10212	1 Indep.Coy.	CollegePark, S.A.	01.07.42	37
Seater, Pte. L.L.	NX. 28414	1 Indep.Coy.	Bega, NSW	01.07.42	25
Shands, Gnr. R.D.	VX.129355	Hvy.Bty., RAA	Melbourne, Vic.	01.07.42	37
Shaw, Pte. G.G.	VX. 37445	2/22 Bn.	Kew, Vic.	01.07.42	20
Shaw, Pte. T.A.	SX. 8367	1 Indep.Coy.	Plympton, S.A.	01.07.42	24
Shaw, Sgt. W.F.	VX.129350	Hvy.Bty. RAA	Collingwood, Vic.	01.07.42	35
Sherwin, Pte. H.V.	QX. 8417	1 Indep.Coy.	Glen Geddes, Qld.	01.07.42	24
Sherwood, Sgt. J.C.	NX. 26627	4 A/Tk. Regt.	Marrickville, NSW	01.07.42	45
Shimmin, Gnr. W.A.	VX. 25676	4 A/Tk. Regt.	Merbein, Vic.	01.07.42	24
Shoobridge, Rfn. Ivan	NGX. 492	New Guin.Vol.Rfls.	Adelaide, S.A.	01.07.42	
Sibraa, Pte. L.S.	NX. 34251	1 Indep.Coy.	Ashfield, NSW	01.07.42	23

Simmonds, Pte. T.R.	VX. 26037	2/22 Bn.	Docker, Vic.	01.07.42	33
Simmons, Cpl. F.W.	VX.129405	Ftrss.Engrs.	Kensington, Vic.	01.07.42	21
Simpson, L/Cpl. J.O.	VX. 23715	2/22 Bn.	Northumberland, UK	01.07.42	41
Skinner, Gnr. F.D.	NX. 55411	4 A/Tk. Regt.	Balgowlah, NSW	01.07.42	24
Slaven, Pte. B.J.	NX. 54368	1 Indep.Coy.	Gooloogong, NSW	01.07.42	25
Small, S/Sgt. F.C.	SX. 11433	Hvy.Bty., RAA	Parkside, S.A.	01.07.42	24
Smalley, Pte. L.P.	VX. 30116	2/22 Bn.	Pascoe Vale, Vic.	01.07.42	21
Smalley, Cpl. P.T.	VX. 30100	2/22 Bn.	Preston, Vic.	01.07.42	23
Smeaton, L/Cpl. John	VX. 44168	2/22 Bn.	Neerim Junction, Vic.	01.07.42	37
Smith, Cpl. D.F.	VX. 44521	2/22 Bn.	Dunolly, Vic.	01.07.42	30
Smith, Cpl. D.S.	VX. 38091	2/22 Bn.	Dunolly, Vic.	01.07.42	34
Smith, Pte. E.D.	NX. 16030	1 Indep.Coy.		01.07.42	21
Smith, Pte. F.W.	NX. 27430	1 Indep.Coy.	Hurstville, NSW	01.07.42	23
Smith, Pte. H.P.	VX. 48510	1 Indep.Coy.	Camperdown, Vic.	01.07.42	30
Smith, Cpl. J.A.	VX. 29573	2/22 Bn.		01.07.42	38
Smith, Gnr. K.M.	NX. 52916	4 A/Tk. Regt.	Roseville, NSW	01.07.42	25
Smith, Pte. L.S.	VX. 26947	2/22 Bn.	Heidelberg, Vic.	01.07.42	26
Smith, Pte. N.S.	VX. 37494	2/22 Bn.	Tenterfield, NSW	01.07.42	30
Smith, L/Cpl. W.A.G.	VX. 37739	2/22 Bn.	Malvern, Vic.	01.07.42	40
Snell, Bdr. J.T.	NX. 34004	4 A/Tk. Regt.	Chatswood, NSW	01.07.42	42
Somerville, Gnr. Francis	VX. 23783	4 A/Tk. Regt.	Nth. Melbxnne, Vic.	01.07.42	28
Soutar, Pte. George	VX. 47702	2/22 Bn.	Glasgow, Scot.	01.07.42	35
Sparks, Gnr. A.J.	VX.129368	Hvy.Bty., RAA	North Carlton, Vic.	01.07.42	19
Spears, Pte. J.M.	VX. 19322	2/22 Bn.	Shepparton, Vic.	01.07.42	24
Spence, Pte. J.D.	VX. 37019	2/22 Bn.	Sth. Melbourne, Vic.	01.07.42	34
Spencer, Gnr. A.E.	VX. 31527	4 A/Tk. Regt.	Shepparton, Vic.	01.07.42	30
Spensley, Cpl. G.W.	NGX. 490	New Guin.Vol.Rfls.	Glen Iris, Vic.	01.07.42	38
Spriggs, L/Cpl. R.A.	VX. 23954	2/22 Bn.	Flemington, Vic.	01.07.42	24
Spunner, Sgt. R.L.	VX. 23667	2/22 Bn.	Mentone, Vic.	01.07.42	25
Squire, Pte. J.B.	QX. 10246	1 Indep.Coy.	Springsure, Qld.	01.07.42	25
Stanley, Pte. Allan	VX. 36738	2/22 Bn.	LaPerouse, NSW	01.07.42	33
Stanton, L/Cpl. E.C.	NX. 19908	1 Indep.Coy.	Artarmon, NSW	01.07.42	26
Starkey, Sgt. A.G.	NX. 59082	1 Indep.Coy.	Brookvale, NSW	01.07.42	41
Steer, Gnr. T.F.	VX.129367	Hvy.Bty., RAA	Boundary Bend, Vic.	01.07.42	41
Stephens, Spr. D.K.	VX.129371	Ftrss.Engrs.	McKinnon, Vic.	01.07.42	27
Stevens, Gnr. B.J.	TX. 4391	Hvy.Bty., RAA	New Town, Tas.	01.07.42	21
Stewart, Bdr. A.D.	NGX. 499	New Guin.Vol.Rfls.	Warburton, Vic.	01.07.42	23
Stewart, Cpl. G.D.	NGX. 498	NewGuin.Vol.Rfls.	Point Piper, NSW	01.07.42	
Stewart, Pte. J.McN.	VX. 38168	2/22 Bn.	Abington, Scotland	01.07.42	34
Stewart, Pte. L.W.	NX. 25683	1 Indep.Coy.	Bankstown East, NSW	01.07.42	26
Stewart, Sgt. Lionel	VX. 24609	4 A/Tk. Regt.	Hawthorn, Vic.	01.07.42	23
Stillman, Pte. E.C.	VX. 44240	2/22 Bn.	Alexandra, Vic.	01.07.42	35
Stokes, L/Bdr. G.S.	NX. 22874	4 A/Tk. Regt.	Roseville, NSW	01.07.42	23
Street, Gnr. C.L.	VX. 25487	4 A/Tk. Regt.	Eaglehawk, Vic.	01.07.42	29
Stuart, L/Cpl. H.J.	VX. 47695	2/22 Bn.	Sandford, Vic.	01.07.42	37
Stubberfield, Pte. L.F.	VX. 41497	2/22 Bn.	Ascot Vale, Vic.	01.07.42	22
Stubbs, Pte. M.R.	VX. 47681	2/22 Bn.	West Geelong, Vic.	01.07.42	20
Sullivan, Gnr. W.D.G.	TX. 4386	Hvy.Bty., RAA	Sandy Bay, Tas.	01.07.42	21
Supple, Pte. J.G.	VX. 23957	2/22 Bn.		01.07.42	22
Sutherland, Pte. J.P.	VX. 42440	2/22 Bn.		01.07.42	36
Tacey, Sgt. A.P.	QX. 64910	AAOC	Lutwyche, Qld.	01.07.42	36
Tait, Pte. C.A.	VX. 38688	2/22 Bn.	Hawthorn, Vic.	01.07.42	23
Tait, Rfn. R.E.	NGX. 485	New Guin.Vol.Rfls.	Darwin, N.T.	01.07.42	19
Taylor, Bdr. F.S.	SX. 11434	Hvy.Bty., RAA	Lenswood, S.A.	01.07.42	27
Taylor, Gnr. G.E.	SX. 11499	Hvy.Bty., RAA	Nedindie, S.A.	01.07.42	24
Taylor, Spr. H.H.	TX. 4414	Ftrss.Engrs.		01.07.42	23
Taylor, Cpl. W.E.	VX. 39812	1 Indep.Coy.	Geelong, Vic.	01.07.42	24
Thies, Pte. C.H.	VX. 37152	2/22 Bn.	West Footscray, Vic.	01.07.42	24
Thomas, Pte. Albert	VX. 21133	18 Dental Unit	Fitzroy, Vic.	01.07.42	40
Thomas, Cpl. E.J.	VX. 41403	2/22 Bn.	Northcote, Vic.	01.07.42	35
Thomas, Pte. F.M.	VX. 37498	2/22 Bn.	Wst Preston, Vic.	01.07.42	28

Thomas, Pte. George	VX. 45373	2/22 Bn.	Yarram, Vic.	01.07.42	25
Thompson, Pte. J.V.	VX. 44685	2/22 Bn.	Lockhart, NSW	01.07.42	36
Thompson, Pte. J.W.	VX. 24375	2/22 Bn.	Elsterwick, Vic.	01.07.42	38
Thompson, Pte. W.H.	QX. 10964	1 Indep.Coy.	Neutral Bay, NSW	01.07.42	27
Thomson, L/Cpl. D.H.	VX. 24140	2/22 Bn.	Colac, Vic.	01.07.42	27
Thomson, Cpl. J.A.	NX. 60643	1 Indep.Coy.	Wahroonga, NSW	01.07.42	25
Thornell, Gnr. J.F.	VX.129344	Hvy.Bty., RAA	North Fitzroy, Vic.	01.07.42	24
Thornton, Pte. F.E.	VX. 27908	2/22 Bn.	Latrobe, Tas.	01.07.42	29
Thornton, Gnr. G.H.W.	NX. 55060	4 A/Tk. Regt.	Gladesville, NSW	01.07.42	19
Thornton, Pte. Jack	NX. 55649	1 Indep.Coy.	Newtown, NSW	01.07.42	26
Thurst, Pte. J.R.	VX. 47625	2/22 Bn.	Skenes Creek, Vic.	01.07.42	29
Tippetts, Cpl. W.A.	SX. 3594	1 Indep.Coy.	Boronia, Vic.	01.07.42	26
Tole, Pte. J.F.M.	NX. 55921	1 Indep.Coy.	Paddington, NSW	01.07.42	27
Tomlinson, Sigmn. W.J.	VX.129386	Ftrss. Sigs.	Fitzroy, Vic.	01.07.42	22
Toms, Pte. C.H.	VX. 37531	2/22 Bn.	Sale, Vic.	01.07.42	37
Toms, Pte. C.H.	VX. 33107	2/22 Bn.		01.07.42	35
Toogood, L/Cpl. R.F.	VX. 23941	2/22 Bn.	Box Hill, Vic.	01.07.42	41
Traill, Gnr. A.T.	TX. 4427	Hvy.Bty., RAA	NewNorfolk, Tas.	01.07.42	29
Triffett, Gnr. R.C.	TX. 4389	Hvy.Bty., RAA.	Moonah, Tas.	01.07.42	23
Trigg, Gnr. K.A.	NX. 53269	4 A/Tk. Regt.	Tuggerah, NSW	01.07.42	20
Trigg, Cpl. W.E.	VX. 40058	2/22 Bn.	Geelong West, Vic.	01.07.42	28
Tucker, Gnr. E.G.	VX.129396	Hvy.Bty., RAA	Nth.Williamstown, Vic.	01.07.42	20
Tulloch, Pte. Bruce	VX. 45812	2/22 Bn.	Ballarat East, Vic	01.07.42	36
Tummon, Pte. A.S.	QX. 64915	HQ. New Guin. Area	Bundaberg, Qld.	01.07.42	22
Turnbull, Pte. H.P.	QX. 10965	1 Indep.Coy.	Bulimba, Qld.	01.07.42	23
Turner, L/Cpl. C.O.	VX. 30283	2/22 Bn.	Elwood, Vic.	01.07.42	36
Turner, Pte. D.G.	NX. 57051	1 Indep.Coy.	Willoughby, NSW	01.07.42	19
Turner, Pte. D.J.	NX. 57052	1 Indep.Coy.	Willoughby, NSW	01.07.42	22
Turner, L/Cpl. S.S.	NX. 57050	1 Indep.Coy.	Willoughby, NSW	01.07.42	26
Turner, L/Cpl. W.S.J.	NX. 66006	1 Indep.Coy.	French's Foret, NSW	01.07.42	28
Tweddle, Pte. C.J.	VX. 46297	2/22 Bn.	Numurkah, Vic.	01.07.42	26
Twigg, Pte. L.V.	VX. 21240	2/22 Bn.	South Yarra, Vic.	01.07.42	36
Uhlman, Pte. S.G.	VX. 44347	1 Indep.Coy.	Brunswick, Vic.	01.07.42	31
Vale, Spr. A.F.	VX.129409	Ftrss. Engrs.	Balwyn, Vic.	01.07.42	26
Valle, Gnr. Bartholomew	NX.191463	A/A.&Mil.Lndg.Crft. Def.(Rabaul) RAA	Wrightville, NSW	01.07.42	20
Venning, Rfn. F.O.	NGX. 486	New Guin.Vol.Rfls.	Clayfield, Qld.	01.07.42	
Vinen, Pte. E.H.	VX. 46790	2/22 Bn.	Moorabbin, Vic.	01.07.42	22
Vinnell, Pte. A.R.	VX. 47742	2/22 Bn.	Warrnambool, Vic.	01.07.42	22
Wainewright, L/Cpl. W.L.	VX. 24139	2/22 Bn.	Winchelsea, Vic.	01.07.42	30
Wainwright, Sgt. V.E.R.	NX. 54267	4 A/Tk. Regt.	Woollahra, NSW	01.07.42	27
Walker, Cpl. G.E.	NGX. 487	New Guin.Vol.Rfls.	Kew, Vic.	01.07.42	
Walker, L/Bdr. G.W.J.	TX. 4374	Hvy.Bty., RAA	Hobart, Tas.	01.07.42	25
Walker, Pte. J.A.	NX. 56794	8 Div.Sup.Coy.AASC	Randwick, NSW	01.07.42	30
Walker, Pte. R.J.	VX. 47917	2/22 Bn.		01.07.42	34
Walker, L/Cpl. R.H.	VX. 44608	2/22 Bn.	East Prahran, Vic.	01.07.42	25
Walker, Cpl. W.H.	SX. 7253	1 Indep.Coy.		01.07.42	37
Wall, Pte. L.F.	VX. 25486	2/22 Bn.		01.07.42	23
Wallace, Pte. Duncan	VX. 26100	2/22 Bn.	Glen Iris, Vic.	01.07.42	26
Wallis, Pte. R.J.	VX. 45856	2/22 Bn.	Serviceton, Vic.	01.07.42	29
Wallis, Pte. R.E.	QX. 64944	AAOC	KelvinGrove, Qld.	01.07.42	28
Walsh, Pte. Ralph	VX. 32549	2/22 Bn.	Ouyen, Vic.	01.07.42	33
Ward, L/Bdr. A.A.	NX.191447	A/A.&Mil.Lndg.Crft. Def.(Rabaul)RAA	Elizabeth Bay, NSW	01.07.42	20
Ward, L/Bdr. R.E.	VX. 30697	4 A/Tk. Regt.	Emerald, Vic.	01.07.42	22
Warhurst, S/Sgt. William	TX. 4358	Hvy.Bty., RAA	Queenscliff, Vic.	01.07.42	42
Warner, Pte. M.A.	VX. 23455	2/22 Bn.	Semaphore, S.A.	01.07.42	33
Waterman, Rfn. F.A.	NGX. 489	NewGuin.Vol.Rfls.	Chelsea, Vic.	01.07.42	42
Watkins, Pte. G.L.	VX. 36634	2/22 Bn.	Kilburn, S.A.	01.07.42	25

Watkins, Pte. R.J.	VX. 37495	2/22 Bn.	Brunswick, Vic.	01.07.42	24
Watson, Sgt. A.R.	VX. 46166	2/22 Bn.	Melbourne, Vic.	01.07.42	23
Watson, Pte. H.S.	NX. 57063	8 Div.Sup.Coy.AASC	Erskineville, NSW	01.07.42	35
Watson, Pte. T.J.	WX. 7307	1 Indep.Coy.	Mount Lawley, W.A.	01.07.42	27
Wear, Pte. R.W.N.	VX. 30369	2/22 Bn.	Windsor, Vic.	01.07.42	25
Wear, Pte. T.A.	VX. 29099	2/22 Bn.	Box Hill, Vic.	01.07.42	22
Wells, L/Cpl. H.M.	VX. 44740	2/22 Bn.	Belmore, NSW	01.07.42	40
Wells, Pte. W.H.H.	NX. 27623	2/10 Fd.Amb.AAMC		01.07.42	32
Westaway, Pte. C.A.	NX. 28482	8 Div.Sup.Coy.AASC	Tamworth, NSW	01.07.42	31
Westcott, Gnr. W.P.	VX.129357	Hvy.Bty., RAA	Maryborough, Vic.	01.07.42	22
Wharton, Pte. J.W.C.	VX. 23645	2/22 Bn.	Dandenong, Vic.	01.07.42	30
Wheldon, Gnr. Rodolph	NX. 27388	4 A/Tk. Regt.	Croydon, NSW	01.07.42	38
White, L/Bdr. J.W.	SX. 11454	Hvy.Bty., RAA	Torrensville, S.A.	01.07.42	22
White, Pte. J.G.S.	VX. 32827	2/22 Bn.	Oakleigh, Vic.	01.07.42	23
White, Pte. N.E.	VX. 23976	2/22 Bn.	Preston, Vic.	01.07.42	22
White, Pte. William	VX. 22881	2/22 Bn.	Sandringham, Vic.	01.07.42	27
White, Pte. W.R.N.	NX. 59856	8 Div.Sup.Coy.AASC	Bondi, NSW	01.07.42	22
Whitehead, Pte. J.F.	VX. 25084	2/22 Bn.	Hawthorn, Vic.	01.07.42	24
Willding, Pte. L.R.	NX. 32294	1 Indep.Coy.	Forbes, NSW	01.07.42	25
Williams, Gnr. A.E.	NX.191454	A/A.&Mil.Lndg.Crft. Def.(Rabaul) RAA	Woy Woy, NSW	01.07.42	20
Williams, Spr. F.G.	TX. 4411	Ftrss.Engrs.	Lenah Valley, Tas.	01.07.42	22
Williams, Pte. I.C.	VX. 47644	2/22 Bn.	Newtown, Vic.	01.07.42	20
Williams, Cpl. L.L.	VX. 50632	2/22 Bn.	Mornington, Vic.	01.07.42	23
Willis, Pte. V.C.	VX. 37528	2/22 Bn.	Flinders Island Vic.	01.07.42	22
Wilson, Pte. E.R.	VX. 16950	2/22 Bn.	East Brighton, Vic.	01.07.42	39
Wilson, Pte. J.A.	VX. 25043	2/22 Bn.		01.07.42	21
Wilson, Pte. K.A.	VX. 47659	2/22 Bn.	Teesdale, Vic.	01.07.42	23
Wilson, Pte. Phillip	VX. 45975	2/22 Bn.	Oakleigh, Vic.	01.07.42	30
Wilson, Pte. S.R.	VX. 44390	2/22 Bn.	Sandalwood, S.A.	01.07.42	30
Wilton, Cpl. R.MacD.	VX. 41606	2/22 Bn.	Hawthorn, Vic.	01.07.42	35
Wiltshire, Gnr. J.W.	VX.129362	Hvy.Bty., RAA	Sandringham, Vic.	01.07.42	20
Wise, Bdr. G.C.	TX. 4379	Hvy.Bty., RAA	Blackman's Bay, Tas.	01.07.42	24
Wittingslow, Pte. C.T.	VX. 37917	2/22 Bn.	Castlemaine, Vic.	01.07.42	19
Wood, Pte. A.L.	VX. 35018	2/22 Bn.	Sandringham, Vic.	01.07.42	27
Woodford, Pte. Jack	VX. 27701	2/22 Bn.		01.07.42	34
Woodhams, L/Sgt. O.H.	VX. 30687	2/22 Bn.	Chelsea, Vic.	01.07.42	41
Woodhouse, Gnr. A.J.	NX.191451	A/A.&Mil.Lndg.Crft. Def.(Rabaul) raa	Peakhurst, NSW	01.07.42	18
Woodward, L/Cpl. C.J.	NX. 41199	1 Indep.Coy.	Deepwater, NSW	01.07.42	37
Woolley, Pte. F.S.	NX. 66421	1 Indep.Coy.	Earlwood, NSW	01.07.42	29
Wright, Pte. William	VX. 47223	2/22 Bn.	Burwood, Vic.	01.07.42	29
Wyatt, L/Sgt. H.E.	NX.191489	Engrs. Stores Branch, RAE	Kogarah, NSW	01.07.42	23
Wythe, Pte. Basil	VX. 24187	2/22 Bn.	Ballarat, Vic.	01.07.42	23
Wythe, Pte. Rex	VX. 18861	2/22 Bn.	Hamilton, Vic.	01.07.42	23
Yerbury, Pte. R.H.	NX. 66145	1 Indep.Coy.	Swansea, Wales	01.07.42	23
Young, Pte. C.R.	VX. 24362	2/22 Bn.	St. Kilda, Vic.	01.07.42	23
Zanker, L/Cpl. Maxwell	VX. 24914	2/22 Bn.	East Melbourne, Vic.	01.07.42	22

CIVILIANS LOST ON MONTEVIDEO MARU - JULY 1942

Name	*Residence*	*Birthplace*	*D.of Death*	*Age*
Abbott, E.M.	Rabaul, TNG	Waverley, NSW	01.07.42	33
Adams, Harry	Patlangat Pltn.	Bristol, U.K.	01.07.42	49
Allen, A.G.	Mioka, New Brit. TNG	Somerset, U.K.	01.07.42	49
Allen, W.E.	Rabaul, TNG	Lonchen, Nth.England	01.07.42	38
Alley, D.C.	Bouganville, TNG	Clinton, N.2.	01.07.42	35
Anderson, Hugo	M.S. HERSTEIN	Trondheim, Norway	01.07.42	28
Ash, N.E.	Rabaul, TNG	Kent, England	01.07.42	40
Ashby, S.A.	Maramakas Pltn. New Ireland, TNG	Tunbridge Wells, UK	01.07.42	47
Atherton, J.M.	Rabaul, TNC	Rockhampton, Qld.	01.07.42	49
Atkinson, William	Rabaul, TNG	New Lambton, NSW	01.07.42	38
Banks, A.E.D.	Rabaul, TNG	Dublin, Ireland	01.07.42	66
Barnes, C.W.	Rabaul, TNC	Bristol, England	01.07.42	67
Bath, V.G.	Rabaul, TNC	Brisbane, Qld.	01.07.42	53
Beazley, S.C.	Rabaul, TNG	Northam, W.A.	01.07.42	33
Beck, N.R.	Rabaul, TNG	Sth. Melbourne, Vic.	01.07.42	52
Bell, D.J.	Tabar Island, TNG	Herberton, Qld.	01.07.42	30
Berman, R.A.A.	Talasea, TNG	Scone, NSW	01.07.42	24
Bickmann, Niels	MS HERSTEIN	Sweden	01.07.42	25
Bolt, Benn	MS HERSTEIN	Sandefjord, Norway	01.07.42	27
Bowman, Herbert	Rabaul	Adelaide, S.A.	01.07.42	21
Box, W.C.	New Hanover, TNG	London, England	01.07.42	48
Brandal, Peter	MS HERSTEIN	Oslo, Norway	01.07.42	47
Brennan, C.A.	Douglas Park, NSW	Balmain, NSW	0I.07.42	26
Brett, G.L.	Misima, Papua	Kent, England	01.07.42	49
Brinston, H.G.W.	Rabaul, TNG	Mt. Morgan, Qld.	01.07.42	44
Brown, R.A.L.	Rabaul, TNG	Sydney, NSW	01.07.42	64
Brown, T.G.	Rabaul, TNG		01.07.42	
Bruckshaw, A.F.	Rabaul, TNG	London, England	01.07.42	45
Bunney, J.F.	Rabaul, TNG	South Africa	01.07.42	70
Burke, J.D.	Rabaul, TNG	Wooloongabba, Qld.	01.07.42	47
Bye, E.C.	Rabaul, TNG	Finchampstead, Eng.	01.07.42	60
Campbell, C.J.	Shorncliffe, Old.	Toowoomba, Qld.	01.07.42	41
Cannon. C.F.	Rabaul, TNG	Penrith, NSW	01.07.42	42
Carlysle, Lincoln	Kokopo, TNG	Manchester, Eng.	01.07.42	35
Carr, L.A.A.	Kokopo, TNG	Melbourne, Vic.	01.07.42	48
Carson, L.W.	Fead Island, TNG	Yanerathan, Vic.	01.07.42	48
Clark, lvan	Rabaul, TNG	Bunbury, W.A.	01.07.42	43
Clark, J.A.J.(Aka. John Downs)	Rabaul, TNG	Geelong, Vic.	01.07.42	48
Clark, R.L.	Rabaul, TNG	Sydney, NSW	01.07.42	52
Clunn, Colin	Rabaul, TNG	Cooktown, Qld.	01.07.42	62
Cobb, Forbes	Panaras Pltn.,TNG	Ellerston, NSW	01.07.42	53
Coe, P.E.R.	Rabaul, TNG	Naracoorte, S.A.	01.07.42	36
Collett, T.D.	Emira Island, TNG	Wee Waa, NSW	01.07.42	29
Considine, L.A.	Rabaul, TNG	Mount Gambier, S.A.	01.07.42	36
Cook, R.E.	Rabaul, TNG	Annandale, NSW	01.07.42	40
Coomber, Arthur	Rabaul, TNG	Erskineville, NSW	01.07.42	43
Cooper, R.W.	Rabaul, TNG	Toorak, Vic.	01.07.42	40
Coote, Philip	Rabaul, TNC	London, Eng.	01.07.42	54
Crocker, M.C.	Keravat, TNG	Ipswich, Qld.	01.07.42	45
Cruise, J.B.	Rabaul, TNC	Brisbane, Qld.	01.07.42	44
Davies, Roger	Rabaul, TNG	Herne Bay, U.K.	01.07.42	41
Daymond, J.E.	Gasmata, TNG	Launceston, Tas.	01.07.42	
Dockrill, William	Rabaul, TNG	Bedfordshire, U.K.	01.07.42	60
Dodd, Henry	Rabaul, TNG	Ipswich, Qld.	01.07.42	54
Doyle, H.G.	Selapiu Pltn., TNG	Auckland, N2	01.07.42	35

Doyle, N.X.	Rabaul, TNG	Brisbane, Qld.	01.07.42	21
Drane, C.T.	Rabaul, TNG	Brisbane, Qld.	01.07.42	56
Duus, W.L.	Brisbane, Qld.	Brisbane, Qld.	01.07.42	25
Earl, R.B.	Kokopo, TNG	Melbourne, Vic.	01.07.42	47
Edvardsen, Gunnar	MS HERSTEIN	Fredrikstad, Norway	01.07.42	25
Edwards, J.H.	Rabaul, TNG	Terang, Vic.	01.07.42	52
Edwards, M.S.	Kavieng, TNG	Broken Hill, NSW	01.07.42	29
Eglinton, A.M.	Rabaul, TNG	Broken Hill, NSW	01.07.42	36
Einsiedel, E.R.	Rabaul, TNG	Elwood, Vic.	01.07.42	41
Evans, T.E.	Rabaul, TNG	Nelson, N.2.	01.07.42	38
Field, C.T.R.	Rabaul, TNG	Perth, W.A.	01.07.42	47
Filan, S.H.	Rabaul, TNG	Murrurundi, NSW	01.07.42	30
Fogervick, Kare	MS HERSTEIN		01.07.42	
Forsyth, R.N.H.	Rabaul, TNG	Sydney, NSW	01.07.42	44
Fulton, H.B.	Rabaul, TNG	Waverley, NSW	01.07.42	33
Garrett, T.V.	Kokopo, TNG	London, U.K.	01.07.42	54
Gascoigne, C.J.	Rabaul, TNG	Banbury, U.K.	01.07.42	49
Gascoigne, I.N.	Rabaul, TNG	Rabaul, TNG	01.07.42	15
Goad, J.C.	Kavieng, TNG	Lancaster, U.K.	01.07.42	49
Gray, K.M.	Kokopo, TNG	Oaklands, S.A.	01.07.42	21
Green, A.S.	New Britain, TNG	Colac, Vic.	01.07.42	58
Green, E.C.D.	Kerevat, TNG	West Maitland, NSW	01.07.42	37
Greenwood, F.O.	Rabaul, TNG	Yorkshire, U.K.	01.07.42	57
Greenwood, Wilfred	New Britain, TNG	Yorkshire, U.K.	01.07.42	
Gregory, H.A.	Rabaul, TNG	Perth, W.A.	01.07.42	44
Grytnes, Reidar	MS HERSTEIN	Horten, Norway	01.07.42	17
Gustavussen, Gotha	MS HERSTEIN	Sweden	01.07.42	
Hamilton, J.E.	Rabaul, TNG	Hawthorn, Vic.	01.07.42	55
Hamilton, Latham	Djaul Island, TNG	Marlborough, N.2.	01.07.42	55
Hansen, Jack	MS HERSTEIN	Denmark	01.07.42	
Hansen, Kaare	MS HERSTEIN	Vennesla, Norway	01.07.42	26
Hansen, Olaf	MS HERSTEIN	Skudesneshavn, Norway	01.07.42	30
Hawnt, E.M.	Wunawutung, TNG	Warrington, U.K.	01.07.42	60
Hay, Arthur	Kavieng, TNG	Hobart, Tas.	01.07.42	35
Hennessy, J.G.	Buka, TNG	Boston, USA	01.07.42	36
Herket, T.H.	Rabaul, TNG	Nth. Wairoa, N.2.	01.07.42	44
Heron, W.L.	New Britain, TNG	Brighton, Vic.	01.07.42	48
Herron, A.G.	Rabaul, TNG	Sydney, NSW	01.07.42	28
Hogan, G.G.	Rabaul, TNG	Melbourne, Vic.	01.07.42	56
Holden, Harry	Rabaul TNG	Cheshire, U.K.	01.07.42	46
Holland, H.D.	Rabaul, TNG	Clifton Hill, Vic.	01.07.42	49
Hoogerwerff, Jan	Rabaul, TNG		01.07.42	
Hosking, H.C.	Rabaul, TNG	Murtoa, Vic.	01.07.42	47
Jemtland, Alf	MS HERSTEIN	Brevick, Norway	01.07.42	35
Jervis, C.C.	Nissan Island, TNG	London, U.K.	01.07.42	48
Kelly, E.C.	Kavieng, TNG	Ballinasloe, Eire	01.07.42	46
King, A.J.	Rabaul, TNG	Melbourne, Vic.	01.07.42	22
Knudsen, Gunnar	MS HERSTEIN	Oslo, Norway	01.07.42	28
Koinberg, Axel	MS HERSTEIN	Estonia	01.07.42	
Kristiansen, Kristian	MS HERSTEIN	Arendal, Norway	01.07.42	26
Landhaug, Arthur	MS HERSTEIN	Asfjorden, Norway	01.07.42	34
Lie, Ivar	MS HERSTEIN	Larvik, Norway	01.07.42	21
Linggood, W.L.I.	Raluana, TNG	Essex, U.K.	01.07.42	40
Livingstone, W.J.	Kavieng, TNG	Wellington, N.2.	01.07.42	37
Lockhart, Joh	Rabaul, TNG	Nelson, U.K.	01.07.42	44

McArthur, L.A.	Rabaul, TNG	Hawker, S.A.	01.07.42	38
McCheane, G.A.	Rabaul, TNG	Hobart, Tas.	01.07.42	32
McCullagh, D.B.	Sydney, NSW	Boulder, W.A.	01.07.42	31
MacDougall, Donald	Rabaul, TNG	North Uist, Scotland	01.07.42	41
McEvoy, J.T.	Manus, TNG	Auckland, N.2.	01.07.42	46
MacKellar, Colin	New Ireland,TNG	Narellan, NSW	01.07.42	45
McLaren, T.W.	Rabaul, TNG	Newtown, NSW	01.07.42	38
MacLean, C.H.R.	Rabaul, TNG	Sydney, NSW	01.07.42	61
Mcpherson, R.S.	Kavieng, TNC	Brisbane, Qld.	01.07.42	32
Mantle, F.W.	Rabaul, TNG	Magdeburg, Germany	01.07.42	56
Mater, C.S.P.	Rabaul, TNG	Marrickville, NSW	01.07.42	29
Millington, H.N.	Rabaul, TNG	lslington, U.K.	01.07.42	61
Moller, Bjarne	MS HERSTEIN	Arendal, Norway	01.07.42	31
Moore, R.K.P.	New Britain, TNG	Charleville, Qld.	01.07.42	56
Mostad, Knut	MS HERSTEIN	Notteroy, Norway	01.07.42	33
Muggleton, H.A.	Kokopo, TNG	England	01.07.42	37
Mulligan, E.W.C.	Kalgoorlie, W.A.	Coolgardie, W.A.	01.07.42	28
Mulvey, N.W.	Rabaul, TNG	lnvercargill, N.2.	01.07.42	37
Murray, G.H.	Rabaul, TNG	Geelong, Vic.	01.07.42	60
Myhre, Reidar	MS HERSTEIN	Oslo, Norway	01.07.42	38
Naulty, P.G.	Rabaul, TNG	Penola, S.A.	01.07.42	43
Nielsen, Gustav	MS HERSTEIN	Sweden	01.07.42	
Nikolaisen, J.A.	MS HERSTEIN	Slagen, Norway	01.07.42	37
Nunan, F.C.	Mandres, TNG	Moruya, NSW	01.07.42	30
Oakes, W.D.	Pinikidu, TNG	Liverpool, U.K.	01.07.42	36
Oaten, Frederick	Manus, TNG	Seymour, Vic.	01.07.42	30
O'Dwyer, Noel	New Britain, TNG	Brisbane, Qld.	01.07.42	49
Olsen, Gerhard	MS HERSTEIN	Floro, Norway	01.07.42	62
Ormond, J.L.	Djaul Island, TNG	Deveonport, U.K.	01.07.42	64
Page, H.H.	Rabaul, TNG	Grafton, NSW	01.07.42	53
Parry, A.R.	Kokopo, TNG	Burwood, NSW	01.07.42	47
Pearce, E.W.	Rabaul, TNG	Ashfield, NSW	01.07.42	41
Pearson, H.J.	Vunairima, TNG	Kadina. S.A.	01.07.42	29
Perrett, Andrew	Rabaul, TNG		01.07.42	
Pettersen, Egil	MS HERSTEIN	Norway	01.07.42	42
Pickering, M.B.	Rabaul, TNG	Wilmington, S.A.	01.07.42	50
Pinching, Edward	New Britain, TNG	Somerset, U.K.	01.07.42	
Pines, C.M.	Kavieng, TNG	Brisbane, Qld.	01.07.42	46
Plunkett, T.M.	Brisbane, Qld.	Brisbane, Qld.	01.07.42	23
Poole, J.W.	Kalas, TNG	Hurstville, MSW	01.07.42	28
Raff, G.S.	Rabaul, TNG	Gympie, Qld.	01.07.42	24
Rand, D.W.L.	New Ireland, TNG	Førbes. NSW	01.07.42	42
Reed, A.R.	Rabaul, TNG		01.07.42	
Renton, Albany	Rabaul, TNG	London, U.K.	01.07.42	49
Reynolds, J.A.	Rabaul, TNC	Ipswich, Qld.	01.07.42	52
Ringshaug, Arthur	MS HERSTEIN	Tonsverg, Norway	01.07.42	25
Roberts, D.L.	Kavieng, TNG	Durainga, Qld.	01.07.42	29
Robinson, H.E.	Rabaul, TNG	Pyop, S.A.	01.07.42	42
Robinson, Wright	Rabaul, TNG	Northumberland, U.K.	01.07.42	23
Ryan, W.J.	Rabaul, TNG	Tullow, Ireland	01.07.42	51
Saunders, F.V.	Kavieng, TNG	Stanmore, NSW	01.07.42	50
Savage, S.K.	Kavieng, TNG	Newcastle, NSW	01.07.42	50
Sawkins, A.G.	New Ireland, TNG	Essex, U.K.	01.07.42	51
Schmidt, Adolf	Rabaul, TNC	Dayboro, Qld.	01.07.42	37
Scott, H.M.	New Britain, TNG	Suva, Fiji	01.07.42	
Seigers, J.C.	Rabaul, TNG	Arncliffe, NSW	01.07.42	44
Setchell, W.G.	New Britain, TNG	Kent, U.K.	01.07.42	38

Shebler, D.A.	Rabaul, TNG	Carisbrook, Vic.	01.07.42	36
Shelton, H.B.	Duke of York Is.,TNG	Tamworth, NSW	01.07.42	44
Simpson, T.N.	New Hanover, TNG	London, U.K.	01.07.42	
Skaug, Magnus	MS HERSTEIN	Vardal, NOrway	01.07.42	
Smith, D.McD.	Rabaul, TNG	Whangarei, N.2.	01.07.42	39
Smith, J.O.	Rabaul, TNG	Skegness, U.K.	01.07.42	63
Smith, J.W.	Rabaul, TNG	Beechworth, Vic.	01.07.42	43
Snook, Samuel	Rabaul, TNG	London, U.K.	01.07.42	50
Solomon, E.E.	Brighton Bch., Vic.	Victoria, Aust.	01.07.42	26
Solomons, R.L.	Rabaul, TNG	Sydney, NSW	01.07.42	52
Squires, R.T.	Gasmata, TNG	Essex, U.K.	01.07.42	49
Staley, W.G.S.	Rabaul, TNG	Romsey, Vic.	01.07.42	54
Stephen, R.J.	Rabaul, TNG	Petersham, NSW	01.07.42	46
Stevens, R.H.	Rabaul, TNG	Glasgow, Scotland	01.07.42	35
Stewart, James	Rabaul, TNG	Foriarshire, Scotland	01.07.42	60
Strathearn, A.J.	Rabaul, TNG	Adelaide, S.A.	01.07.42	36
Symes, H.H.C.	New Britain, TNG	Portsmouth, U.K.	01.07.42	48
Teien, Hars	MS HERSTEIN	Sardefjord, Norway	01.07.42	26
Thomas, Cecil	Rabaul, TNC	Pilliga, NSW	01.07.42	26
Thompson, L.C.	Kokopo, TNC	Melbourne, Vic.	01.07.42	32
Thorrsen, Finn	MS HERSTEIN	Oslo, Norway	01.07.42	32
Thorsell, K.M.F.	MS HERSTEIN	Gothenburg, Sweden	01.07.42	36
Titchener, J.W.	New Britain, TNC	Witchurch, Bucks.UK	01.07.42	53
Townsend, H.O.	Rabaul, TNG	Brunswick, Vic.	01.07.42	49
Trevitt, J.W.	New Britain, TNG	Murwillumbah, NSW	01.07.42	28
Tritton, A.J.	Rabaul, TNG	Picton, NSW	01.07.42	34
Turnbull, H.F.	Laidley, Qld.	Laidley, Qld.	01.07.42	24
Tynan, James	MS HERSTEIN	Auckland, N.2.	01.07.42	16
Voss, G.H.D.	Rabaul, TNG	Bexhill, U.K.	01.07.42	37
Walker, Thomas	Rabaul, TNG	Vancouver, Canada	01.07.42	55
Wallace, T.V.	Rabaul, TNG	Rutherglen, Vic.	01.07.42	42
Walsh, T.R.	Rabaul, TNG	Paddington, NSW	01.07.42	41
Washington, H.J.	New Britain, TNG	Melbourne, Vic.	01.07.42	55
Wayne, R.N.	Rabaul, TNG	Sydney, NSW	01.07.42	38
Whiteman, A.K.	Rabaul, TNG	East Maitland, NSW	01.07.42	49
Wilkin, W.M.	New Hanover, TNG	Cambridgeshire, U.K.	01.07.42	56
Willmet, W.P.	Kokopo, TNG	Devon, U.K.	01.07.42	46
Youlden, R.M.	Rabaul, TNG	Bendigo, Vic.	01.07.42	48

HONOUR ROLL - TAMAHOKO MARU

Aikman, Pte. M.G.		TX. 5434	2/40 Bn.	Kamona, Tas.	24.06.44	22
Alder, Bdr. S.C.		NX.36956	2/1 Hvy.Bty.,RAA	Campsie, NSW	24.06.44	31
Allen, Pte. Leslie		TX. 3633	2/40 Bn.	Wynyard, Tas.	24.06.44	25
Armstrong, Spr. Robert		SX.14871	2/1Ftress.Coy.RAE	Somerton, S.A.	24.06.44	22
Arnold, Sgt. W.H.W.		TX. 3042	2/3 MC Bn.	Ulverstone, Tas.	24.06.44	40
Ashman, Pte. Geoffrey		TX. 3184	2/3 MG Bn.	Cleveland, Tas.	24.06.44	26
Bailey, Pte. J.H.		TX. 4795	2/40 Bn.	Tiberias, Tas.	24.06.44	24
Bailey, Pte. J.W.		NX.37973	2/12Fld. Amb.	Surry Hills, NSW	24.06.44	24
Bailey, Sgt. W.A.		NX.65888	2/12Fld. Amb.	Grafton, NSW	24.06.44	38
Bailey, Gnr. W.C.		SX.13242	2/1Hvy.Bty., RAA	Wayville, S.A.	24.06.44	29
Bambach, Pte. P.J.		NX.47134	105Gen.Tpt. Coy.	Port Macquarie, NSW	24.06.44	30
Barber, Gnr. S.P.		NX.38491	2/1Hvy.Bty., RAA	Torrensville, S.A.	24.06.44	22
Barr, L/Cpl. M.D.		TX. 5047	2/40 Bn.	Wynyard, Tas.	24.06.44	28
Beard, Pte. G.H.		NX.21319	H.Q.Guard Bn.	Petersham, NSW	24.06.44	42
Bell, Pte. A.M.		NX.39778	2/19 Bn.	Emu Plains, NSW	24.06.44	23
Blake, Pte. L.M.		TX. 4760	2/40 Bn.	North Hobart, Tas.	24.06.44	28
Blizzard, Pte. G.M.		TX. 3725	2/40 Bn.	Smithton, Tas.	24.06.44	25
Bolton, Pte. L.C.		TX. 1502	2/40 Bn.	Triabunna, Tas.	24.06.44	29
Bowden, Gnr. A.P.		VX.57811	2/1Hvy.Bty,,RAA	Albury, NSW	24.06.44	25
Brewer, Pte., C.J.		TX. 5506	2/40 Bn.		24.06.44	29
Bricknell, Pte. W.J.		TX. 8415	2/40 Bn.	Ulverstone, Tas.	24.06.44	19
Briggs, Spr. Mervyn		NX.38680	2/1Ftrress.Coy, RAE	Strathfield, NSW	24.06.44	26
Broome, Pte. A.L.		VX.23081	2/2 Pnr.Bn.	Noorinbee, Vic.	24.06.44	24
Browning, Pte. T.J.M.		TX. 2757	2/40 Bn.	Hobart, Tas.	24.06.44	28
Bucknell, Pte. E.F.W.		SX.11937	2/3 MG Bn.	Camberwell, Vic.	24.06.44	34
Burandt, Pte. E.A.		VX.17846	105GGen. Tpt Coy.	Williamstown, Vic.	24.06.44	22
Byrth, Pte. W.K.		SX.10326	2/3 MG Bn.	Mannum, S.A.	24.06.44	38
Callow, Pte. L.H.		VX.54322	2/40 Bn.		24.06.44	26
Castle, Pte. R.H.		TX. 2628	2/40 Bn.	Bellerive, Tas.	24.06.44	33
Clarke, Cpl. J.E.		TX. 3737	2/3 MG Bn.	Warringa, Tas.	24.06.44	25
Conley, Pte. R.A.		TX. 2603	2/40 Bn.		24.06.44	24
Cooper, Pte. J.A.H.		TX. 3873	2/40 Bn.	Lower Wilmot, Tas.	24.06.44	28
Cooper, Pte. W.P.		TX. 3759	2/40 Bn.	Lower Wilmott, Tas.	24.06.44	24
Corvan, Cpl. G.C.		TX. 4649	2/40 Bn.	New Town, Tas.	24.06.44	22
Cowle, Pte. R.P.		TX. 4791	2/40 Bn.	Runnymede, Tas.	24.06.44	32
Crawford, Pte. S.A.		TX. 3751	2/3 MG Bn.	South Riana, Tas.	24.06.44	26
Cunningham, Cpl. C.B.		TX. 2845	2/40 Bn.	Gretna, Tas.	24.06.44	29
Cunnington, Pte. P.O.		VX.33903	2/3 MG Bn.	Bamawm, Vic.	24.06.44	29
Daft, Pte. L.C.		TX. 5026	2/40 Bn.		24.06.44	38
Darling, Pte. E.W.		TX. 2733	2/40 Bn.		24.06.44	38
Davis, Pte. A.N.		TX. 2958	2/40 Bn.	Melton Mowbray, Tas.	24.06.44	33
Dawson, Pte. L.H.		TX. 4677	2/40 Bn.	Hobart, Tas.	24.06.44	28
Dayman, Spr. W.R.J.		NX.18537	2/6Fld. Coy.,RAE	Chullora, NSW	24.06.44	34
Dean, Pte. L.C.		TX. 2902	2/40 Bn.	Sandford, Tas.	24.06.44	24
Dennis, Pte. J.W.		TX. 8386	2/40 Bn.	Nabowla, Tas.	24.06.44	21
Doherty, Pte. Harry		VX.34041	2/29 Bn.	East Kew, Vic.	24.06.44	25
Donavan, Pte. Jeremiah	(i)	SX. 6351	2/3 MG Bn.		24.06.44	43
Doran, Pte. E.J.		WX.10551	2/3 MG Bn.	Mount Lawley, W.A.	24.06.44	33
Dow, Spr. C.McL.		NX.29994	2/6Fld. Coy.,RAE	Lithgow, NSW	24.06.44	29
Dowd, Pte. Milton		VX.63689	2/40 Bn.	Coburg, Vic.	24.06.44	23
Draper, Pte. E.T.		QX. 5752	1 Coy.AASC	Beaudesert, Qld.	24.06.44	26
Eagling, Pte. C.H.		TX. 3637	2/40 Bn.	Myalla, Tas.	24.06.44	29
Ellis, Sgt. J.W.E.		SX. 8486	2/3 MG Bn.	St.Peters, S.A.	24.06.44	32

(i) Served as West, Pte. J.

Ellis, Gnr. Charles	NX.55825	4 A/Tk.Regt.	Arncliffe, NSW	24.06.44	41
Esler, Pte. L.E.	VX.33734	2/3 MG Bn.		24.06.44	25
Farrell, Pte. J.A.	VX.34988	2/40 Bn.	Ormond, Vic.	24.06.44	24
Featherstone, Pte. A.L.	TX. 4794	2/40 Bn.	Sorell, Tas.	24.06.44	28
Ferris, Pte. B.T.	QX,10692	1 Coy.AASC	Nambour, Qld.	24.06.44	31
Fletcher, Pte. H.R.G.	TX. 2688	2/40 Bn.	Dunalley, Tas.	24.06.44	33
Flitton, Sigmn. D.L.	VX.60285	8 Div.Sigs.	Apollo Bay, Vic.	24.06.44	20
Fraser, Pte. F.V.	VX.34928	2/2 Pnr.Bn.	Ormond, Vic.	24.06.44	46
Freeman, Pte. H.G.	TX. 2220	2/40 Bn.	Lindisfarne, Tas.	24.06.44	24
Fridlington, Pte. J.C.	SX. 6066	2/3 MG Bn.	Minlaton, S.A.	24.06.44	25
Gardiner, Pte. L.G.	TX. 5102	2/40 Bn.	Ulverstone, Tas.	24.06.44	25
Garrett, Pte. W.J.	TX. 5854	2/40 Bn.	Launceston, Tas.	24.06.44	35
Garvin, Cpl. J.S.	VX.35769	2/2 Pnr.Bn.	Moonee Ponds, Vic.	24.06.44	43
Geason, Pte. A.J.	TX. 3688	2/40 Bn.	Deloraine, Tas.	24.06.44	31
Gilbert, Spr. H.M.	NX.38845	2/1 Ftress Coy.,RAE	Chullora, NSW	24.06.44	27
Gleadall, Pte. J.A.	NX.12070	2/3 MG Bn.	Fremantle, W.A.	24.06.44	23
Goesch, Bdr. J.R.	NX.39401	2/1Hvy. Bty.,RAA	Glebe, NSW	24.06.44	40
Graham, Cpl. Archie (MM)	VX.20201	2/2 Pnr. Bn.	Albert Park, Vic.	24.06.44	34
Gregory, Pte. William	VX.32280	2/40 Bn.	Dandenong, Vic.	24.06.44	39
Griffiths, Pte. W.C.	TX. 5015	2/40 Bn.Bridport, Tas.		24.06.44	33
Gunton, Pte. K.G.	TX. 3049	2/3 MG Bn.	Sandy Bay, Tas.	24.06.44	31
Haggblom, Pte. L.W.	VX.24568	2/40 Bn.	Sea Lake, Vic.	24.06.44	28
Hamilton, Lt. Richard	WX. 3336	2/3 MG Bn.	Moora, W.A.	24.06.44	28
Harrison, Pte. F.J.	TX. 2660	2/40 Bn.	Parattah, Tas.	24.06.44	25
Hedger, Pte. W.R.	SX. 5121	2/3 MG Bn.	Mount Compass, Tas.	24.06.44	25
Henderson, Pte. E.C.	TX. 5317	2/40 Bn.	Dilston, Tas.	24.06.44	23
Hibbert					
Hill, Pte. M.J.	TX. 5420	2/40 Bn.	Launceston, Tas.	24.06.44	24
Hockings, Pte. O.A.	QX/20774	3Res.MTCoy,	New Farm, Qld.	24.06.44	36
Hoffman, Pte. Samuel	SX.11964	2/3MG Bn.		24.06.44	24
Howe, Pte. F.W.	TX. 3449	2/40 Bn.	Fern Tree, Tas.	24.06.44	29
Huntington, Cpl. C.D.	TX. 4039	2/40 Bn.	Launceston, Tas.	24.06.44	34
Jacob					
Jamie, Gnr. David	QX.19756	2/1 HvyBty.,RAA	Gympie, Qld.	24.06.44	29
Jones, Pte. S.J.	NX.69578	3Res.MT Coy.	Bankstown, NSW	24.06.44	26
Jones, Spr. A.B.	SX.15008	2/1 Ftress.Coy.,RAE	Woodville North, S.A.	24.06.44	27
Keating, Pte. B.E.	TX. 4809	2/40 Bn.	Campania, Tas.	24.06.44	26
Keating, Pte. M.S.	TX. 4101	2/40 Bn.	Campania, Tas.	24.06.44	24
Kerin, Pte. A.W.	SX. 7822	2/3 MG Bn.	Brighton, S.A.	24.06.44	24
King, Pte. D.A.	TX. 5451	2/40 Bn.		24.06.44	34
Kingston, Pte. D.H.	TX. 2612	2/40 Bn.	Moonah, Tas.	24.06.44	25
Klye, Pte. Reginald	TX. 8123	2/40 Bn.	Battery Point, Tas.	24.06.44	25
Knowles, Pte. R.W.	TX. 4821	2/40 Bn.	New Town, Tas.	24.06.44	24
Knox, Pte. A.S.	NX.60544	2/12Fld.Amb.	Tahmoor, NSW	24.06.44	26
Lake, Cpl. P.P.	NX.38710	2/1 Ftress. Coy.,RAE	Mosman, NSW	24.06.44	22
Leckie, Pte. J.M.	WX. 9813	2/3 MG Bn.	Claremont, W.A.	24.06.44	36
Ling, Pte. L.T.	TX. 5386	2/40 Bn.	Penguin, Tas.	24.06.44	24
Ling, Pte. V.A.	TX. 5121	2/40 Bn.	Railton, Tas.	24.06.44	23
Lockett, Pte. J.S.	TX. 4879	2/40 Bn.	Wynyard, Tas.	24.06.44	21
Longbottom, Pte. R.J.	NX.59104	3 Res.MT Coy.	Rockdale, NSW	24.06.44	29
Longbottom, Pte. Theodore	NX.69615	3 Res.MT Coy.	Rockdale, NSW	24.06.44	26
Lunn, Pte. H.P.	SX. 6133	2/3 Mg Bn.	Unley Park, S.A.	24.06.44	29
Mackintosh, Sgt. I.V.	VX.39873	2/1Hvy.Bty., RAA	Brighton, Vic.	24.06.44	28
Magnussen, Gnr. H.J.	NX.36856	2/1Hvy.Bty., RAA	Wentworthville, NSW	24.06.44	22
Margison, Pte. W.H.	TX. 3683	2/40 Bn.	Cornwall, Tas.	24.06.44	29

Marks, Gnr. G.A.J.	NX.41226	4 A/Tk.Regt.	Bondi, NSW	24.06.44	30
Marks, Pte. R.E.	VX.56053	2/2 Pnr.Bn.	Tabilk, Vic.	24.06.44	24
Matthews, Pte. M.J.	TX. 5084	2/40 Bn.	Wynyard, Tas.	24.06.44	29
Maynard, Pte. V.T.	TX. 5433	2/40 Bn.	Flinders Island, Tas.	24.06.44	25
McCurdy, Gnr. D.V.	WX.14456	2/3Hvy.Bty.,RAA	Fremantle, W.A.	24.06.44	22
McGregor, Pte. J.D.	VX.48268	2/3 MG Bn.	Koyuga, Vic.	24.06.44	27
McKerlie, Pte. A.J.	SX. 6344	2/3 MG Bn.	Murray Bridge, S.A.	24.06.44	25
McNamara, Capt. M.J.	NX.71018	5 Gen. Hosp.	Mosman, NSW	24.06.44	39
Medlin, Sgt. A.J.	SX.15009	2/1 Ftress. Coy.,RAE	Kurralta Park, S.A.	24.06.44	23
Milne, Pte. Adrian	TX. 5073	2/40 Bn.	West Hobart, Tas.	24.06.44	26
Morris, Maj. J.D. (MID)	VX.16925	2/2 CCS	Oakleigh, Vic.	24.06.44	30
Murray-Williams, L/Cpl. Denis	TX. 3897	2/40 Bn.	Hobart, Tas.	24.06.44	25
Nangle, Gnr. J.J.	NX.36857	2/1 Hvy. Bty., RAA	Rose Bay, NSW	24.06.44	19
Nas, Pte. Bertram	TX. 2969	2/40 Bn.	West Hobart, Tas.	24.06.44	25
Nix, Cpl. A.J.	QX. 1739	2/11 Fld. Coy.,RAE	Annerley, Qld.	24.06.44	32
Norman, Pte. W.G.	WX. 6228	H.Q. Guard Bn.		24.06.44	40
O'Hehir, Pte. J.J.	NX.41885	Sparrow Fce.,AASC	Goulburn, NSW	24.06.44	33
O'Keefe, Sgt. L.C.	QX.19761	2/1Hvy.Bty.,RAA	New Farm, Qld.	24.06.44	24
O'Reilly, L/Cpl. P.J.	NX.38686	2/1Ftress.Sigs.	Canberra, ACT	24.06.44	23
Oliver, Pte. H.J.	TX. 3238	2/3 MG Bn.		24.06.44	32
Payne, Pte. Charles	TX. 5948	2/40 Bn.	South Forest, Tas.	24.06.44	22
Paxton, Pte. Robert	VX.48508	2/40 Bn.	Williamstown, Vic.	24.06.44	24
Phillips, Pte. George	VX.60565	2/40 Bn.	Brighton, Vic.	24.06.44	21
Phillips, L/Cpl. R.A.	VX.64545	Sparrow Fce.,AASC	Calulu, Vic.	24.06.44	24
Phillips, Pte. W.A.	VX.26564	2/3 MG Bn.	Kensington, Vic.	24.06.44	29
Pickett, Pte. C.W.	TX. 2728	2/40 Bn.	Tunbridge, Tas.	24.06.44	24
Pulham, Pte. Noah	NX. 6602	Sparrow Fce.,AASC	Coonabarrabran, NSW	24.06.44	25
Pyke, Pte. Neil	TX. 2957	2/40 Bn.	Cranbrook, Tas.	24.06.44	27
Rice, Pte. K.T.	TX. 5085	2/40 Bn.	Mowbray Hts, Tas.	24.06.44	24
Richards, Pte. C.W.	TX. 5910	2/40 Bn.	Launceston, Tas.	24.06.44	28
Robotham, Pte. L.D.	TX. 3430	2/40 Bn.	Ridgley, Tas.	24.06.44	27
Rolley, Gnr. F.H.	QX.19760	2/1Hvy.Bty.,RAA	Nundah, Qld.	24.06.44	23
Ross, Cpl. D.E.	VX.29169	2/40 Bn.	Orbost, Vic.	24.06.44	28
Rowe, Pte. J.A.	VX.54669	2/40 Bn.	West Footscray, Vic.	24.06.44	2$
Sayer, Pte. W.J.	TX. 3199	2/3 MG Bn.	Launceston, Tas.	24.06.44	39
Searle, Pte. R.W.	TX. 5345	2/40 Bn.	Launceston, Tas.	24.06.44	23
Shannon, Cpl. T.A. (MM)	VX.42260	2/2 Pnr. Bn.	24.06.44	44	
Simpson, Pte. Ebenezer	TX. 2678	2/40 Bn.	Oakleigh, Vic.	24.06.44	36
Simpson, Pte. Andrew	SX. 7391	2/3 MG Bn.	Adelaide, S.A.	24.06.44	27
Smith, Pte. E.A.	TX. 4803	2/40 Bn.	Woodbridge, Tas.	24.06.44	23
Smith, Pte. T.G.	TX. 5075	2/40 Bn.	Sandy Bay, Tas.	24.06.44	25
Smith, Pte. W.G.	NX.45070	3Res.MICoy.	Quirindi, NSW	24.06.44	24
Smith, Pte. T.G.	VX.60256	2/2 Pnr. Bn.	Richmond, Vic.	24.06.44	27
Stacey, Pte. H.J.	TX. 3197	2/40 Bn.		24.06.44	36
Stagg, Gnr. E.R.	SX.13241	2/1 Hvy.Bty.,RAA	Kadina, S.A.	24.06.44	24
Stephens, Pte. A.A.	TX. 3577	2/40 Bn.	Sheffield, Tas.	24.06.44	27
Strachan, Pte. J.A.	VX.37344	2/40 Bn.	Nth Geelong Vic.	24.06.44	41
Sullivan, Pte. W.B.	VX.18035	2/2 Pnr.Bn.	Epsom, N.2.	24.06.44	36
Tarr, Pte. Arnold	VX.34809	2/40 Bn.	Chilwell, Vic.	24.06.44	24
Thomas, Pte. N.L.	VX.27973	2/40 Bn.	Sth Melbourne, Vic.	24.06.44	24
Thompson, Pte. F.W.	TX. 5912	2/40 Bn.	Launceston, Tas.	24.06.44	21
Tully, Pte. F.W.	VX.22871	2/2 Pnr. Bn.	Sth Richmond, Vic.	24.06.44	33
Wall, Gnr. B.A.	NX.36889	2/1Hvy. Bty.,RAA	Manly, NSW	24.06.44	25
Walsingham, Bdr. S.A.	VX.57812	2/1 Hvy. Bty.,RAA	Highett, Vic.	24.06.44	23
Wardlaw, Pte. G.G.	TX. 3684	2/40 Bn.	Swansea, Tas.	24.06.44	23

Warren, Pte. E.A.	TX. 4883	2/40 Bn.	South Arm, Tas.	24.06.44	22
Whitmore, Pte. Wesley	TX. 3632	2/40 Bn.	Creek, Tas.	24.06.44	25
Willard, Spr. A.W.	NX.42423	2/6Fd. Coy., RAE	Enfield, NSW	24.06.44	31
Williams, Pte. R.H.	TX. 4714	2/40 Bn.	Dunalley, Tas.	24.06.44	25
Williams, Pte. W.R.	IX. 3124	2/40 Bn.		24.06.44	29
Williams, Pte. L.F.	SX. 7850	2/3 MG Bn.	Woodville, S.A.	24.06.44	37
Wilson, Pte. G.F.	VX.36326	2/40 Bn.	Ballendella, Vic.	24.06.44	25

Royal Australian Navy

Ferguson, Stkr.	HMAS PERTH	24.06.44
Mellish, C.P.O.	HMAS PERTH	24.06.44

Royal Australian Air Force

Binnie, LAC. N.A.	33659	R.A.A.F.	Bathurst, NSW	24.06.44	29
Brown, LAC. R.E.	17047	R.A.A.F.	Boulder, W.A.	24.06.44	22
Buchhorn, AC.1. M.H.	8594	R.A.A.F.	Gilberton, S.A.	24.06.44	25
Gibbins, Cpl. B.A.	3353	R.A.A.F.	CroydonPark, S.A.	24.06.44	26
Green, W.O. J.J.	400951	R.A.A.F.	Brunswick, Vic.	24.06.44	24
Hooper, W.O. D.R.	404280	R.A.A.F.	Ipswich, Qld.	24.06.44	26
Joel, LAC. R.E.	8814	R.A.A.F.	Bunbury, W.A.	24.06.44	27
Landsberg, W.O. J.W.	404759	R.A.A.F.		24.06.44	24
Lewis, Sgt. H.V.	406146	R.A.A.F.	Leederville, W.A.	24.06.44	35
McKean, Cpl. G.N.	5651	R.A.A.F.	Bentleigh, Vic.	24.06.44	31
Pittendrigh, LAC. J.L.	15398	R.A.A.F.	Mallanganee, NSW	24.06.44	23
Potts, AC.1. C.D.	39872	R.A.A.F.	Gilberton, S.A.	24.06.44	35
Stanford, AC.1. E.F.	27978	R.A.A.F.	Cobdogla, S.A.	24.06.44	22
Toohey, W.O. B.A.	402758	R.A.A.F.		24.06.44	23

S.S. VAN WAERWIJCK – SUNK OFF SUMATRA

AUSTRALIAN PRISONERS OF WAR LOST

Allen. Pte. L.R.	NX.55719	2/20 Bn.	Wynyard, Tas.	26.06.44	24
Clancy, Pte. James	NX.26032	2/18 Bn.		26.06.44	34
Deery, Pte. J.S.	NX.72937	2/20 Bn.	Lidcombe, NSW	26.06.44	34
Emmerson, Pte. William	QX.23480	2/26 Bn.	Rosewood, Qld.	26.06.44	38
Lucas, Pte. E.A.	QX.23487	2/26 Bn.	Tempe, NSW	26.06.44	37
Maughan, Pte. E.C.	QX.24004	2/29 Bn.	Warwick, Qld.	26.06.44	42
McDonald, Pte. C.J.W.	TX. 8237	2/29 Bn.	North Hobart, Tas.	26.06.44	35
Nunn, Pte. J.F.	VX.41048	2/29 Bn.	St. Kilda, Vic.	26.06.44	39
Richards, Cpl. J.N.	VX.43928	2/29 Bn.	Warwick, Qld.	26.06.44	38

Roberts, Pte. Herbert	NX.35661	2/19 Bn.	Leeton, NSW	26.06.44	40
Salter, Pte. D.B.	TX. 8178	2/29 Bn.	Hobart, Tas.	26.06.44	21
Sargent, Spr. R.F.	VX.30106	2/10 Fd.Coy.	Preston, Vic.	26.06.44	32
Willms, Pte. Bjarne	QX.23493	2/26 Bn.	Oslo, Norway	26.06.44	36

HONOUR ROLL – RAKUYO MARU

Adams, Pte. A.H.	NX.73334	2/19 Bn.	Arncliffe, NSW	13.09.44	24
Adams, Cpl. W.J.	SX. 5457	2/3 MG Bn.	Ravenshoe, Qld.	12.09.44	38
Aiken, Dvr. T.A.	TX. 4481	2/3 M.A.C.	Campbell Town. Tas.	12.09.44	40
Aitken, Pte. T.W.	QX.14637	2Bde.Coy.AASC	Scarborough, Qld.	12.09.44	26
Allen, Gnr. T.C.	QX.10932	2/10 Fd.Rgt.	Wondai, Qld.	14.09.44	29
Allison, L/Cpl. W.M.	NX.33374	HQ.8 Div.Sigs.	North Sydney, NSW	12.09.44	28
Altshuler, L/Sgt. Evsick	NX.38958	M.L.F.D.U.	North Bondi, NSW	14.09.44	26
Annesley, Sgt. F.J.	WX. 7905	2/4 MG Bn.	Scarborough, W.A.	16.09.44	28
Argus, Pte. E.H.	VX.52408	2/10 Ord.Wksp.	Daysdale, NSW	12.09.44	24
Armstrong, W.O.II D.C.	NX.65777	2/15 Fd.Rgt.	Surrey Hills, Vic.	13.09.44	30
Asher, Pte. K.R.	VX.26180	27 Bde.Co.AASC	Caulfield, Vic.	14.09.44	26
Aston, Gnr. Norman	NX.28634	2/15 Fd.Rgt.	Five Dock, NSW	12.09.44	33
Atkin, Sgt. M.N.P.	NX.55753	2/18 Bn.	Punchbowl, NSW	12.09.44	35
Auricht, Bdr. R.J.	VX.37822	4 A/T. Rgt.	Murrayville, Vic.	15.09.44	32
Aust, Spr. A.T.	VX.34165	2/10 Fd.Coy.	Burnley, Vic.	12.09.44	38
Austin, Pte. A.J.	VX.52747	27 Bde.Coy.AASC		12.09.44	25
Baggs, Pte. R.J.	WX. 9864	2/4 MG Bn.	Suviaco, W.A.	14.09.44	34
Baguley, Gnr. J.L.	VX.32497	4 A/T. Rgt.	West Preston, Vic.	12.09.44	27
Bailey, Pte. N.H.	NX.24081	2/30 Bn.	Burwood, NSW	14.09.44	31
Baird, Pte. J.H..	NX.47812	2/30 Bn.	S. Murwillumbah, NSW	12.09.44	37
Baker, Spr. A.R.	NX.68076	2/12 Fd.Coy.	Mayfield West, NSW	12.09.44	26
Baker, Pte. A.J.	WX. 8720	2/4 MG Bn.	Mount Lawley, W.A.	12.09.44	30
Baker, Gnr. H.T.	NX.38221	2/15 Fd.Rgt.	Dunoon, NSW	12.09.44	23
Baker, Pte. W.R.S.	WX. 8682	2/4 MG Bn.	Cannington, W.A.	12.09.44	25
Barnes, Pte. C.K.	TX. 5463	2/40 Bn.	King Island	12.09.44	22
Barnes, Pte. F.G.	VX.28968	2/2 Pnr. Bn.	Lwr.Ferntree Gully, Vic.	12.09.44	25
Barrett, Sgmn. Ambrose	NX.50664	8 Div. Sigs.	Strathfield, NSW	12.09.44	22
Barrow, L/Cpl. J.A.	TX. 4216	2/4 C.C.S.	Pontville, Tas.	13.09.44	25
Bateman, Pte. Kenneth	VX.36712	H.Q. 27 Inf.Bde.	East Kew, Vic.	12.09.44	30
Beathe, Pte. H.S.	NX.29291	2/19 Bn.	Cundletown, NSW	12.09.44	25
Beatty, L/Cpl. N.E.	QX.10756	1 Coy. AASC	Pialba, Qld.	14.09.44	25
Bell, Pte. H.C.	NX.30969	1 Fd. Bakery	Adamstown, NSW	12.09.44	29
Bell, Pte. R.J.	WX.16389	2/4 MG Bn.	Pingaring, W.A.	14.09.44	24
Bellamy, Pte. G.J.	QX. 7564	2/26 Bn.	Atherton, Qld.	12.09.44	30
Berry, Pte. E.W.	QX.20032	2/3 Ord.StoreCoy.	Sherwood, Qld.	12.09.44	26
Blacket, Pte. S.B.	NX.38928	H.Q. 8Div. AASC	Hurstville, NSW	12.09.44	23
Board, Sgt. A.D.	QX.17846	8 Fd.Cash.Off.	Toowoomba, Qld.	12.09.44	25
Boese, Gnr. R.S.	NX.71390	2/15 Fd. Rgt.	Arncliffe, NSW	12.09.44	24
Boland, Sgt. J.A.	QX.20572	3 Res. MT	Leichhardt, NSW	15.09.44	37
Booth, L/Cpl. Malcolm	NX.26483	2/12 Fd. Coy.	Gladesville, NSW	13.09.44	27
Bostock, Cpl. W.R.	NX.34111	2/19 Bn.	Taralga, NSW	13.09.44	27
Bould, Pte. K.A.	VX.44138	2/2 Pnr. Bn.	Dandenong, Vic.	12.09.44	26
Bourke, Spr. J.H.	NX.42014	2/6 Fd. Coy.	Murwillumbah, NSW	14.09.44	26
Bowden, Pte. T.K.	QX.14638	2 Coy. AASC	Brisbane, Qld.	12.09.44	29
Bowe, Pte. J.P.	NX.40638	2/18 Bn.	Bondi, NSW	14.09.44	29
Bower, Dvr. J.E.	VX.18712	1 PetrolPark	Auburn, Vic.	12.09.44	25
Bowkett, Pte. E.J.	QX.12062	2/26 Bn.	Mount Isa, Qld.	13.09.44	26
Box, Pte. R.J.	VX.22788	2/2 Pnr. Bn.	Carnegie, Vic.	13.09.44	25
Boyd, Pte. F.R.	VX.39862	27Bde.Ord.Wksp.	Pomborneit Nth., Vic.	12.09.44	29
Brady, L/Cpl. P.F.	NX.46278	3 Res. MT Coy.		12.09.44	29
Breen, Pte. P.A.	VX.48239	2/29 Bn.	Romsey, Vic.	12.09.44	29

Breen, Pte. P.A.	VX.48239	2/29 Bn.	Romsey, Vic.	12.09.44	29
Bresnan, Pte. J.L.	NX.55259	27Bde.Coy.AASC	Waterloo, NSW	12.09.44	32
Brettell, Pte. Edward	VX.30486	2/4 C.C.S.	Birmingham, U.K.	13.09.44	42
Brimage, Pte. R.V.	SX. 5391	2/2 MT Coy.	Port Adelaide, S.A.	12.09.44	31
Brock, Pte. W.G.	SX.10257	2/2 Res. MT	Orroroo, S.A.	12.09.44	24
Brown, Pte. A.M.	VX.21517	2/2 Pnr. Bn.	Nth. Carlton, Vic.	12.09.44	37
Brown, Pte. L.C.	VX.56623	2/2 Pnr. Bn.	Paddington, NSW	12.09.44	22
Browne, Sgt. E.A.	VX.55103	22 Ord.Fd.Pk.	Hartwell, Vic.	12.09.44	35
Burke, Lieut. J.A.	NX.25608	2/lO Fd. Am.	Bondi, NSW	12.09.44	34
Burnet, Pte. A.J.F.	QX.23829	2/26 Bn.	Toorak, Vic.	12.09.44	42
Burtenshaw, Cpl. R.P.	NX.31922	74 LAD. ACEME	Inverell, NSW	12.09.44	22
Butler, Dvr. A.F.W.	NX.52134	22 Bde.Coy.AASC	Woy Woy, NSW	12.09.44	28
Butler, Pte. L.V.	VX.41324	2/2 Pnr.Bn.	Oakleigh, Vic.	13.09.44	39
Byford, S/Sgt. C.H.	QX.17593	8 Fd. Cash Office	Oxley, Qld.	12.09.44	36
Camm, Pte. Richard	VX.51879	2/2 Pnr. Bn.	Launceston, Tas.	14.09.44	22
Campbell, Gnr. A.H.	QX.10519	2/10 Fd.Rgt.	Wooroonden, Old.	14.09.44	30
Campbell, Pte. J.F. (iii)	VX.51738	2/29 Bn.	Fitzroy, Vic.	13.09.44	24
Campbell, Gnr. Lang	NX.28995	2/15 Fd.Rgt.	Chatswood, NSW	13.09.44	28
Carne, Pte. William	VX.20748	2/2 Pnr. Bn.	Kew, Vic.	15.09.44	38
Carter, Pte. A.M.	VX.62603	A.I.F. Admn.H.Q.	Ballarat, Vic.	13.09.44	24
Carter, Pte. A.H.	WX. 9326	2/4 MG Bn.	Dangin, W.A.	12.09.44	24
Cassidy, Pte. H.A.	NX.50614	H.Q. 27 Inf.Bde.	Bondi, NSW	12.09.44	24
Chalmers, Major J.S.	TX. 2150	2/4 C.C.S.	Manly, NSW	14.09.44	34
Chambers, Gnr. Leo	QX. 9816	2/10 Fd. Rgt.	Mungallala, Qld.	13.09.44	29
Charles, Pte. G.B.	SX. 5143	8 Div.Salv.Unit	Semaphore, S.A.	13.09.44	25
Cherry, Pte. K.A.	OX.16938	2/26 Bn.	Barnsley, NSW	12.09.44	26
Chippendale, Pte. George	NX.34378	2/18 Bn.	Kurri Kurrii, NSW	12.09.44	26
Christie, Pte. D.E.	VX.21306	2/2 Pnr. Bn.	St. Kilda, Vic.	12.09.44	24
Christie, Pte. E.R.	VX.35469	2/29 Bn.	Koondrook, Vic.	12.09.44	28
Clark, Pte. G.T.	QX.17039	2/26 Bn.	Nambour, Qld.	12.09.44	28
Clark, Cpl. Robert	QX.15385	3 Res. MT	Mossman, Qld.	12.09.44	39
Clarris, Pte. A.R.G.	QX.20007	2/30 Bn.	Wooloongabba, Qld.	12.09.44	23
Cobon, Gnr. J.J.	QX.14419	2/10 Fd. Rgt.	Crows Nest, Qld.	12.09.44	26
Cobon, Gnr. T.B.	QX.14418	2/10 Fd. Rgt.	Crows Nest, Qld.	12.09.44	26
Cochrane, Sgt. W.R.	NX.68768	3 Res. MT	Paddington, NSW	12.09.44	43
Colquhoun, Pte. A.J.	WX. 9109	2/4 MG Bn.	Sawyers Valley, W.A.	15.09.44	38
Connan, S/Sgt. A.D.	VX.14855	2/2 Pnr. Bn.	Coburg, Vic.	14.09.44	33
Connors, Pte. S.J.	VX.33988	2/2 Pnr. Bn.	East Brunswick, Vic.	12.09.44	30
Constable, Gnr. G.A.	QX. 9851	2/10 Fd. Rgt.	Woodenbong, NSW	12.09.44	25
Cook, Gnr. W.C.Q.	VX.42904	4 A/Tk. Rgt.	Camperdown, Vic.	12.09.44	31
Cook, Pte. W.S.	NX.42352	2/19 Bn.	ForestLodge, NSW	12.09.44	39
Coon, Cpl. L.J. (MID)	NX36283	2/12 Fd. Am.	Cowra. NSW	12.09.44	34
Cooper, S/Sgt. A.L.	NX.25599	2/12 Fd. Coy.	Armidale, NSW	12.09.44	36
Cooper, Pte. F.W.	SX. 9699	2/2 Res. MT	Kadina, S.A.	14.09.44	27
Cooper, Pte. G.J.	VX.58019	2/2 Pnr. Bn.	Box Hill, Vic.	13.09.44	23
Cooper, Pte. N.C.	NX.52182	22 Rnf. AASC	Merrylands, NSW	12.09.44	32
Cooper, W.O.II. T.C.	QX. 1838	2/10 Fd. Rgt.	Sth Townsvillelle, Qld.	13.09.44	31
Cornelius, Pte. W.B.P.	VX.43452	2/29 Bn.	Mildura, Vic.	12.09.44	25
Cottam, Pte. A.E.	NX.35853	2/19 Bn.	Tumbarumba, NSW	13.09.44	30
Cousins, Pte. A.V.	WX. 9092	2/4 MG Bn.	Mount Helea, W.A.	14.09.44	30
Crammer, Pte. W.A.	VX.33271	1 Fd. Bakery	Nth Melbourne, Vic.	13.09.44	25
Crawford, Pte. N.E.	NX.42392	2/18 Bn.	Berry, NSW	12.09.44	24
Cripps, Pte. D.C.	WX.15783	2/4 MG Bn.	Northampton, W.A.	12.09.44	22
Crocker, Pte. R.A.	VX.65455	25/27 Ind.Bde. Wksp.	Ballarat, Vic.	13.09.44	26
Crocombe, Sgt. H.A.	QX.10796	2/26 Bn.	Walloon, Qld.	12.09.44	33
Cruttenden, Pte. R.F.T.	VX.51877	2/29 Bn.	Northcote, Vic.	12.09.44	22
Dare, Pte. R.W.	VX.55006	2/29 Bn.	Nth Melbourne, Vic.	12.09.44	25
Dart, Pte. R.W.	VX.60684	2/10 Ord. Wksp. ACEME	Frankston, Vic.	16.09.44	24

(iii) Served as Case, Pte. J.F.

Davidson, Pte. G.C.	TX. 2885	2/40 Bn.	Triabunna, Tas.	13.09.44	25
Davies, Dvr. B.F.T.	VX.30002	1 Petrol Pank	Coburg, Vic.	12.09.44	25
Davies, Sgt. D.C.	VX.13698	2/lO Fd. Rgt.	Toowong, Qld.	12.09.44	25
Davies, Pte. W.H.R.	VX.59875	Ord. Wksps.		12.09.44	24
Dawson, Gnr. A.R.	QX.14028	2/lO Fd. Rgt.	Kangaroo Point, Old.	12.09.44	26
Deacon, Pte. T.P.	NX.10913	2/20 Bn.	Annandale, NSW	12.09.44	25
Dean, Cpl. William	VX.23496	2/2 Pnr. Bn.		12.09.44	29
Delaporte, Pte. H.T.	WX. 8011	2/4 MG Bn.	Boyanup, W.A.	12.09.44	30
Denmead, Cpl. W.C.	VX.55797	27 Ord. Wksp.	Ballarat, Vic.	12.09.44	34
Dent, Spr. T.B.	NX.67299	H.Q. 8Div. RAE	Forbes, NSW	12.09.44	24
Deuchar, Gnr. D.S.	NX.46123	2/15 Fd. Rgt.	Codrington, NSW	12.09.44	25
Dewsbury, Pte. A.DeF.	VX.44281	2/2 Pnr. Bn.	Sale, Vic.	12.09.44	24
Dick, Sgt. C.D.	QX.14602	2/10 Fd. Rgt.	West End, Qld.	12.09.44	24
Diggins, Gnr. W.A.J.	NX.81705	2/1 Hvy. Bty.	Willoughby, NSW	18.09.44	33
Dorrington, Pte. H.M.	NX.42823	G.B.D.	Tabulam, NSW	12.09.44	33
Doyle, Pte. C.J.	NX.31449	2/2O Bn.	West Wyalong, NSW	13.09.44	28
Drummond, Pte. A.McD.D.	WX. 8830	2/4 MG Bn.	East Perth, W.A.	15.09.44	33
Duncan, Pte. A.W.	QX.12286	2/26 Bn.	Highgate Hill, Qld.	12.09.44	30
Dunstan, Pte. W.J.	VX.47008	2/29 Bn.	Williamstown, Vic.	12.09.44	25
Du Ross, Sgt. S.C.M.	NX.24909	2/30 Bn.	Manly, NSW	12.09.44	27
Easton, Pte. L.W.	NX.56128	AIF HQ Malaya	Woy Woy, NSW	12.09.44	29
Edwards, S/Sgt. A.D.	NX.46355	2/20 Bn.		14.09.44	37
Edwards, Pte. A.A.	SX. 3849	2/2 Res. MT	Birkenhead, S.A.	15.09.44	24
Edwards, Pte. H.C.	VX.27881	27Bde. Coy. AASC	Frankston, Vic.	12.09.44	24
Eley, Pte. I.S.	WX. 9646	2/2 Pnr. Bn.	Geraldton, W.A.	12.09.44	30
Engel, Dvr. A.E.	NX.47202	3 Res. MT Coy.	Port Stephens. NSW	14.09.44	24
Eva, Sgt. C.S.	VX.30683	2/2 Pnr. Bn.	Canterbury, Vic.	12.09.44	26
Ewin, Pte. L.A.	NX.32289	2/10 Ord.Wksp..	Lewisham, NSW	12.09.44	24
Fallows, Spr. L.G.	WX. 6361	2/6Fd.Pk.Coy.	Goosebury Hill, W.A.	12.09.44	25
Farrell, Gnr. M.J.	NX.33866	2/15 Fd. Rgt.	Lakemba, NSW	12.09.44	24
Faust, Pte. J.F.	QX.11292	2/26 Bn.	Proserpine,Qld.	15.09.44	27
Flanagan, Pte. A.J.	QX.23093	2/26 Bn.	Longreach	14.09.44	24
Flannery, Spr. R.A.	TX. 5185	2/10 Fd.Coy.	Don, Tas.	14.09.44	30
Fleming, Pte. James	WX.10963	4 Res. MT	Merredin, W.A.	14.09.44	39
Flynn, Cpl. J.L.	NX.158!5	2/6 Fd. Coy.	Marrickville, NSW	12.09.44	30
Fogo, L/Sgt. George	NX.52967	2/12 Fd. Coy.	Canterbury, NSW	13.09.44	29
Foot, Dvr. P.M.	NX.49400	3 Res. MT	Kingsiord, NSW	14.09.44	26
Forbes, Pte. J.H.	VX.14293	1 Petrol Park	Carnegie North, Vic.	12.09.44	37
Ford, L/Sgt. R.A.H.	NX.58361	9 Sup. Pers. Sec..	Arncliffe, NSW	13.09.44	27
Fordham, Gnr. K.O.	VX.38361	4 A/Tk. Rgt.	Highett, Vic.	14.09.44	24
Forrest, Pte. H.A.	VX.33714	1 Petrol Park	Red Cliffs, Vic.	12.09.44	37
Forrest, Dvr. J.G.	VX.53389	105 AGT	Mildura, Vic.	12.09.44	25
Francis, Spr. C.F.	VX.23469	2/10 Fd. Coy.	Warragul, Vic.	12.09.44	34
Gale, Pte. N.H.	NX.58165	2/10 Fd. Amb.	Chatsworth, NSW	12.09.44	24
Gallagher, Pte. J.E.	VX.50018	4 Res. MT	Windsor, Vic.	12.09.44	38
Gardner, Gnr. Harry	NX.10962	2/15 Fd. Rgt.	New Lambton, NSW	12.09.44	24
Garland, Sgt. C.W.C.	NX.52118	2/18 Bn.	Perth, W.A.	12.09.44	35
Garner, Sgt. E.G.	QX.14018	2/26 Bn.	Yass, NSW	12.09.44	28
Gibbs, Pte. L.G.	WX.16407	2/4 MG Bn.	Wanneroo, W.A.	14.09.44	27
Gibbs, Pte. W.H.	WX. 8958	2/4 MG BN.	Wanneroo, W.A.	12.09.44	28
Gillan, Pte. L.C.	WX.10060	2/9 Fd. Amb.	Fremantle, W.A.	12.09.44	33
Gillespie, Sigmn. M.S.	NX.59824	8 Div. Sigs.	Kincumber, NSW	12.09.44	24
Gillespie, Pte. T.M.S.	NX.50824	H.Q. 8 Div.	Kincumber, NSW	12.09.44	33
Gilmour, Cpl. K.H.C.	NX.58727	HQ.22 Inf. Bde.	Belmore, NSW	13.09.44	31
Goffage, Pte. F.C.P.	NX.71655	3Res. MT. Coy.	Parramatta, NSW	12.09.44	32
Goodman, Cpl. G.J.P.	VX.21001	2/2 Pnr. Bn.	Cobram, Vic.	12.09.44	26
Gordon, Pte. G.E.	VX.37662	1 Perol Park	Sth Melbournene, Vic.	13.09.44	34
Gordon, Pte. G.W.	VX.29476	2/29 Bn.	Fairfield, Vic.	12.09.44	30
Gorman, Pte. J.A.	QX.18663	2/26 Bn.	Mackay, Qld.	12.09.44	32

Goss, Cpl. G.B.		TX. 4490	2/3 M.A.C.	Hobart, Tas.	12.09.44	31
Gove, Pte. K.J.		VX.51079	2/29 Bn.	Ballarat, Vic.	12.09.44	26
Graham, Sgt. Robert		NX.47103	3 Res. MT	Cooks Hill, NSW	12.09.44	40
Gratton, Sgt. J.W.		QX.16802	3 Res. MT	Toowoomba, Qld.	12.09.44	39
Greaves, Pte. W.K.		NX.59292	HQ. 22 Inf. Bde.	Clovelly, NSW	12.09.44	29
Griffiths, Sgt. A.J.D.		QX.17552	2/10 Fd. Rgt.	Silkstone, Qld.	12.09.44	35
Grout, Pte. L.J.		QX.12958	3 Res. MT	Nanango, Qld.	12.09.44	41
Guy, Pte. H.A.		QX.11294	2/26 Bn.	Ardlethan, NSW	12.09.44	27
Hamilton, Pte. O.R.		VX.30489	4 Res, MT	KorongVale, Vic.	13.09.44	48
Hampton, Pte. R.J.		VX.56533	2/2 Pnr. Bn.	South Yarra, Vic.	12.09.44	30
Handebo, Cpl. E.A.	(ii)	NX. 2133	8 Div. Prov.		12.09.44	39
Handley, Pte. Thomas		QX.19994	2/26 Bn.	Alderley, Qld.	12.09.44	40
Hands, Pte. Richard		VX.36558	2/2 Pnr. Bn.	Seddon, Vic.	15.09.44	24
Hanlin, L/Cpl. L.G.F.		SX.10814	8Div.Amn.S/Pk.	Sefton Park, S.A.	13.09.44	35
Harding, Sgt. A.J.		QX.12041	2/10 Fd. Rgt.	Epping, NSW	13.09.44	43
Harvey, Gnr. E.R.		QX.13037	2/10 Fd. Rgt.	Hamilton, Qld.	12.09.44	24
Harvey, Cpl. L.J.		WX.10822	2/4 MG Bn.	West Perth, W.A.	12.09.44	24
Hawkes, Pte. E.C.		NX.27022	1 Coy. AASC	Ashiield, NSW	12.09.44	34
Hayes, Pte. A.G.		WX. 8408	2/4 MG Bn.		12.09.44	33
Hayes, Pte. E.A.G.		NX.72673	2/3 M.A.C.	Awaba, NSW	14.09.44	23
Hayes, Gnr. G.P.		NX.30333	2/15 Fd. Rgt.	Hay, NSW	13.09.44	29
Hayward, Pte. V.C.		NX.44799	3 Res. MT	Casino, NSW	12.09.44	23
Head, Cpl. F.E.		VX.23525	2/2 Pnr. Bn.	Osborne's Flat, Vic.	12.09.44	23
Head, Pte. F.J.A.		QX.23538	2/3 0rd.Store Coy.	Valley, Qld.	12.09.44	38
Heasman, Bdr. V.F.		NX.33124	2/15Fd. Rgt.	Homebush, NSW	14.09.44	26
Hedley, L/Sgt. G.R.		VX.31807	4 A/Tk. Rgt.	Geelong, Vic.	14.09.44	24
Hedrick, L/Cpl. S.J.		VX.53549	8 Div. Sigs.	Armadale, Vic.	12.09.44	29
Heffernan, Cpl. F.O'R.		QX.10493	2/26 Bn.		12.09.44	34
Heidke, Pte. R.E.		QX15281	2/26 Bn.	Balmain, NSW	12.09.44	24
Helsin, Cpl. J.F.		WX.10095	2/4 MG Bn.	Palmyra, W.A.	12.09.44	25
Henderson, Pte. A.C.		NX.55785	H.Q. 8 Div.	Maroubra, NSW	12.09.44	25
Henderson, Gnr. C.M.		VX.47063	4 A/Tk. Rgt.	Murtoa, Vic.	12.09.44	25
Herringe, Gnr. W.J.		NX.30644	2/15 Fd. Rgt.	Cowra, NSW	12.09.44	24
Hobson, Pte. Clifford		WX.16446	2/4 MG Bn.	Kippax, LeedsYorks.UK	12.09.44	38
Hocken, Pte. S.B.		QX.18795	2/30rd.Store Coy.	North Mackay, Qld.	12.09.44	20
Hodson, Pte. George		SX. 92l1	8 Div. Am. S/Pk.	Streaky Bay, S.A.	12.09.44	37
Holder, Sgt. G.H.		NX.51726	2/26 Bn.	Ramsgate, NSW	12.09.44	32
Horsburgh, Pte. R.J.		VX.45055	2/29 Bn.	Hilgay, Vic.	14.09.44	22
Hounsell, Pte. A.J.		NX.72062	3 Res. MT	Urana, NSW	12.09.44	36
Hounsell, Dvr. H.T.		NX.72064	3 Res. MT	Wagga Wagga, NSW	12.09.44	36
Howard, Pte. B.J.		NX.73270	88 LAD	Quirindi, NSW	12.09.44	29
Howse, L/Bdr. R.A.		NX.27998	2/15 Fd. Rgt.	Orange, NSW	12.09.44	25
Hoy, Spr. F.V.		VX.29382	2/10 Fd.Coy.	East Brunswick, Vic.	15.09.44	36
Hughes, Pte. E.G.		VX.56048	2 Res. MT	Coleraine, Vic.	13.09.44	39
Hughes, Pte. R.F.		WX.10795	2/4 MC Bn.	Maylands, W.A.	12.09.44	24
Hunt, Spr. J.R.		NX.67516	2/12 Fd. Coy.	Clovelly, NSW	13.09.44	27
Hutchinson, Pte. H.A.	(iv)	VX.65868	2/10 Ord.Fd.Pk.	Port Melbourne, Vic.	12.09.44	25
Hutchison, Pte. R.B.		WX. 7646	2/4 MG Bn.	Subiaco, W.A.	12.09.44	32
Ide, Bdr. W.P.J.		QX.13648	2/10 Fd. Rgt.	Northbridge, NSW	12.09.44	29
Iredale, Spr. F.W.		VX.65143	2/10 Fd. Coy.	Wonthaggi, Vic.	12.09.44	31
Isaacs, Sigmn. W.J.		NX. 7360	Ftress. Sigs.	Weston Super Mare, Somerset, UK	12.09.44	24
Jackson, Bdr. P.A.		VX.42827	4 A/Tk. Rgt.	Mount Dundeed, Vic.	12.09.44	25
Jackson, L/Cpl. W.F.		NX.29942	27 Bde. Coy. AASC	Bowral, NSW	12.09.44	34
Jacobs, Pte. O.E.		SX. 9628	8 Div. Amn. S/Pk.	Mount Compass, S.A.	15.09.44	27
James, Pte. H.T.		VX.55577	2/2 M.A.C.	Eaglehawk, Vic.	12.09.44	24
Jamieson, Cpl. T.J.		NX.54371	8 Div.Sigs.	Queanbeyan, NSW	12.09.44	29

(ii) Served as Braggs, Cpl. A.W.
(iv) Served as Francis, Pte. H.A.

Jeffery, Pte. G.F.	NX.65537	HQ. 22 Inf.Bde.	Chatswood, NSW	16.09.44	24
Jeffrey, Pte. E.G.	VX.59960	2/2 M.A.C.	Broadiord, Vic.	14.09.44	22
Jennings, Cpl. J.C.	QX. 5348	69 LAD	Chelmer, Qld.	12.09.44	29
Jinks, Pte. W.C.	QX.10496	1 Coy. AASC		12.09.44	31
Johnson, Dvr. C.J.	VX.36298	Petrol Park	Laanecoorie, Vic.	12.09.44	26
Johnson, Pte. H,E.	VX.33654	2/2 Pnr. Bn.	Geelong West, Vic.	14.09.44	31
Johnstone, Pte. J.J.	VX.50919	2/2 Pnr. Bn.	Chelsea, Vic.	12.09.44	25
Jones, Sigmn. F.A.	NX.49740	8 Div.Sigs.	Maclean, NSW	12.09.44	23
Jones, Pte. F.F.	QX.12941	1 Coy. AASC	Dagun, Qld.	12.09.44	27
Jones, Pte. C.S.	VX.40430	2/2 Pnr. Bn.	South Yarra, Vic.	!2.09.44	24
Jones, Pte. L.H.	VX.41948	2/29 Bn.	Traralgon, vic.	14.09.44	32
Jones, Sgt. W.A.	VX.22752	1 Petrol Park	Merbein, vic.	14.09.44	34
Joyner, Spr. A.E.	NX.72260	2/12 Fd. Coy.	Kiama, NSW	12.09.44	29
Kelleher, Pte. C.F.	NX.34347	2/10 Fd. Amb.	Neutral Bay, NSW	12.09.44	30
Kelly, Cpl. V.L.	NX.21980	2/6 Fd. Coy.	Mosman, NSW	12.09.44	32
Kendall, S/Sgt. R.C.	VX.63398	27 Bde. Ord. Fd. Pk.	Preston, Vic.	17.09.44	27
Kenna, Pte. F.J.	QX.12735	3 Res. MT	Rockhampton, Qld.	12.09.44	38
Kennedy, Gnr. J.L.	QX.10310	2/10 Fd. Rgt.	Roma, Qld.	14.09.44	27
Kilpatrick, Pte. I.D.	VX.45040	2/29 Bn.	Coleraine, Vic.	12.09.44	27
King, Pte. G.F.	VX.64359	2/10 Ord. Fd. Wksp.	Werribee, Vic.	13.09.44	35
King, Gnr. J.A.S.	QX. 1878	2/10 Fd. Rgt.	Townsville,Qld.	12.09.44	32
Kinniburgh, Pte. Gerald (v)	NX.64639	2/29 Bn.	Daylesford, Vic.	12.09.44	27
Knight, Pte. J.E.	QX. 9754	2/20 Bn.	Rockhampton,Qld.	12.09.44	35
Lack, Sigmn. C.G.	NX.69082	8 Div. Sigs.	Condong, NSW	12.09.44	23
Laing, Sigmn. J.O.D.	NX.51517	8 Div. Sigs.	Essendon, Vic.	12.09.44	24
Laurenti, L/Cpl. J.D.	SX.10624	27 Ind. Bde. Co. Wksp.	Menindee Gardens, S.A.	12.09.44	32
Laverty, Pte. Allan	NX.60329	2/19 Bn.	Laggan, NSW	12.09.44	28
Lechmere, Pte. A.R.	WX. 221	2/2 Pnr. Bn.	Subiaco, W.A.	12.09.44	24
Leeson, Sigmn. C.W.L.	VX.60142	8 Div. Sigs.	Surrey Hills, Vic.	13.09.44	25
Leeson, Sgt. R.M.	VX.15156	1 Pet. Pk. AASC	Riverstone, NSW	12.09.44	28
Lennard, Pte. Robert	VX.18278	2/2 Pnr. Bn.	Hampton, Vic.	12.09.44	24
Leschke, Pte. W.W.	SX. 9347	8 Div. Salv..	Croydon, S.A.	12.09.44	28
Lester, Spr. A.D.	NX.33286	H,Q. 8 Div.		14.09.44	26
Lewcock, Dvr. G.S.	VX.37259	1 Petrol Park	Barham, NSW	12.09.44	28
Lewis, Spr. J.V.	NX.21633	2/6 Fd. Coy.	Amiens, Qld.	12.09.44	29
Lewis, Pte. M.G.	NX.71872	AIF. H.Q. Malaya	Lismore, NSW	12.09.44	28
Limbrick, Pte. L.G.	VX.21427	2/2 Pnr. Bn.	Lilydale, Vic.	12.09.44	32
Linnane, Pte. V.P.P.	NX.43764	2/2 MG Bn.	Lismore, NSW	15.09.44	22
Lister, Sigmn. R.J.	VX.33250	8 Div. Sigs.	Richmond, Vic.	12.09.44	36
Lloyd, Pte. Arthur	NX.32414	2/30 Bn.	Jerry Bailey, NSW	12.09.44	30
Love, Gnr. J.T.	QX.17589	2/10 Fd. Rgt.		14.09.44	23
Loveday, Pte. Ralph	QX.16334	1 Coy. AASC	Pittsworth, Qld.	15.09.44	24
Lovering, Spr. J.R.	WX.11949	2/6 Fd. Pk.	Hyden, W.A.	12.09.44	27
Lowe, Pte. H.E.	VX.43441	2/2 Pnr. Bn.	Carrum, Vic.	12.09.44	28
Loxton, L/Cpl. W.T.	SX. 9690	2/2 Res. MT		12.09.44	25
Lye, Pte. A.J.	QX.12298	2/26 Bn.	Monto, Qld.	12.09.44	24
Lynch, Spr. M.M.	VX.27139	2/10 Fd. Coy.	Sunshine, Vic.	15.09.44	29
Lynch, Gnr. R.R.	NX.10318	2/15 Fd. Rgt.	Camperdown, NSW	12.09.44	24
Lynch, Pte. R.T.	VX.15768	2/2 Pnr. Bn.	Bacchus Marsh, Vic.	12.09.44	25
Lynn, Cpl. K.H.	VX.19291	2/2 Pnr. Bn.	Thornbury, Vic.	12.09.44	30
McAuley, Pte. F.C.	NX.72960	Reinforcements, AASC	Cremorne, NSW	12.09.44	28
McCabe, Pte. A.J.	QX.12244	2/26 Bn.		12.09.44	24
McCauley, Pte. J.J.G.	NX.50337	2/19 Bn.		12.09.44	28
McCracken, Pte. R.D.	WX. 5584	2/4 MG BN.	Maylands, W.A.	15.09.44	24
McDonald, Dvr. W.E.	QX.16203	1 Coy. AASC	Gatton, Qld.	12.09.44	30
McDowall, Cpl. M.W.	NX.40997	H.Q. RAE	Torrington, NSW	14.09.44	26
McFarland, Pte. W.J.	VX.34255	105 Gen.Tp.Co.	Hawksburn, Vic.	12.09.44	29

(v) Served as Ryan, Pte. Gerald

MacFarlane, Spr. L.R.	NX.36754	2/6 Fld.Coy.	Cootamundra, NSW	12.09.44	28
McGrath, Pte. E.J.	QX.18378	2/26 Bn.	Wallangarra, Qld.	12.09.44	26
McGrath, Cpl. Frank	VX.30028	2/2 Pnr. Bn.	East Brunswick, Vic.	14.09.44	37
McGrath, L/Cpl. J.M.	NX.45789	2/30 Bn.	Waratah, NSW	12.09.44	28
McGrath, Pte. S.L.	QX.17247	HQ. 8 Div. AASC	Windsor, Qld.	12.09.44	30
McGregor, Pte. M.R.	NX.40324	2/18 Bn.	North Barraba, NSW	12.09.44	24
Macheson, Pte. Claude	QX.14544	2/26 Bn.	Valley, Qld.	12.09.44	26
Mclnnes, L/Cpl. lan	NX.44535	8/10 Reinf. 8 Div. Sgs.	Campbelltown, NSW	12.09.44	26
MacKay, Pte. James	NX.41920	73 LAD	Kogarah, NSW	12.09.44	25
McKellar, Spr. R.K.	NX.67951	HQ 8 Div. RAE	Katoomba, NSW	12.09.44	24
McKelvey, Gnr. R.H.	QX.19540	2/10 Fd. Rgt.	Taringa, Qld.	15.09.44	33
McKinnis, L/Cpl. Roy	VX.22165	2/2 Pnr. Bn.	Arat, Vic.	12.09.44	32
NcLean, Gnr. K.A.	QX. 9764	2/10 Fd. Rgt.	South Brisbane, Qld.	12.09.44	24
McLennan, Pte. K.W.	VX.33101	2/2 Pnr. Bn.	Fawkner, Vic.	12.09.44	26
McLeod, Cpl. T.K.	NX.20550	2/30 Bn.	Concord, NSW	12.09.44	29
McMahon, Pte. T.M.	WX. 8760	2/4 MG Bn.	Byford, W.A.	14.09.44	24
McManus, L/Cpl. Richard	NX.18445	8 Div. MLFDU	Kogarah, NSW	12.09.44	22
McNae, W.O.II. W.C.	QX.13590	2/10 Fd. Rgt.	Bowen Hills, Qld.	14.09.44	28
McNamara, Cpl. Jack	QX.10734	2/26 Bn.	Nanango, Qld.	12.09.44	32
Mann, Cpl. K.R.	QX.10069	2/26 Bn.	Goondawindi, Qld.	13.09.44	29
Manners, Cpl. J.E.	VX.37281	2/29 Bn.	Koondrook, Vic.	12.09.44	28
Martin, L/Cpl. A.E.	VX.21231	2/2 Pnr. Bn.	Cheltenham, Vic.	12.09.44	33
Martin, Spr. D.J.	VX.55262	2/10 Fd.Coy.	Moama, NSW	12.09.44	35
Mavrothalasitis, Pte. George	NX.69998	2/20 Bn.	Acracia, Greece	14.09.44	27
Maxwell, Pte. W.K.	NX.36907	2/20 Bn.	Woodburn, NSW	12.09.44	23
Maxwell, Spr. W.H.	NX.72711	2/12 Fd.Coy.	Woodburn, NSW	12.09.44	30
May, Pte. F.G.	NX. 7248	2/30 Bn.	Lennox Head, NSW	12.09.44	23
May, Cpl. R.J.	OX. 5602	8 Div.Prov.	Greenmount, Old.	12.09.44	33
Mead, Spr. A.G.	NX.44744	8 Div.Engrs.	Willoughby, NSW	14.09.44	24
Mears, Spr. J.F.	NX.15879	2/6 Fd. Coy.	Randwick, NSW	12.09.44	27
Mellett, Gnr. D.S.	NX.49488	2/15 Fd. Rgt.	Randwick, NSW	12.09.44	22
Meredith, Pte. L.S.Y.	SX.10986	2/2 Res. MT	Mylor, S.A.	13.09.44	27
Mewitt, Gnr. Ronald	VX.45754	4 A/Tk. Rgt.		12.09.44	30
Millard, Cpl. W.G.	NX.56101	2/19 Bn.	Young, NSW	17.09.44	26
Miller, L/Cpl. J.M.	VX.14639	2/2 Pnr. Bn.	Albury, NSW	16.09.44	27
Minchin, Cpl. A.R.	WX. 7662	2/4 MG Bn.	Dangin, W.A.	15.09.44	30
Mitchell, Pte. A.W.	VX.59033	2/2 Pnr. Bn.		12.09.44	36
Moller, Pte. T.C.	NX.33640	HQ. 22 Inf. Bde.	Dulwich Hill, NSW	14.09.44	30
Moon, Spr. C.W.	NX.29172	2/12 Fd.Coy.	Brookvale, NSW	12.09.44	39
Moore, Pte. F.C.	WX. 8076	2/4 MG Bn.	Shenton Park, W.A.	12.09.44	33
Morgan, Gnr. W.R.H.	QX.10437	2/10 Fd.Rgt.	Cunnamulla, Qld.	13.09.44	39
Moritz, Cpl. J.L.	SX. 9416	2/2 Res. MT		12.09.44	39
Moritz, Pte. T.R.	SX. 9417	2/2 Res. MT	Magill, S.A.	12.09.44	36
Mossley, Spr. J.J.	WX. 7553	2/6 Fd.Pk.	Albany, W.A.	12.09.44	36
Moxham, Gnr. H.W.	NX.19749	2/15 Fd. Rgt.	Waverton, NSW	16.09.44	30
Moyle, Sgt. L.G.	VX.23878	105 Gen. Tpt.	Black Rock, Vic.	12.09.44	27
Moynihan, Sgt. W.J.	NX.32703	2/30 Bn.	Moss Vale, NSW	12.09.44	25
Mudford, Dvr. J.B.	VX.50766	4 Res. MT	Albury, NSW	14.09.44	23
Mudford, Pte. K.M.	QX.16336	2/26 Bn.	Wootton, NSW	13.09.44	33
Mulford, Cpl. R.W.E.	NX.13948	2/6 Fd. Coy.	Newtown, NSW	12.09.44	30
Munn, Gnr. Frank	VX.45341	4 A/Tk. Rgt.			
Munro, Cpl. James	NX.30299	2/6 Fd. Coy.	Maclean, NSW	12.09.44	39
Murphy, Bdr. R.W.	VX.38350	4 A/Tk. Rgt.	Oakleigh, Vic.	12.09.44	26
Murrell, Pte. J.P.M.	VX.41152	2/29 Bn.		13.09.44	35
Mutter, Gnr. F.F.	QX.22039	2/l0 Fd. Rgt.	Woody Point, Qld.	12.09.44	29
Mutton, Pte. Charles	WX. 7181	2/4 MG Bn.	St. Kilda, Vic.	12.09.44	31
Myers, Pte. G.E.	NX.40440	2/18 8n.	Tamworth, NSW	12.09.44	38
Myers, Gnr. J.R.	NX.30917	2/15 Fd. Rgt.	Orange, NSW	13.09.44	42
Newby, Pte. Kenneth	NX.69115	3 Res. MT	Kogarah, NSW	15.09.44	35
Newnham, Sgt. S.F.	VX.20455	2/29 Bn.	Berwick, Vic.	13.09.44	43
Nichol, Pte. J.N.	NX.72411	9Sup. Pets. Sec.	Leichhardt, NSW	12.09.44	27

Nicholas, Pte. Tony	QX.21979	2/26 Bn.	Samis Is. Greece	14.09.44	38
Nicholson, Pte. W.G.	WX. 7940	2/4 MG Bn.	Mount Hawthorn, W.A.	13.09.44	36
Nicolson, L/Sgt. D.I.	VX.28950	2/10 Fd. Coy.	Warrigul, Vic.	12.09.44	29
Nightingale, Pte. J.K.	VX.21441	2/2 Pnr. Bn.	Footscray, Vic.	13.09.44	28
Nolan, Pte. E.L.	WX. 7659	2/4 MG Bn.	South Perth, W.A.	12.09.44	34
Nugent, Pte. J.D.S.	VX.26520	2/2 Pnr. Bn.	Moonee Ponds, Vic.	12.09.44	31
Nuss, Pte. F.T.	QX.18066	2/3 Ord. Store Coy.	Roma, Qld.	12.09.44	26
O'Hara, Gnr. Geoffrey	NX.38239	2/15 Fd. Rgt.	Hambledon Hill, NSW	13.09.44	26
Olsen, Pte. P.V.	NX.67028	3 Res. MT	Granville, NSW	14.09.44	
Page, Pte. E.C.	VX.42400	2/2 Pnr. Bn.	Preston, Vic.	12.09.44	30
Page, Spr. Merrick	NX. 1189	2/12 Fd. Coy.	Maclean, NSW	13.09.44	24
Parker, Pte. J.H.	VX.18781	2/2 Pnr. Bn.	Hawthorn, Vic.	12.09.44	24
Parkyn, Pte. R.V.	SX. 9315	2/2 Res. MT	Blinman, S.A.	15.09.44	26
Paterson, Cpl. W.A.	VX.20509	105 Gen. Tpt.	Albert Park, Vic.	12.09.44	37
Pearce, Pte. A.L.	NX.72217	HQ. 8 Div. AASC	Wentworth Falls, NSW	12.09.44	29
Pearce, Pte. E.H.	VX.63613	2/26 Bn.	Footscray, Vic.	12.09.44	19
Pearce, Pte. H.W.	WX. 8856	2/4 MG Bn.	Beaconsfield, W.A.	12.09.44	30
Penaluna, L/Cpl. J.S.	VX.45849	2/2 Pnr. Bn.	Ballarat, Vic.	12.09.44	31
Pepper, Dvr. W.E.	NX.71943	3 Res. MT		12.09.44	23
Perry, Spr. B.G.	NX.44820	8/10 Reinf. RAE	Crows Nest, NSW	14.09.44	25
Perry, Spr. L.G.	NX.44821	8/10 Reinf. RAE	Crows Nest, NSW	14.09.44	24
Peters, Pte. E.J.	QX.16817	3 Res. MT	Manly, NSW	13.09.44	38
Phillips, Lieut. L.J.	VX.37564	8 Div. Pet. Pk.	Albert Park, Vic.	12.09.44	29
Phorson, Spr. E.E.	NX.50325	2/12 Fd. Coy.	Double Bay, NSW	12.09.44	35
Picton, Pte. C.G.	NX.68902	2/18 Bn.	Croydon, NSW	14.09.44	23
Plant, Pte. R.A.B.	VX.57701	2/10 Ord.Wksp.	Trentham, Vic.	14.09.44	31
Pocock, Pte. G.F.	VX.39201	22 Bde. Ord. Wksp.	North Fitzroy, Vic.	12.09.44	24
Portbury, Bdr. K.R.	VX.30124	4 A/Tk. Rgt.	Coburg, Vic.	12.09.44	31
Powis, Gnr. R.A.	VX.53436	4 A/Tk. Rgt.		12.09.44	24
Raft, Sigmn. Stanley	NX.53310	8 Div. Sigs.	Sydney, NSW	12.09.44	25
Raine, Spr. Holmes	WX. 7684	2/6 Fd. Pk.	West Perth, W.A.	12.09.44	36
Randall, Pte. E.E.	WX.16356	2/4 MG Bn.	Ajana, W.A.	12.09.44	36
Rayment, Pte. K.G.	VX.25927	2/2 Pnr. Bn.	Surrey Hills, Vic.	15.09.44	22
Read, Sigmn. V.H.	NX.55747	8 Div. Sigs.	Sydney, NSW	12.09.44	23
Redgrave, Pte. E.J.W.	NX.59145	2/19 Bn.	Balmain, NSW	12.09.44	28
Reed, Pte. H.E.	NX. 8319	2/19 Bn.	Delegate, NSW	13.09.44	24
Rees, Pte. Donald	QX. 5698	2/26 Bn.		12.09.44	38
Reeves, Pte. J.W.	VX.56962	4 Res. MT	Spotswood, Vic.	12.09.44	28
Rehn, Pte. G.L. (i)	NX.48495	3 Res. MT		14.09.44	39
Richards, Spr. Walter	VX.33680	2/10 Fd. Coy.	Hampton, Vic.	15.09.44	31
Roach, Bdr. A.E.	NX.30592	2/15 Fd. Rgt.	Tooraweenah, NSW	12.09.44	28
Roberts, Pte. Donald	VX.59952	2/2 Pnr. Bn.	Murrumbeena, Vic.	12.09.44	22
Robertson, Cpl. H.S.	VX.29954	2/2 Pnr. Bn.	West Brunswick, Vic.	12.09.44	23
Robertson, L/Sgt. J.B.	NX.54338	2/12 Fd. Coy.	Coniston, NSW	12.09.44	26
Robertson, L/Sgt. J.H.	QX. 5968	2/10 Fd. Rgt.	Stanthorpe, Qld.	14.09.44	33
Robin, Spr. A.C.	NX.53050	2/12 Fd. Coy.	West Ryde, NSW	12.09.44	29
Robinson, Cpl. J.F.	VX.59883	2/10 Ord. Wksp.		12.09.44	22
Rohrlach, Pte. M.C.	SX. 9439	8 Div. Amn. S/Pk.	Swan Reach, S.A.	15.09.44	28
Rolfe, Pte. S.B.	NX.72410	2/30 Bn.	Lidcombe, NSW	12.09.44	32
Romey, Pte. Norman	NX.51667	2/19 Bn.	Hamilton, Qld.	14.09.44	29
Rosenbrock, Spr. R.G.	VX.29189	2/10 Fd.Coy.	Bairnsdale, Vic.	12.09.44	30
Rowley, Pte. W.R.	VX.23934	27 Bde.	Elwood, Vic.	12.09.44	38
Rudd, Gnr. W.B.	QX.12055	2/10 Fd.Rgt.	Aramac, Qld.	!3.09.44	24
Russell, Cpl. D.W.	NX.16829	8 Div.Prov.	Condobolin, NSW	12.09.44	24
Russell, Pte. R.G.S.	NX.72923	2/20 Bn.	Hurstville, NSW	14.09.44	40
Russell, L/Bdr. Thomas	NX.27327	2/15 Fd. Rgt.	Concord, NSW	12.09.44	33
Ryan, L/Bdr. F.T.P.	VX.32994	4 A/Tk. Rgt.	Flemington, Vic.	12.09.44	26

(i) Served as Barnett, Pte. L.A.

Ryan, Pte. J.W.	VX.50393	2/10 Ord.Fd.Pk.	Karrawinna North, Vic.	15.09.44	24
Ryan, Pte. R.L.	NX.73960	2/19 Bn.	Nth. Parramatta, NSW	12.09.44	22
Ryan, L/Sgt. W.A.G. (MM)	VX.18252	2/2 Pnr. Bn.	Brunswick, Vic.	12.09.44	33
Salcole, Pte. R.E.	NX. 4738	3 Res. MT	Nyngan, NSW	12.09.44	32
Sanger, Pte. S.J.R.	VX.36218	27 Bde. Coy. AASC		12.09.44	36
Sanson, Pte. R.A.	NX. 594	2/30 Bn.	StrathField, NSW	12.09.44	27
Sargent, Cpl. Joseph	NX.69499	3 Res. MT	West Ryde, SW	12.09.44	34
Savage, Pte. S.W.	NX.44407	8 Div. MLFDU	Tempe, NSW	12.09.44	23
Sawyer, Pte. H.W.	QX.23933	2/3 Ord.Store Coy.	Dulwich Hill, NSW	12.09.44	33
Scaife, Gnr. Stanley	NX.53978	2/15 Fd. Rgt.	Padstow, NSW	13.09.44	25
Scarpella, Gnr. W.T.	VX.57052	4 A/Tk. Rgt.	North Carlton, Vic.	15.09.44	32
Schofield, Pte. F.W.	OX.15303	2/26 Bn.	Stratiord, Qld.	12.09.44	25
Scott, L/Cpl. Thomas	NX.20054	8 Div. MLFDU	Peakhurst, NSW	12.09.44	25
Scott, Pte. T.B.	VX.44379	2/2 Pnr. Bn.	Merlynston, Vic.	13.09.44	25
Sexton, Gnr. B.M.	QX.13955	2/10 Fd. Rgt.		12.09.44	28
Shannahan, L/Sgt. E.J.	VX.21112	2/2 Pnr. Bn.	Geelong, Vic.	13.09.44	23
Simpson, Pte. W.J.	NX.72654	1 Coy. AASC	Bankstown, NSW	12.09.44	23
Sinclair, Cpl. W.C.	NX.39776	2/19 Bn.	Balmain, NSW	12.09.44	24
Skene, Spr. A.J.	NX.19903	2/12 Fd. Coy.	Woy Woy, NSW	14.09.44	39
Skinner, Sgt. F.K.H.	WX. 9282	2/4 MG Bn.	Koorda, W.A.	12.09.44	40
Smith, Lieut. C.E.	VX.39037	4 A/Tk. Rgt.	Bacchus Marsh, Vic.	12.09.44	28
Smith, Pte. L.R.	QX.22609	2/26 Bn.	Wooloowin, Qld.	12.09.44	23
Smith, Pte. Maurice (vi)	VX.67225	2/29 Bn.	Strathmerton, Vic.	12.09.44	21
Smith, Pte. P.C.	VX.60590	2/2 Pnr. Bn.	Red Cliffs, Vic.	12.09.44	32
Smith, Pte. R.H.	VX.55254	4 Res. MT	East Geelong, Vic.	12.09.44	24
Smith, Sgt. Robert	QX. 8450	2/10 Fd. Rgt.	Mackay, Qld.	12.09.44	41
Smith, Gnr. R.E.	NX.51490	2/15 Fd. Rgt.	Gloucester, NSW	12.09.44	22
Snell, Pte. H.A.	QX.21253	2/26 Bn.	Gunalda, Qld.	13.09.44	25
Snelling, S/Sgt. C.W.	VX.39665	72 Sp. Dental Unit	Hungerford, NSW	18.09.44	26
Somerville, Spr. William	WX.12500	2/6 Fd. Pk.		12.09.44	29
Spooner, L/Cpl. Alex	WX. 7337	2/4 MG Bn.	Carlisle, W.A.	14.09.44	33
Standen, Bdr. R.R.	NX.52286	2/15 Fd. Rgt.	Abbotsford, NSW	16.09.44	24
Stedman, Cpl. J.N.	NX.55682	2/18 Bn.	Artarmon, NSW	14.09.44	22
Stephens, Sgt. W.J.	WX. 2618	2/3 MG Bn.	Collie, W.A.	14.09.44	27
Stidolph, Pte. G.S.J.	QX.21631	2/26 Bn.	Warwick, Qld.	12.09.44	23
Stillwell, S/Sgt. W.B.	VX.16152	1 Petrol Park	Hawthorn, Vic.	12.09.44	26
Stirling, Pte. Leslie	QX.15841	2/18 Bn.	Julia Creek, Qld.	14.09.44	27
Straughen, Pte. S.G.	VX.19543	1 Petrol Park	East Brunswick, Vic.	12.09.44	28
Stupart, Lieut. H.L.	QX. 6321	2/10 Fd. Rgt.	Wavell Heights, Qld.	12.09.44	30
Suggate, Sig. N.F.	NX.50941	8 Div. Sigs.	Mortdale, NSW	13.09.44	35
Sumner, Capt. A.B. (MID)	VX.39013	2/29 Bn.	Geelong, Vic.	13.09.44	29
Sunderland, Gnr. A.G.	NX.27932	2/15 Fd. Rgt.	Nimbin, NSW	16.09.44	26
Sykes, Pte. R.E.R.	VX.32773	27 Bde.Coy. AASC		12.09.44	25
Sylvander, Spr. F.J.B.	NX.20352	2/13 Fd. Coy.	Hay, NSW	12.09.44	28
Tate, Sgt. Bertie (DCM)	NX.28467	2/15 Fd. Rgt.	Bondi, NSW	15.09.44	38
Taylor, Pte. A.P.	NX.59562	22 Bde. Coy AASC	Petersham, NSW	12.09.44	28
Taylor, Cpl. C.R.	NX.52482	2/19 Bn.	The Clump, NSW	12.09.44	25
Thomas, Pte. D.W.	WX. 6623	2/4 MG Bn.	Perth, W.A.	12.09.44	23
Thomas, Pte. William	NX.21431	2/10 Fd. Amb.	Wingham, NSW	13.09.44	39
Thompson, Pte. R.A.	VX.17847	2/2 Pnr. Bn.	Port Melbourne, Vic.	14.09.44	32
Titmarsh, Gnr. A.C.	QX.12553	2/10 Fd. Rgt.	Bundamba, Qld.	14.09.44	28
Todd, Cpl. G.B.	VX.21924	2/2 Pnr. Bn.		12.09.44	33
Tome, Sgt. Frank	NX.32743	2/30 Bn.	Inverell, NSW	12.09.44	40
Tome, Cpl. M.J.M.	NX.32742	2/19 Bn.	Inverell, NSW	13.09.44	33
Toms, Pte. F.W.	WX. 7664	2/4 MG Bn.	New Bradwell, Bucks.,UK	14.09.44	40
Toogood, Pte. R.W.	VX.60984	2/2 Pnr. Bn.	Box Hill, Vic.	12.09.44	26
Travers, Pte. Keith	NX.35205	2/19 Bn.	Harden, NSW	13.09.44	38
Tresham, Spr. L.G.	NX.52907	2/12 Fd. Coy.	East Sydney, NSW	12.09.44	38

(vi) Served as Hocking, Pte. J.

Tresham, Spr. L.G.	NX.52907	2/12 Fd. Coy.	East Sydney, NSW	12.09.44	38
Trigwell, Pte. V.C.	WX.17863	2/4 MG Bn.	Donnybrook, Vic.	14.09.44	24
Tucker, Pte. W.J.	WX. 7484	2/4 MG Bn.	Bassendean, W.A.	12.09.44	38
Tumeth, Cpl. N.W.	NX.31930	8 Div. Prov.	Tamworth, NSW	12.09.44	35
Turnbull, Pte. Kenneth	QX.22722	2/26 Bn.	St. Lucia, Qld.	12.09.44	23
Turnbull, Pte. William	QX.23514	2/26 Bn.	St. Lucia, Qld.	12.09.44	27
Tyler, Pte. Allan	QX.16822	3 Res. MT	Kangaroo Point, Qld.	13.09.44	39
Underhill, Dvr. Henry	NX.71940	3 Res. MT	Randwick, NSW	14.09.44	27
Underwood, Pte. D.G.	SX. 8884	2/2 Res. MT	Myrtle Bank, S.A.	17.09.44	24
Valmadre, Pte. R.J.	QX.11305	2/26 Bn.	Proserpine, Qld.	12.09.44	25
Varley, Brig. A.L. (MC,MID)	NX.35005	H.Q. 22 Inf. Bde.	Inverell, NSW	13.09.44	50
Vary, Pte. R.S.	QX.19514	2/3 Ord. Store Coy.	Brookstead, Qld.	14.09.44	39
Venemore, Pte. N.J.	WX. 9292	2/4 MG Bn.	Shackleton, W.A.	15.09.44	28
Verdon, Pte. P.J.	NX.35262	2/19 Bn.		15.09.44	29
Verney, Pte. W.C.	NX.52877	H.Q. 22 Inf. Bde.	North Bondi, NSW	14.09.44	33
Vidal, Spr. G.R.	NX.67418	2/12 Fd. Coy.	New Lambton, NSW	12.09.44	22
Vidler, Dvr. V.N.	NX. 1196	3 Res. MT	Nth.Arm,Tweed Rvr.,NSW	14.09.44	23
Walker, Pte. W.N.	VX.63237	2/l0 Ord. Wksp.	Albury, NSW	16.09.44	30
Wallis, Sgt. J.C.	QX. 8942	69 LAD	Ipswich, Qld.	12.09.44	28
Walsh, Gnr. J.O'N.	VX.41094	4 A/Tk. Rgt.	Ballarat, Vic.	14.09.44	26
Walsh, Pte. L.P.	WX. 8776	2/4 MG Bn.	Shenton Park, W.A.	12.09.44	36
Want, Cpl. Harold	NX.71195	3 Res. MT	Paddington, NSW	12.09.44	34
Ward, Sigmn. E.W.	VX.35797	8 Div. Sigs.	South Yarra, Vic.	14.09.44	26
Wark, Spr. J.J.P.	VX.30136	2/lO Fd. Coy.	Prahran, Vic.	12.09.44	37
Wark, Pte. T.J.	NX.56139	2/19 Bn.	Coonabarrabran, NSW	12.09.44	33
Watson, Crftsmn. J.R.	VX.62875	2/10 Ord. Wksp.	Richmond, Vic.	12.09.44	39
Webb, Pte. F.W.	WX. 9829	2/4 MG Bn.	Claremont, W.A.	12.09.44	22
Welldon, Pte. R.A.	QX.20521	2/26 Bn.	Sans Souci, NSW	15.09.44	34
White, Pte. W.L.	QX.23671	2/3 Ord. Store Coy.	Windsor, Qld.	14.09.44	28
Wighton, Spr. J.J.	VX.26529	2/10 Fd. Coy.	Albert Park, Vic.	15.09.44	38
Willard, Pte. A.J.	VX.13211	2/2 Pnr. Bn.		12.09.44	38
Willey, Spr. H.N.	VX.41357	2/10 Fd. Coy.	Essendon, Vic.	12.09.44	24
Williams, L/Cpl. B.J.	NX.51285	8 Div. Sigs.	Manly, NSW	17.09.44	35
Williams, Pte. J.H.	SX. 8715	2/2 Res. MT	Millicent, S.A.	12.09.44	30
Williams, Sigmn. J.H.	NX.41612	8 Div. Sigs.	Wagga Wagga, NSW	12.09.44	22
Williams, Pte. V.H.P.	SX. 4059	2/4 Fd. Wksp.	Holmesdale, S.A.	12.09.44	24
Willis, Pte. Alphonsus	VX.32917	1 Fd.Bakery	West Brunswick, Vic.	12.09.44	34
Wilson, Spr. G.S.	NX. 7073	2/12 Fd. Coy.	Blackheath, NSW	13.09.44	43
Wilson, Cpl. R.A.	SX.10963	2/4 Fd. Wksp.	Rose Park, S.A.	12.09.44	24
Wilson, Cpl. Vivian	VX.41946	2/l0 Fd. Coy.	Moe, Vic.	12.09.44	25
Winters, Pte. L.J.	NX. 596	2/30 Bn.	Queanbeyan, NSW	12.09.44	26
With, Bdr. J.W.H.	QX.17209	2/10 Fd. Rgt.	Newmarket, Qld.	12.09.44	24
Wood, Pte. C.P.	QX.13460	2/26 Bn.	New Farm, Qld.	12.09.44	29
Woodard, Pte. N.F.	TX. 5703	2/29 Bn.	Natone, Tas.	12.09.44	36
Woodhead, Pte. J.A.	VX.62147	2/2 Pnr. Bn.	Richmond, Vic.	14.09.44	20
Young, Dvr. J.McK.	NX.69184	3 Res. MT Coy.		12.09.44	33
Young, Pte. William	NX.68341	27 Bde. Coy. AASC	Concord, NSW	13.09.44	32

HMAS PERTH CASUALTIES - RAKUYO MARU

PA.1311	Bell, C.L.	A/g Leading Seaman
H. 1511	Bessell, L.D.	Stoker II
W. 1199	Campbell, F.C.	Able Seaman
21120	Casserly, E.E.	Stoker
23163	Dvorak, G.L.	Stoker
20055	Gebhardt, R.A.	Leading Seaman
19356	Hogman, W.F.	Stoker Petty Officer
23005	Hosking, T.M.	Able Seaman
21788	Jackson, N.F.L.	A/G Leading Signalman
22047	Johnson, F.D.	A/g Leading Signalman
F. 3316	Johnston, W.J.	Ordinary Seaman
18298	Jones, A.T.	Leading Stoker
20835	Keith, H.A.	Leading Telegraphist
22989	Likiard, Socrates	Leading Supply Assistant
23824	MacPherson, L.G.	Able Seaman
S. 1984	Maher, R.D.	Able Seaman
W. 2255	Martin, Vernon	Stoker 11
F. 3455	McCall, W.T.P.	Ordinary Seaman
23097	McDonnell, W.C.	Stoker
13959	Milne, William	Petty Officer
F. 3060	Nagle, H.L.	Able Seaman
19076	Parks, J.B.	Able Seaman
W. 2164	Pethebridge, C.A. (AM)	Stoker 11
S. 4094	Ritchie, F.E.	Able Seaman
S/V. 69	Rix, D.G.	Telegraphist
23025	Rosevear, A.J.	Stoker
24925	Slattery, F.J.	Stoker 11
B. 2832	Smith, R.J.	A/g Able Seaman
20401	Turnbull, J.J.S.	A/g Stoker Petty Officer
PA.1776	Williams, R.S.W.	Able Seaman
S. 4360	Wilson, L.A.T.	Able Seaman
24382	Winnett, C.l.	Able Seaman
S. 5523	Wright, F.B.	Sick Berth Attendant II

R.A.A.F. PERSONNEL on RAKUYO MARU

18951	Begg, C.B. AC.1		17.09.44	28
207782	Bonnett, R.J. Cpl.	Rockdale, NSW	14.09.44	26
13091	Gill, J.T. LAC	West Geelong, Vic.	15.09.44	25
19690	Kendall, R.D. LAC	Nth Fitzroy, Vic.	12.09.44	23
19190	McClelland, R.W. LAC	Camberwell, Vic.	12.09.44	26
11813	Meredith, A.C. Cpl.	Thornbury, Vic.	16.09.44	28
404155	Wood, K.R. W/O.	Potts Point, NSW	12.09.44	25

EPILOGUE

USS PAMPANITO was commissioned in 1943 when she represented the height of submarine development. After World War II had ended she was de-commissioned and became one of the ships in the Navy scrap-heap.

In the late 1970s she was discovered by a young officer from the San Francisco National Maritime Museum who thought she would be a valuable acquisition to the Museum's fleet of old ships. Due to his energy and enthusiasm and with professional help from the U.S. Navy Department together with hard-working members of the Maritime Museum Association, in 1982 PAMPANITO was opened to the public at Pier 45 Fisherman's Wharf.

She generated great public interest which continued to grow and in May 1985 she was nominated for National Historic Landmark status. Further interest was created when in August 1985 her war-time crew members held their first Reunion in 40 years aboard her.

In January 1986 the Museum's Board of Trustees were delighted to receive news that PAMPANITO had been officially declared a "National Historic Landmark of the U.S.A.", and on 14th November a special ceremony was held to mark PAMPANITO's new status and to dedicate her to the Memory of those who gave their lives while serving in submarines during World War 11. During this Service two Plaques were unveiled, one commemorating the Dedication, the other to recognize and commend the work and efforts of all those who had contributed to her restoration.

On a recent visit, her war-time Skipper, Rear Admiral Paul Summers, USN (Retd.), paid tribute to those responsible for restoring his old command to her 1943 appearance and also admitted he had never seen her so 'ship-shape'!. He also mentioned how proud he and his crew were to have served on her and of her battle honours which are emblazoned on her conning tower.

On 23 July 1990 the Australian Government presented a Plaque to the USS PAMPANITO commending the humanity and gallantry shown by her officers and men while rescuing, while deep within enemy waters, 73 Allied POWs of whom 47 were Australian and expressing the deep gratitude of those rescued and the thanks of the Nation.

When Frank Coombes' Motor Transport Unit crossed on to Singapore before being shipped to Java, he towed a car carrying a Chinese family. When he got it to safety the Chinese presented him with some jewellery as a reward. He carried the jewellery up to the time his shirt was cut away from him on the deck of the PAMPANITO and it was tossed overboard. He still had a diamond studded earring and he presented these to his three new American friends in the engine room. When Frank Farmer visited United States in 1990, he met one of the crew and he said, "Tell Frank Coombes my wife is still wearing the diamond he gave me on the PAMPANITO."

Norman Hunter, formerly of SEALION, made his second trip to Australia to visit survivors who had been rescued by SEALION. He travelled to Perth, W.A. to see Alf Sing, stayed with Tony Clive in Sydney, visited friends in Melbourne and went to Queensland to see Norm Nutley and Norm Calvert.

Former Torpedoman Don Miller of the BARB visited Jack Flynn in 1990, it was a great reunion. Miller went home and persuaded his fellow veterans to finance a trip to the United States for Jack and Sandy Flynn. Jack said the Americans gave them a wonderful time – it was as unbelievable as the rescue.

ACKNOWLEDGEMENTS

Several survivors wrote their own accounts for their families and with their kind permission I have used extracts. Some survivors preferred not to be interviewed, many agreed things happened in the final hours of survival while in a state of delirium they preferred to forget.

It was not my intention to pierce the emotional barrier to explore these events – the Honour Roll says it all.

I would like to thank all the survivors to whom I spoke and who made a contribution to this account, especially Tim Bowden, A.B.C. Social History Department for access to his Survival transcripts; Arthur Bancroft for permission to use extracts from his unpublished "Mikado's Guests"; Jack Flynn for use of his private records; Mrs. Sacey Thams; Carole Skoljerev for her father, Harry Weigand's record written at Saipan; Allan Pollock and Lance Gibson for the TAMAHOKO MARU records; Roy Cornford, Les Miller and Frank Jesse; Bill Harry, 2/22 Bn. Association; John Hocking, 2/2 Pnr. Bn. Association; Frank Farmer for use of his written records, for information used in Epilogue on USS PAMPANITO, and for photographs; Phil Beilby, Les Bolger, Reg Bullock, Norm Calvert, Bob Collins, Frank Coombes, Bill Cunneen, Tony Clive, Ross Dunbar; Elizabeth Duncan for permission to use extracts of Vic Duncan's written records; Cliff Farlow and his friends at the Bowling Club at Hay, NSW.; Dave Flinn, George Hinchy, Reg Harris, John Langley, Doug Mayers, Lloyd "Darby" Munro, Harold Martin, Bill McKitterick, Ian MacDiarmid, Norm Nutley, Don McArdle, Frank McGovern, Bob Farrands, Ron Miscamble, Bill Mayne, Harold Ramsey, Ross Smith, Russell Savage, Reg Stewart, John Wade, Ken Williams, Wal Williams, Bert Wall, Ray Wheeler; Marion Holmes, Custodian, Jim Campbell records; Mrs. Nancy McGrath-Kerr for use of Peter McGrath-Kerr's written records.

Special thanks to Alex Dandie for his meticulous checking of the Honour Roll and Allan Wild for proof reading; Bert McKay for R.A.A.F. information.

And to the many people I spoke to who answered my queries and assisted in every way possible, my thanks.

DON WALL

REFERENCES

Australian War Memorial Records Department:
A.I.F. List of survivors rescued by Japanese. Ref. Echelon Records 144/1/124-128
American and Japanese Accounts of sinking of MONTEVIDEO MARU. Ref. 779/1/26.
Kitchener Loughnan Statements. AWM.54/10/10 Series.
John Dwyer Statements.

Australian Archives, Brighton, Victoria.

MP.729/6	Items	63/901/728
MP.742/1	Items	255/15/579
MP.1049/5	ltems	1951/2/99
MP.1587/1	ltems	20.S.

BIBLIOGRAPHY

Return from River Kwai – Joan and Clay Blair.
Silent Victory – Clay Blair.
United States Submarine Operation World War II – Theodore Roscoe.
Japanese Thrust – Lionel Wigmore.
Singapore and Beyond – Don Wall
Clear The Bridge – Richard O'Kane.

SUMMARY

LOST ON RAKUYO MARU		
	A.I.F.	503
	R.A.N.	33
	R.A.A.F.	7
		543

RESCUED BY JAPANESE		
	A.I.F.	71
	R.A.N.	8
	R.A.A.F.	3
		82

RESCUED BY U.S. SUBMARINES		
	A.I.F.	87
	R.A.N.	4
	R.A.A.F.	1
		92

	TOTAL	717

NOTE: There was a report that there were two Australian Merchant Seaman captured in Java who were also lost.

POWs RESCUED BY JAPANESE – SINKING OF "RAKUYO MARU"

KAWASAKI GROUP

VX.36401	Amoore, Pte. J.	2/2 Pnr. Bn.
TX. 5662	Bassett, Cpr. J.E.	2/10 Fld.Coy.
NX.58088	Brooks, Pte. M.K.	2/19 Bn.
VX.59998	Carroll, Pte. G.P.	2/2 Pnr.Bn.
NX.10358	Clayden, Pte. S.R.	2/4 M.G. Bn.
WX. 4927	Climie, Pte. A.W.	2/4 M.G. Bn.
QX. 8219	Craig, Pte. L.F.	2/26 Bn.
NX67939	Curtis, Pte. O.E.	87 L.A.D.
QX.12737	Desailly, Pte. H.V.A.	3 Res.M.T.Coy.
VX. 9845	Downes, W.O.}I. W.	2/2 Pnr. Bn.
QX.14995	Dwyer, Pte. J.M.	Admin. H.Q.
VX.32739	Goninon, Dvr. W.B.	4 Res. M.T. Coy.
NX.25711	Hann, Pte. I.G.	2/30 Bn.
NX.26890	Harper, Pte. A.J.	2/19 Bn.
NX.13013	Henderson, Cpr. R.R.	2/6 Fld.Coy.
VX.39162	Heywood, W.O.I. W.S.	2 Coy. A.A.S.C.
NX.37380	Hicks, Pte. D.A.	2/30 Bn.
VX.56918	Hock, Pte. L.J.	2/2 Pnr. Bn.
QX.10205	Hyde, Pte. K.J.	2/26 Bn.
SX.14943	Hodder, Dvr. R.W.	8 Div.Ammn.Sub.Pk.
VX.31460	Hubbard, Gnr. W.N.	4 A/Tk. Regt.
NX.46875	Hunt, Dvr. A.S.	13 Res.M.T.Coy.
NX.59469	Johnson, Dvr. F.B.	H.Q. A.A.S.C.
NX.44871	Kay, Pte. A.W.	2/18 Bn.
NX.57812	Langley, Pte. J.R.	2/30 Bn.
NX.34300	Lawrence, Pte. F.W.	2/20 Bn.
NX.69606	Luke, Dvr. L.C.	3 Res.Tpt.Coy.
VX.16237	Matthews, Pte. H.L.	2/2 Pnr. Bn.
VX.21145	Mayers, Dvr. D.C.	105 Tpt.Coy.
VX.55477	Mayne, Dvr. W.E.J.	2/1 Fld.Survey A.I.F.
NX.31777	McNeill, Cpl. W.	2/30 Bn.
QX.13095	Porter, Pte. J.E.M.	2/26 Bn.
VX.17827	Ramsey, Pte. H.G.	2/2 Pnr.Bn.
NX.27158	Rigelsford, Dvr. R.L.	2/10 Fld.Amb.
VX.48448	Smith, Dvr. W.B.	2/2 Res.M.T.Coy.
QX.12962	Webb, A/Cpl. W.P.	3 Res.M.T.Coy.
VX.22430	White, Pte. J.J.	2/2 Pnr.Bn.
NX.57223	Williams, Pte. G.W.	2/20 Bn.
NX.56234	Wright, Pte. A.G.	2/18 Bn.

HMAS PERTH

S. 5787	Campbell, Ord.Seaman H.M.
21589	Duncan, C.P.O. V.R.
21945	Johnson, A/g.P.O. T.C.
PM. 3870	Major, Ord.Seaman P.W.
24251	Matson, Ord.Seaman S.C.
S. 3478	McGovern, Able Seaman F.J.
S. 4074	Mills, Able Seaman K.W.E.
13891	Thomas, P.O. A.J.R.

R.A.A.F.

Burrell, K.
McKay, A.
Quick, D.

POWs RESCUED BY JAPANESE – SINKING OF "RAKUYO MARU"

MOJI

NX.65914	Burridge, Pte. R.	2/12 Fld.Coy.
TX.61535	Keating, Pte. T.	4 Res.M.T. Coy.
NX.48102	West, Pte. W.H.	2/19 Bn.

SAKATA

QX.22678	Anderson, Pte. E.W.	Postal Corps.
VX.41477	Attrill, Gnr. F.	4 A/Tk.Regt.
V#.64170	Clark, Pte. D.H.	Postal Rfts.
NX.53198	Dorman, L/Cpl. W.M.	2/12 Fld.Coy.
NX.41072	Dowd, Cpr. C.H.	H.Q. 8 Div.Engr.
NX.30330	Dunbar, A/Bdr. R.	2/15 Fld.Regt.
QX.13145	Hall, Sgt. A.W.	2/10 Fld.Regt.
QX.17595	Hodgson, Gnr. H.J.	2/10 Fld.Regt.
NX.29485	Kelk, Pte. R.J.	Gen.Base Depot
VX.32162	Lewin, Pte. F.A.	2/2 M.A.C.
QX.10108	Loughnan, Gnr. K.M.	2/10 Fld.Regt.
QX.16526	MacDiarmid, Gnr. I.A.	2/10 Fld.Regt.
VX.12548	Macauley, Sgt. G.	105 Tpt.Coy.
NX.28252	McKone, Gnr. J.	2/15 Fld.Regt.
VX.61564	Manning, Pte. #.J.	2/10 Ord.W/Shps.
NX.68567	Martin, Cpl. K.H.N.	2/15 Fld.Regt.
NX.19827	Moxham, Gnr. T.R.	2/15 Fld.Regt.
NX.37793	Mullens, Gnr. J.R.	2/15 Fld.Regt.
NX.70273	Richards, Capt. C.R.B.	2/15 Fld.Regt.
SX.18426	Robinson, Pte. A.A.	2/10 Ord.W/Shps.
QX.17752	Savage, Gnr. W.L.	2/10 Fld.Regt.
QX.17590	Savage, Gnr. J.R.	2/10 Fld.Regt.
SX.10989	Schwerdt, Pte. J.N.	2/2 Res.M.T.Coy.
VX.57046	Smith, Gnr. J.A.	14 A/Tk.Refts.
NX.32933	Wade, A/Sgt. E.J.	2/15 Fld.Regt.
NX.26519	Wade, Gnr. J.	2/15 Fld.Regt.
WX.12989	Wall, Pte. H.J.	2/4 M.G. Bn.
QX. 9975	Wilson, Gnr. C.C.	2/10 Fld.Regt.
NX.33836	Weekes, Sgt. S.	8 Div.Sigs.

BRITISH RESCUED BY USS PAMPANITO

Number	Name and Rank	Regiment	Home
5949038	Anderson, C. L/Cpl.	5 Bdfs.& Herts. Regt.	Bedfordshire, UK
5952591	Baldwin, G. Pte.	5 Bdfs.& Herts. Regt.	London, UK
5774196	Barker, H.J. Pte.	4 Royal Norfolk Regt.	Norfolk, UK
	Brierley, T.B. Gnr.	32 Coast Bty., 9 Coast Rgt.	Kent, UK
1103020	Costello, S. Gnr.	148 Fld. Regt., R.A.	York, UK
1787132	Cray, W. Pte.	16 Advance Regt., R.A.	Hull, UK
	Cresswell, D.A. Gnr.	148 Fld. Regt., R.A.	Surry, UK
	Everitt, W.		London, UK
872495	Fieldhouse, E. Gnr.	9 Coast Regt., R.A.	Isle of Man, UK
4865795	Harrison, J. Pte.	1st Bn., Leics. Regt.	Lincolnshire, UK
4204143	Hughes, E. Pte.	16 MBU, Sherwood Frstrs.	Wrexham, Wales
1110409	Jay, C. Gnr.	148 Fld. Regt., R.A.	Essex, UK
2323445	Jones, H. Sgt.	Royal Corp. of Signals	Lancashire, UK
5030966	Kidman, W. Pte.	5 Suffolks, Royal Inf.	Ely, Cambshire, UK
5134120	Mandley, W.A. Gnr.	8(S) Coastal Bty., R.A.	Northampton, UK
1115656	Nobbs, A. Pte.	80th Fld. Regt., R.A.	Yorkshire, UK
	Ogden, A. Gnr.	88 Fld. Regt., R.A.	Nr. Rotherham, UK
907794	Perry, C.A.	125th A.T. Regt., R.A.	Durham, UK
10562139	Smethurst, H. Pte.	R.A.O.C.	Lancashire, UK
910824	Smith, T. Pte.	125th A.T. Regt., R.A.	Durham, UK
4278586	Smith, D. Fusilier	Royal Northumb. Fusiliers	Yorkshire, UK
3859126	Taylor, T. Pte.	18th Recon. Corps.	Blackpool, UK
4974795	Ward, G. Pte.	5 Bn., Sherwood Frstrs.	Nottingham, UK
5830703	Whiley, S. Pte.	4th Bn., Suffolk Regt., R.I.	Staffordshire, UK
5955652	Wiles, F.E. Pte.	5 Bn.,Bdfs. & Herts. Regt.	Surrey, UK
Deceased			
	Campbell, John	2 Gordon Bn. Gordon Highlanders	Aberdeen, Scotland

BRITISH RESCUED BY USS QUEENFISH

Number	Name and Rank	Regiment	Home
812905	Carter, F. Dvr.	R.A.8.C. 196 Fld.Amb.	Yorkshire, UK
	Grice, 'Darky'	88th Fld. Regt.	Yorkshire, UK (Decd)
977758	Harrison, W. Gnr.	9 Coast Regt., R.A.	Durham, UK
1092740	Hudson, R.A. Bdr.	85th A/Tk. Regt. R.A.	Derbyshire, UK
7648536	Jones, H. Pte.	14th Sect., R.A.O.A.	Lancashire, UK
	Winters, W. (Came on board in a delirium, no one else had seen him before.)		England (Decd)

BRITISH RESCUED BY USS BARB

Number	Name and Rank	Regiment	Home
915449	Allbury, A.	118 Fld. Regt.	London, UK
853661	Carr, T.	9th Coast Regt.	Durham, UK
879065	Fullar, A.C.	499th Battalion	Kent, UK
1432144	Johnson, J.	llth Bty., 7th Coast Rgt.	Yorkshire, UK

SURVIVORS – "TAMAHOKO MARU"

* Davies, S.E. Sgt.	NX.30489	18th A/Tk.Bty.	West Ryde, NSW
* Nimmo, R.W. Bdr.	NX.30453	18th A/Tk.Bty.	Petersham, NSW
Jobling, E.M. Gnr.	VX.Z5508	18th A/Tk.Bty.	Appin, Vic.
Ericksson, C. Dvr.	NX.48379	2/3Res. MT	Auburn, NSW
Moore, M. Dvr.	VX.688Z6	2/3Res. MT Coy.	Narromine, NSW
Montefiore, A.E. Sgt.	WX.1855Z	A.H.Q.	West Perth, WA
Johnson, F.J. Sgt.	A.1152301	R.A.A.F.	Chelsea, Vic.
Barnes, J.D. Sgt.		R.A.A.F.	Auchenflower, Qld.
Downie, R.B. LAC	Aus.34226	R.A.A.F.	Stockton, NSW
Fitzmaurice, F.W. Bdr.	NX.32416	2/1 Hvy.Bty.	
Louds, E. Gnr.		2/1 Hvy.Bty.	
Willington, E.R. Gnr.	NX.34626	2/1 Hvy.Bty.	Yenda, NSW
Howard, C.E. GNr.	TX. 48 3	2/1 Hvy.Bty.	Newtown, Tas.
McConnell, R. GNr.	NX.38462	2/1 Hvy.Bty.	Wyong, NSW
Picton, G.E. Gnr.	NX.38540	2/1 Hvy.Bty.	Collarenebri, NSW
Edmiston, G. Gnr.	VX.57239	2/1 Hvy. Bty.	Nth Essendon, Vic.
Pollock, Q. Gnr.	NX.81329	2/1 Hvy.Bty.	Randwick, NSW
McMillan, J. GNr.	VX.57833	2/1 Hvy.Bty.	Caulfield, Vic.
Long, A.E. Dvr.	NX. 2896	A.A.S.C.	Arncliffe, NSW
* Hearne, W.J. Dvr.	NX. 4059	A.A.S.C.	Hurlstone Park, NSW
* Mitchell, W.D. Pte.	VX. 5450		Rushworth, Vic.

Snowden, E.R. Cpl.	NX.47101	2/2 Fld. Amb.	Lake Macquarie, NSW
Russell, A.J. Pte.	NX.50978	2/2 Fld. Amb.	Ashfield, NSW
Craine, V.W. Cpl.	NX.38664	2/2 Fld. Eng.	Bankstown, NSW
Nelligan, M.R. Cpl.	NX.38661	2/2 Fld. Eng.	Canterbury,, NSW
Griffiths, I.E. Spr.	NX.38665	2/2 Fld. Eng.	Warwick, Old.
Lockyer, A.E. Spr.	NX.38693	2/2 Fld. Eng.	Longueville, NSW
Segal, N.E. Sigmn.	NX.4357Z	8 Div.Sig.	Wilton, NSW
Anderson, D.R.G. Cpl.	VX.31555	2/2 Pioneers	Barnawatha, Vic.
Thorne, J. Cpl.	VX.18389	2/2 Pioneers	Kew, Vic.
Hooper, E.E. Pte.	VX.23630	2/2 Pioneers	Goorambat, Vic.
Boyd, W. Pte.	VX.41403	2/2 Pioneers	Wonthaggi, Vic.
Ross, G. Pte.	WX.11771	2/2 Pioneers	Subiaco, W.A.
Powell, L. Pte.	VX.60676	2/2 Pioneers	Bendigo, Vic.
Hayes, W.H. Pte.	VX.21929	8 Div.A.A.S.C.	Bendigo, Vic.
Gibson, L. Lieut.	VX.45741	2/3 MG Rgt.	Rochester, Vic.
parkin, C.O. Cpl.	WX. 2844	2/3 MG Bn.	Perth, W.A.
Reed, W.C. Pte.	VX.45894	2/3 MG Bn.	Bendigo, Vic.
Smythe, P.J. Pte.	VX.25701	2/3 MG Bn.	Mildura, Vic.
Dare, E.C. Pte.	TX. 2348	2/3 MG Bn.	Levendale, Tas.
McDonald, G.S.J. Pte.	WX. 9911	2/3 MG Bn.	Wickepin, W.A.
Johnson, G.C.	WX. 5300	2/3 MG Bn.	Bunbury, W.A.
Tickle, L.J. Pte.	WX. 9943	2/3 MG Bn.	Beverley, W.A.
*Reid, T.K. Pte.	TX. 3984	2/40 Bn.	
Banks, M.W. Pte.	TX. 2986	2/40 Bn.	Launceston, Tas.
Chick, A.C. Pte.	TX. 3350	2/40 Bn.	St. Helens, Tas.
Grieg, C.R. Pte.	TX. 5853	2/40 Bn.	Cressy, Tas.
*O'Keefe, B.D. Pte.	VX.53494	2/40 Bn.	Sth. Melbourne, Vic.
Kerr, P.McG. Sgt.	TX. 3994	2/40 Bn.	Launceston, Tas.
Miller, H.D. Sgt.	TX. 2717	2/40 Bn.	Hobart, Tas.
Marshall, J.J. L/Cpl.	VX.29554	2/40 Bn.	Mulwala, NSW
Marshall, N.J. L/Cpl.	VX.38121	2/40 Bn.	Preston, Vic.
Tyson, G.G. L/Cpl.	TX. 3926	2/40 Bn.	Princeton, Tas.
Curtis, L.K. Pte.	TX. 5736	2/40 Bn.	Fingal, Tas.
Atkison, W.C. Pte.	TX. 3046	2/40 Bn.	Cressy, Tas.
Gleeson, C.J. Pte.	TX. 3914	2/40 Bn.	Yolla, Tas.
Campbell, R. Pte.	TX. 2559	2/40 Bn.	Hobart, Tas.
Prendergast, L. Pte.	VX.41147	2/40 Bn.	Rochester, Vic.
Lewis, D.R. Pte.	TX. 8441	2/40 Bn.	Hobart, Tas.
Lean, L.B. Pte.	VX.45816	2/40 Bn.	Maryborough, Vic.
Garlick, W.D. Cpl.	TX. 2959	2/40 Bn.	New Norfolk, tas.
Lyons, P. Pte.	TX. 3932	2/40 Bn.	Launceston, Tas.
Hamilton, J. Pte.	TX. 2604	2/40 Bn.	Sth. Hobart, Tas.
McMahon, K.P.J. Pte.	TX. 3817	2/40 Bn.	
Prosser, J.T. Pte.	TX. 5456	2/40 Bn.	Launceston, Tas.
Kevin, A.W. OTE.	TX. 7822		

* Survived the atomic bomb at Nagasaki.

A.I.F. PERSONNEL RESCUED BY JAPANESE AND DIED IN JAPAN.

WX. 4927	Climie, Pte. A.N.	2/4 M.G.		13.07.45.	
NX.51198	Dorman, L/Cpl. W.M.	2/12 Fld. Coy.	Died pneumonia	21.05.45	
NX.41072	Dowd, Spr. C.H.	8 Div.HQ. Eng.	Died beri-beri	21.05.45	
NX.25741	Hann, Pte. I.G.	2/30 Bn.	Died pneumonia	18.02.45	27
NX.26890	Harper, Pte. A.J.	2/19 Bn.	Died pneumonia	19.02.45	38
VX.39162	Heywood, W.O.I. W.S.	27 Bde.Coy.AASC	Killed air raid	13.07.45	34
SX.14943	Hodder, Dvr. R.W.	2/2 Res.MT.AASC		13.07.45	26
NX.37793	Mullens, Gnr. J.R.	2/15 Fd.Rgt.RAA	Died dysentery	28.10.44	22
NX.27158	Rigelsford, Pte. R.L.	2/10 Fld. Amb.	Killed air raid	13.07.45	27
QX.17752	Savage, Gnr. W.L.	2/10 Fd.Rgt.RAA	Died pneumonia	01.03.45	36
SX.10989	Swerdt, Pte. J.N.	2/2 Res. M.T.	Killed air raid	16.05.45	

R.A.N. PERSONNEL KILLED IN ALLIED AIR RAID

21945	Johnson, A/g Petty Officer, T.C.
PM. 3870	Major, Ord.Seaman, P.W.
S. 4074	Mills, Able Seaman, K.W.E.

SUMMARY OF THOSE RESCUED BY JAPANESE

A.I.F.	71
R.A.N.	8
RA.A.F.	3
	82

DIED IN JAPAN - TAMAHOKO MARU SURVIVORS

TX. 2706	Bailey, Pte. J.L.	2/40 Bn.	Woodbridge, Tas.	24.12.44	31
TX. 3511	Connors, L/Cpl. K.	2/40 Bn.	South Yarra, Vic.	13.12.44	30
TX. 5104	Haywood, Pte. A.L.	2/40 Bn.	Somerset, Tas.	10.11.44	25
NX. 4059	Hearne, Dvr. W.J.	Sparrow Fce.,AASC	Hurlstone Pk.,NSW	15.12.44	21
VX. 5650	Mitchell, Pte. D.W.	H.Q. Guard Bn.		17.11.44	38
TX. 2937	Pickett, Pte. H.H.	2/40 Bn.	Tunbridge, Tas.	15.09.44	26
TX. 3703	Prior, Pte. F.K.	2/40 Bn.	Young Town, Tas.	13.12.44	23
NX.50978	Russell, Pte. A.J.	2/2 Fld. Amb.	Ashfield, NSW	12.02.45	38
TX. 2802	Smith, L/Cpl. E.T.	2/40 Bn.	Sandy Bay, Tas	07.12.44	33
WX.9943	Tickle, Pte. H.L.	2/3 M.G. Bn.	Claremont, W.A	10.12.44	24

BRITISH RESCUED BY USS SEALION

Number	Name and Rank	Regiment	Home
1606836	Armstrong, C.J. Gnr.	85th A/Tk.Regt., R.A.	Liverpool, UK
982862	Ainsworth, N. Gnr.	148th Fld. Regt., R.A.	Lancashire, UK
4974519	Bagmall, J. Pte.	1/5 Sherwood Forstrs.	Staffordshire, UK
590132	Bambridge, L. Pte.	85th Bedfs. & Herts.	Bedford, UK
1103042	Barnett, W. Gnr.	148th Fld. Regt., R.A.	Yorkshire, UK
902473	Castro, R. Bdr.	135th Fld. Arty., R.A.	Kent, UK
937103	Coward, W.l. Gnr.	125th A/Tk. Regt., R.A.	Yorkshire, UK
6028812	Deighton, J. Sig.	R.O. Corps Signalman	London, UK
862267	Emmett, W.H.R. Gnr.	148th Fld. Regt., R.A.	Bedfordshire,UK
1427178	Fuller, W.H. Bdr.	31/7th Coast Rgt., Fix Defs.	London, UK
1087781	Getzes, A. Gnr.	18th Divn., 88th Fld.Arty.	Yorkshire, UK
7635854	Gould, G. Cpl.	R.A.O.C., 14th Sect. R.A.	Birmingham, UK
4981054	Halfhide, E.D. Cpl.	1/5th Sherwood Frstrs.	Hertfordshire, UK
962445	Hall, A. Gnr.	148th Fld. Regt., R.A.	Shropshire, UK
964404	Halligan, J. Gnr.	118th Fld. Regt.	Nthn. Ireland
1437767	Howland, R.E.A. Gnr.	9th Coast Regt.	Sheeraces, UK
3059601	Leslie, A.H. Sig. Divn., R.A.	18th Fld.Rgt., llth Indian	East Lothian, Scot.
842476	Leighton, W.A. Gnr.	9 Coast Regt., R.A.	Monmouthshire, UK
896993	Lowden, C.M. Gnr.	88th Fld. Regt.	Lancashire, UK
7639917	Pharoah, H.C. Cpl.	R.A.O.C., BOC, Malay Comd.	Portsmouth, UK
5989149 (Died 19.09.44)	Rolph, D. Pte.	5 Bedfs. & Herts.	Hertfordshire, UK
11001011	Simpson, S.G. Gnr.	16th Def.Regt., Malay	Leicester, UK
948854	Smith, L.W. L/Bdr.	148th Fld.Regt., R.A.	Hertfordshire, US
947001	Starkey, R.G. Cnr.	125th A/Tk. Regt.	Yorkshire, UK
1115610	Stone, W.H. Gnr.	88th Fld. Regt.	Nottinghamshire, UK
840625	Wheeler, M. Gnr.	H.Q., 9th Corps.	Edinburgh, Scot.
4755432	Wilson, H.E. Drummer	1/5th Sherwood Frstrs.	London, UK
4620751	Wyllie, A. Pte.	1/5th Sherwood Frstrs.	Lanarkshire, Scot.

INDEX